LEADING FOR MISSION

Integrating Life, Culture and Faith in Catholic Education

Jim and Therese D'Orsa

THE BROKEN BAY INSTITUTE
MISSION AND EDUCATION SERIES

Published in Australia by
Vaughan Publishing
32 Glenvale Crescent
Mulgrave VIC 3170

Vaughan Publishing
A joint imprint of Broken Bay Institute and Garratt Publishing

© 2013 Copyright James D'Orsa and Therese D'Orsa
All rights reserved. Except as provided by Australian copyright law, no part of this publication may be reproduced in any manner without prior permission in writing from the publisher.

Designed by Cristina Neri, Canary Graphic Design
Cover image – Thinkstock.com

Nihil Obstat: Reverend Gerard Diamond MA (Oxon), LSS, D. Theol
            Diocesan Censor

Imprimatur: Monsignor Greg Bennet
            Vicar General

Date: 15 April 2013

The Nihil Obstat and Imprimatur are official declarations that a book or pamphlet is free of doctrinal or moral error. No implication is contained therein that those who have granted the Nihil Obstat and Imprimatur agree with the contents, opinions or statements expressed. They do not necessarily signify that the work is approved as a basic text for catechetical instruction.

DEDICATION

This book honours those leaders who, during major transition periods in Catholic education, have charted—and continue to chart—a course responsive to the challenges of a demanding context.

As Catholic educators move into the fourth era of Catholic education in this country, an era shaped by globalisation and post-modernity, there is much encouragement to be gained from those who negotiated similar transitions in the past. Their success in leading the Catholic community from one era to the next secured the mission and identity of Catholic schools in their time and place.

We celebrate in particular the leadership of Monsignor John Slowey, Br Kelvin Canavan, Fr Frank Martin and Monsignor Tom Doyle; in whose leadership journeys we have been privileged to share.

Jim and Therese D'Orsa
February 2013.

ACKNOWLEDGEMENTS

Financial Support

Since the inception of the program, the Mission and Education series has received financial support from a number of Catholic Education authorities. Their assistance with research and publication costs is gratefully acknowledged:

Queensland – the Catholic Education Offices of Brisbane, Cairns, Rockhampton, Toowoomba, and Townsville

New South Wales – the Catholic Education Offices of Armidale, Broken Bay, Maitland-Newcastle, Parramatta, Sydney, Wagga and Wollongong

Australian Capital Territory – the Catholic Education Office of Canberra-Goulburn

Victoria – the Catholic Education Offices of Ballarat, Sale and Sandhurst

South Australia – *Catholic Education South Australia (Archdiocese of Adelaide and Diocese of Port Pirie)*

Tasmania – the Catholic Education Office of Hobart

Northern Territory – the Catholic Education Office of Darwin

Religious Congregations – Good Samaritan Sisters, Marist Brothers (Sydney Province), Marist Brothers National, Edmund Rice Education Australia.

Graphics

The assistance of Br Ben Boonen cfc with the production of the graphics is much appreciated.

Advice on aspects of the text

The authors are grateful to the following for their expert advice on aspects of the text: Sr Catherine Clark rsj, Fr Noel Connolly ssc, Mgr Tom Doyle, Fr Bruce Duncan cssr, Br John Luttrell fms, Fr Francis Moloney sdb, Dr Peter Price, Dr Anne O'Brien, Fr David Ranson. Any errors remain the responsibility of the authors.

Editorial

Ms Kate Ahearne for patiently assisting the authors in finalising the text.

RECOMMENDATIONS

This book is a MUST for the Catholic Church's leaders and educators. The authors correctly argue that "the Catholic school remains the only plausibility structure for faith that many young people and their parents encounter." Faith development programs of yesterday are ineffective because needs have dramatically changed. Our schools desperately call for imaginative mission-thinkers and practitioners, who understand the radically changed cultural school environment, and are able to create relevant transformative responses. If the insights of this book are not read and implemented our schools have no future as Catholic institutions.

> (Gerald A. Arbuckle, sm. Co-founder of the Re-founding and Development Unit Sydney, Author of many studies including Culture, Inculturation, and Theologians, 2011).

At a time when government funding policies are causing Catholic education system and school leaders to focus on the future economic prospects for Catholic schooling across Australia, Jim and Therese D'Orsa have written a book that represents the canary in the coal mine. In what they refer to as this liminal era, Catholic schooling faces new and serious risks to the integrity of its mission. This is a challenge that must engage all leaders in Catholic education if our schools are to be places where Jesus' message of the kingdom is a lived reality not a history lesson. What is required is leaders who are skilled not only in strategic and operational leadership but also in mission leadership which is the focus of this outstanding book. Mission leadership utilizes theological reflection to enhance mission thinking which assists Catholic school leaders to respond to the multi-dimensional challenges of secularisation. The book is both sophisticated and practical which has great appeal for Catholic school and system leaders who are seeking imaginative and thought-provoking ways to develop a sure-footedness in their leadership in these uncertain times. This is certainly a book for the times and all those who treasure the mission that engages the hearts and minds of Catholic educators/leaders in our efforts to create the Kingdom spaces which transform death dealing post-modern culture into life-giving God-giftedness.

> (Dr Cathy Day, Director of Catholic Education, Diocese of Townsville).

We live in a liminal time when the old certainties have been eroded and the new is yet not convincing. Teachers, parents and students are subject to many postmodern cultural forces. This book argues that evangelisation in this context is not just a matter of greater zeal or effort. We have to understand our culture and the powerful influence it has on us, mostly unconsciously. Jim and Therese D'Orsa give leaders insights and tools to make sense [meaning] of these times and to effectively hand on the faith to postmodern students. This book is excellent in clarifying contemporary missiological themes and ground-breaking in its emphasis on "meaning-making". It is an important addition to current missiological literature, and a good read.

>   (Noel Connolly SSC, Columban Mission Institute Sydney,
>   Formerly Vicar General of St. Columban's Mission Society).

In *Leading For Mission: Integrating Life, Culture and Faith* Jim and Therese D'Orsa, together with the other contributors, have given us a sterling account of a striking story, one of a never-ending journey of leadership for mission and vision. The reflection on the terrain which the Church, and particularly its educational mission, has traversed in this country leaves no room for complacency. The assessment of where we are now impels us to continually revise, renew and amend, our mission and our vision. This is because ours is a mission never finally achieved, but always remains the goal of pilgrimage, and of a vision both Spirit-filled and open to the realities of the world. Insightful, challenging, and constructive, this book is a "must-read" for those involved in today's Church, and especially for its leaders, and those responsible for the ever-adapting processes of Catholic education.

>   (Monsignor Tom Doyle, A.O. Former Director of Catholic
>   Education, Archdiocese of Melbourne).

THE BROKEN BAY INSTITUTE MISSION AND EDUCATION SERIES

The purpose of the Mission and Education Series is to explore aspects of contemporary Catholic education in the light of the Church's official teaching on mission, and of the experience of those who attempt to embrace this mission in their personal and professional lives.

The richness of the resources now at the disposal of those who seek to explore education theologically can come as a surprise. Because the faith held by the Catholic community is a living faith, Catholic Church teaching on mission has developed, and continues to develop, in the light of contemporary societal and cultural changes. Similarly, Scripture continues to yield its treasures. Only now, for example, is the Bible being widely recognised as a witness to God's purpose or mission in the created universe, and as an account of human response to the unfolding of that mission.

We live in a period of rapid cultural change driven by global dynamics. This has its impact on how we understand what knowledge is, how it is acquired, and how schools are best led and organised so as to maximise student learning and the economic and social benefits that are presumed to flow from sound educational policies. Very often the emphasis in such developments shifts from 'the learning student' to the more abstract concept of 'student learning'. This sits uneasily with the concept of a Catholic education.

The consequence of rapid societal change is that, in our time, new areas of mission present themselves with real urgency. It is now clearly necessary to include within the mission agenda both the processes of knowledge construction and meaning-making, and the modes of Christian participation in the new public space created by both globalisation and the communications media. These new areas of mission take their place alongside those fields already familiar to the faith community.

The Mission and Education Series seeks to bring together, in the one conversation, the light that human experience, culture and faith throw on particular topics now central to the future development of Catholic education. It also seeks to honour the significant efforts that Catholic educators make, on behalf of young people, to address the contemporary mission agendas within the total process of education. It provides a forum designed to stimulate further conversation about the 'what' and the 'how' of Catholic Education as a work of the Gospel in our complex society and culture.

It is the hope of the Mission and Education Editorial Board that Catholic educators, both in Australia and beyond, will view the series as an invitation to contribute their own creativity to this vital conversation.

Therese D'Orsa
Commissioning Editor
Mission and Education Series
Broken Bay Institute

Also in this series
Explorers, Guides and Meaning-makers: Mission Theology for Catholic Educators
Catholic Curriculum: A Mission to the Heart of Young People

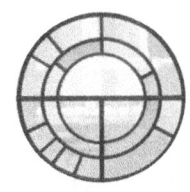

CONTENTS

INTRODUCTION

1 Leading for Mission — 1
Leading in a Liminal Era — 1
Determining the Contours of Mission Thinking — 5
Mission in Catholic School Systems: Generic and Contextual Understandings — 9
'Being Catholic'—Three Paradigms — 12
Leading for Mission — 13
Structure of the Book — 14

PART A
CATHOLIC EDUCATION AS SOCIAL DRAMA: NEGOTIATING LIMINALITY 16

Introduction to Part A

2 Leading for Mission in a Liminal Era — 19
The Experience of Liminality — 19
Common Responses to Leading in a Liminal Era — 21
Liminality and the Catholic School: Negotiating Change — 23
Mission and the Crisis of Liminality — 25
Leadership as a Ministry of Meaning-Making — 25

3 First Transition Era: From 'Schools for Catholics' to 'Catholic Schools' — 28
Mission Expands in Transition Eras — 28
Leading for Mission: The Foundation Era — 30
'Catholic Without Compromise' — 38
Reclaiming the Founding Mythology of Catholic Education — 42

4 Second Transition Era: Catholic Education in the late 20th Century — 46
Life within the 'Catholic Wall' — 47
The Approaching Storm: Catholic Life in the 1960s — 48
Life Beyond the Wall: Catholic Schooling in the 1960s and 1970s — 52
The Catholic Landscape after the Storm — 59

PART B
RESOURCES IN LEADING FOR MISSION: WISDOM OF OUR FAITH TRADITION 64

Introduction to Part B

5	**New Testament Leadership Heritages Emerge: The Suffering Servant**	**67**
	Emergence of Leadership Heritages	68
	Leadership in the Apostolic Era—the Challenge of Meaning-Making	71
	Servant Leadership as Eschatological and Cultural Ideal	78
6	**Leadership Heritages in Luke–Acts, Matthew and John**	**80**
	Leadership Tradition In Luke–Acts	81
	Leadership Tradition in the Gospel of Matthew	84
	Leadership Tradition in the Gospel of John	88
	Leadership in the New Testament Sources	92
7	**Mission as Integrating Agent in Catholic Education**	**95**
	Mission as a Religious Construct	95
	Recent Developments In Catholic Mission Theology	100
	Modalities of Mission	105
	Forms of Mission	107

PART C
RESOURCES IN LEADING FOR MISSION: WISDOM OF OUR CULTURAL TRADITION 111

Introduction to Part C

8	**What Leaders Need to Know About Culture: the Modern Construction**	**113**
	What Is Culture?	113
	Classicist View of Culture	115
	Modern Model of Culture	117
	Conceptualising Culture: Iceberg Model	121
	Culture in School and System Leadership	124
9	**What Leaders Need to Know About Culture: the Post-modern Construction**	**128**
	Working Models of Culture	128
	Post-modern Approach to Culture	131
	Theme and Counter-theme—Two Illustrations	133
	Changes in Cultural Configuration	135
	Theme and Counter-theme in New Testament Leadership Heritages	137
	Post-modern Model: Re-engaging with Pluralism	138

10	**The Leader as Meaning-Maker**	**142**
	Meaning-Making in a Liminal Era	142
	Personal Worldview and Its Role in Meaning-Making	143
	Public Worldviews	145
	How People Make Sense of Their Experiences	148

PART D
LEADING FOR MISSION: CONTEMPORARY PRACTICES AND PERSPECTIVES 155

Introduction to Part D

11	**Hermeneutics and the Mission of the Catholic School: ECSIP as a Case Study** (**Paul Sharkey**)	**158**
	Hermeneutics and Religion: Making Sense of Human Experience	159
	Post-Critical Belief	162
	Play and Dialogue in Meaning-making	165
	Hermeneutics: Between Strangeness and Familiarity	168
12	**Charismic Contributions in Liminal Times** (**Michael Green fms**)	**173**
	Liminality and the Church's Spiritual 'Families'	175
	Re-imagining Marist Life and Mission	180
	Conclusion	186
13	**A Ministry to Meaning-making and to the Imagination: Teaching Catholic System Leadership at ACU** (**Anne Benjamin and Michael Bezzina**)	**189**
	Evolution of the Master of Educational System Leadership	190
	Liminality in the Master of Educational System Leadership	193
	Complex Adaptive Systems Thinking	197
	Conclusion	200
14	**Models, Frameworks and Processes in School Improvement: A Case Study** (**Christopher Barrett**)	**203**
	NSW: a Unique Educational Culture	203
	CEO Sydney Model of School and System Improvement	205
	Incorporation of Evidence-based Approaches to Effectiveness	208
	Determining the Dimensions of Excellence in Catholic Schooling	212

PART E
LEADING FOR MISSION: PROCESSES AND PRIORITIES 217

Introduction to Part E

15 Evangelising the Culture of Catholic Schools and Systems   220
   Evangelisation in Catholic Discourse   220
   Sources of Secularisation   224
   Secularisation and Evangelisation   228
   Evangelising Cultures—Imperative in Leading for Mission   229

16 Doing Theology: A Process of Meaning-making   232
   Model for Doing Theology   233
   Process for Doing Theology   237

17 Securing Mission: The Enduring Challenge   244
   Recontextualising Mission   244
   Mission Thinking, Strategic Thinking, Operational Thinking   247
   Mission Thinking: Vital Elements   249

1
LEADING FOR MISSION

Catholic school and system leaders today face the daunting task of leading as Catholic education enters a new, and as yet undefined, era. The catalyst for the change of era is a fundamental shift in the way people see the world and the impact this is having on the relationships by which they define their life-world. Many taken-for-granted assumptions about what constitutes family, about our culture, about our faith community, and about our relationships to the natural world are under challenge, and people find this disconcerting.

The changes underway, driven by the media and developments in technology, impact on all levels of society, and bring about institutional responses that seek to address a pervasive sense of uncertainty and anxiety by seeking to control more and more of people's lives. The changes have a major impact on the culture in which we live, and so on how we make sense of the world. In a transition era many people perceive life as insecure—as having lost its moorings—because things that were once taken as givens now seem uncertain. As a consequence, they feel disoriented. Finally, the changes underway have their impact on how faith is understood and lived, even on how people now construe what it means 'to be Catholic'.

LEADING IN A LIMINAL ERA

As we discuss in Chapter two, anthropologists describe an historical period in which there is profound unease about the fundamental assumptions that hold a culture together as *a liminal period*, and the experience as that of 'liminality': of living in an 'in-between stage', or 'standing at a threshold'. In this liminal stage people are never clear about what the future will hold. Optimists live in the hope that things will improve, while others turn to various forms of escapism and even despair. Liminal periods contain catalysts for important new developments in a culture.

Leading in a liminal period is never easy, because meanings that were once taken for granted can no longer be assumed. In a liminal period the 'glue' that holds a community together can easily become unstuck because people lose their sense of purpose as meanings begin to change. At the school level, a community's sense of mission and identity—matters which were once unproblematic—now become contested. In such a situation, teachers can easily become unsettled and lose confidence in the worth of what they are doing, particularly as the use of institutional power becomes more pervasive. In a liminal period, being a top class operational thinker, or even a sound strategic thinker, is insufficient, because in most cases these forms of thinking assume and require that meaning is stable. A liminal period calls for *mission thinking* which places a premium on both meaning and on helping staff, parents and students make sense of what is happening in their world.

Negotiating transition periods in Catholic education

The history of Catholic education in this country indicates that it is no stranger to the experience of liminality. Its leaders have already negotiated two major liminal periods, both of which marked important turning points in its development. As today's leaders face an uncertain future, there is much to be learned from these earlier experiences.

Era 1: Schools for Catholics.[1]

The first transition period occurred in the 1870s when the bishops, dissatisfied at having to make major compromises about matters they saw as integral to Catholic schooling, walked away from a system of 'Schools for Catholics' funded by government and established independent Catholic school systems under the charge of religious congregations. The era of schools for Catholics had run for over half a century prior to this, and in that time hundreds of lay teachers had worked under the supervision of parish priests to educate young Catholics, often in very trying conditions.

Era 2: Era of the religious congregations.

The action of the bishops opened the way for a second era—*the era of the religious*—to commence, and this ran until roughly the mid-1960s, when it became clear that the Catholic schools could no longer respond to the demand for places posed by population growth. This second era was based on an assumption which was subsequently disproved: that the identity of the

---

1   This phrase is used of the schools which, during the first era of Catholic education, were established to cater predominantly (but not exclusively) for Catholics, but which functioned within the normal provision of schooling of that time. These schools were not separate from the schooling available to other children and were funded from the same sources. This was not to be the case in the era of the religious congregations.

Catholic school is dependent on the presence of religious. However, such was the success of the second period, and so deeply did the template of a Catholic school as *a school run by religious* find its place in the worldview of Catholics during that time, that Catholic identity had to be seriously re-negotiated in the transition period that heralded the arrival of a third era: *that of the educated lay Catholic leader.*

Era 3: Era of the educated lay Catholic leader.

This era began in the late 1960s when young lay women (and subsequently men) entered the teaching staff of Catholic primary schools in significant numbers after having been trained in Catholic teacher training colleges. The era continued until the mid-2000s, by which time Catholic education had been professionalised and institutionalised, and become the major avenue for lay ministry within the Catholic Church.

A transition period is usually brought to closure when what caused the underlying anxiety and uncertainty has been identified and addressed. The transition periods that preceded the second and third eras in Catholic education were characterised by a pervasive sense that something bearing on the Catholic identity of the Catholic school was becoming problematic. In both cases noted above (as we shall see later) this involved important developments in how the mission of the school was construed and how Catholic education was organised. Negotiating these transitions proved painful, as there is a human cost involved in expanding the framework from which Catholic education draws its meaning. This seems an unavoidable consequence of change, and something that contemporary leaders will soon have to face.

As the new millennium has unfolded, there is again clear evidence of the sense of unease that characterises transition periods. While the sources are multiple, much seems centred on the assumptions that different groups within the Church now hold about what it means 'to be Catholic'. System and Church leaders have responded to this development in a number of ways. For instance, the Brisbane Archdiocese sought to explore the matter in a wide-ranging research project called 'Who's Coming to School Today?' that was concerned to chart changes in the demography of the schools and the attitudes of parents and students.[2] The Catholic Education Commission of Victoria has joined forces with the Catholic University of Leuven, Belgium, to undertake a major project, the 'Enhancing Catholic School Identity Project' (ECSIP), which seeks to provide school leaders with solid data on

---

2   Report: *Who's Coming to School Today?*: Summary of Research Findings Catholic Education Office, Archdiocese of Brisbane, 2009. The research was conducted in collaboration with the Australian Centre for Educational Research (ACER).

the attitudes students and parents bring to Catholic schooling. The goal of the project is that the mission of the schools can be made more responsive to the actual faith situation of the school communities. In the absence of such an initiative, the belief of the Leuven academics driving this project, based on their own experience, is that Catholic schools in this country will gradually become secularised to the point that they lose their Catholic identity.[3] The bishops of New South Wales and the Australian Capital Territory (ACT) have sought to provide guidance to Catholic educators in the face of a pervasive anxiety about the Catholic identity of Catholic schools in their 2007 policy statement *Catholic Schools at a Crossroads*.[4]

What seems unique about the present transition period is *the range of factors that are converging* to produce and sustain a sense of anxiety and uncertainty. While some are peculiar to the Church at the present time, most result from the major cultural changes, and the impact of the megatrends now driving those changes. Among the factors that can be named are:

From the faith arena:

- the unstable nature of the Catholic community
- erosion of confidence in Church authority
- uncertainty among the parent body about what it means to be Catholic, and the impact this has on students' religious development
- the impact of pluralism within the community and the way this now plays out in educational policies and practices.
  From the cultural arena:
- changing aspirations of parents and teachers with respect to the outcomes of schooling
- pervasive loss of confidence in society about what can be taken as true and good.

Added to these general factors are other institutional factors which impact more specifically on the work of schools and educational systems, such as:

- rapid increase in government control over education exercised through statutory regulation and control of funding
- professionalisation of teaching and the transfer of teacher development from employing authorities to statutory bodies
- escalation of accountability provisions for the outcomes of schooling, often quite narrowly defined

---

3   Dr Paul Sharkey discusses this project in detail in Chapter 11.
4   Published by the bishops of NSW and the ACT August 2007, with the assistance of the Catholic Education Office Sydney.

- increased dependence of schools and systems on technology and the skewing of priorities that often accompanies the development and maintenance of technology systems.

All of the above factors now converge to render Catholic schools' contexts fraught with major organisational, educational, ethical and religious challenges.

In liminal periods meaning is at a premium

As we shall see later, anthropologists hold that, in the liminal period between cultural eras, meaning is always at a premium. In the eras of Catholic education referred to above, as meanings expanded, so too did the mission of the Catholic school. The experience has been that, when meaning and mission again more clearly coincide, then school communities gain added confidence in their own identity. A new set of understandings comes to be taken for granted, and with this the anxiety associated with always having to think things through decreases.

The real challenge of leading for mission in a liminal period is to help members of the school community make sense of the context in which teaching and learning occur so that what they are doing becomes more meaningful, and so has added significance for them.

This requires high quality mission thinking, and it is the contours of this thinking that we want to pursue in this book, calling on the resources available in the wisdom of our cultural and faith traditions, and the lived experience of leading for mission.

DETERMINING THE CONTOURS OF MISSION THINKING

Mission thinking, like its cousins operational thinking and strategic thinking, involves skills which leaders now have to master. Mission thinking requires a framework at the heart of which lies the leader's conception of mission. This understanding, of necessity, draws on both religious and secular sources. This introduces ambiguity, and the possibility of mission thinking becoming secularised. This possibility reflects the simple fact that Catholic school and system leaders work at the interface of the Church and society and so are influenced by the aspirations and demands each now make on schools. While there is much about the future shape of Catholic education that remains to be determined, what we do know is that, in order to go beyond the present transition period, there is need for a common project for which responsibility will have to be shared *across the whole Catholic community*.

What is at stake is the re-creation of the Catholic tradition in a qualitatively new context. This will require leaders—lay clerical and religious—to work and dialogue together, mindful of each other's gifts, experience and wisdom. A second necessary component is to construe mission in terms of Jesus' project of making present the Kingdom of God, or as Australian biblical scholar Francis Moloney suggests, 'the reigning presence of God'.[5] This presence has the power to transform the relationships that define a person's life-world—with God, family and friends, culture, faith community—and also the natural environment. Anything less than this re-creation will not take us where we must go in the coming era of Catholic education. *A mission framework embracing both these elements calls for serious renewal.*

Mission thinking is not for the faint-hearted. It is complex because terms like mission, that have explanatory power, tend to be overused almost to the point of incomprehensibility. It is here that missiology, which is vitally concerned with the interplay of faith and culture, has an important contribution to make to the contemporary concerns of Catholic school and system leaders.

Cultural construction of mission

The cultural construction of mission is associated with the ideas of 'purpose' and 'direction'. The common understanding is that the leaders of a group need to define *the preferred future* of the group and so determine in which directions the group needs to move, so as to make this preferred future a reality. Secondly, the leader needs to establish the criteria by which decisions about 'directions' are to be determined. The 'preferred future' constitutes 'the vision' of the organisation, and the criteria used in determining directions are the group's 'values'. Vision and values play an important role in determining the purpose or mission of the group. Groups then seek to articulate and communicate their mission in terms of a 'mission statement'. This statement is meant to convey to constituents the *aspirations of the organisation and the directions in which it seeks to move.* A mission statement is the expressed outcome of the group's mission thinking.[6]

---

5   This is an alternative wording for the phrase used by Jesus to describe his mission commonly translated as 'Kingdom of God' or 'reign of God'. See Francis Moloney *Mark: Storyteller, Interpreter, Evangelist* (Peabody Massachusetts: Hendrickson, 2004), 126. In the view of some scholars, this wording captures the dynamism of Jesus' image better than do the alternatives.

6   The above way of construing 'mission' was popularised in the early 1980s by organisational consultant, Gerard Egan. Egan, a priest of the Chicago diocese and adjunct professor of Loyola University in Chicago, is also well known for his work on counselling. Now in its ninth edition, with a tenth about to be released, his book *The Skilled Helper: A Problem-Management and Opportunity-Development Approach to Helping* (Belmont: Brooks/Cole Cengage Learning, 2010) is regarded as a seminal work in the field.

Religious constructions of mission: two paradigms

The religious construction of mission has a long history within Catholicism. At present there are two competing paradigms of mission in official Catholic thinking. Each has validity and complements the other.

'Mission' is what the Church does.

In the first paradigm, mission is understood in terms of 'what the Church does'. Used in this sense, the paradigm holds that *God's Church has a mission*. This understanding of 'mission' is framed in terms of the 'mission command' found in Matthew 28:18–19. Here, the Gospel writer concludes his reflection on the life of Jesus by having Jesus, depicted as the new Moses, exhort his community as follows:

All authority in heaven and on earth has been given to me. Go therefore and make disciples of all nations, baptizing them in the name of the Father and of the Son and of the Holy Spirit, and teaching them to obey everything that I have commanded you. And remember, I am with you always, to the end of the age.

While all four Gospel writers include a post-resurrection 'mission command' in their account of Jesus' life,[7] this one has been the most influential in determining the meaning of 'mission' within the Christian tradition, and in many ways has come to define the essential 'mission' of the Church. As a consequence, 'mission' is often understood as proclaiming and being a witness to the message of Jesus with the ultimate aim of building up the Church. Used in this way, 'mission' can become synonymous with what the official Church does in spreading the Gospel to peoples who have not heard it (or in the case of the 'new evangelisation' re-proclaiming it to those who have heard it but have ceased to be influenced by what they have heard). Under this paradigm, the official Church 'commissions' people, that is, it sends people out 'on mission' and so legitimises it.[8] This way of interpreting mission, at least in the Catholic tradition, results in mission being taken for granted at the local level as 'what Church professionals do'. This is unsatisfactory in today's context and, as we shall see in Chapter 7, does not of itself fully do justice to the recent magisterial teachings on mission which guide the Church community.

---

7   Matt 28:18–20; Mk 16:15–16; Lk 24:47–49; Jn 20:21–23.
8   The idea of a 'new evangelisation' currently receiving much official attention within the Church is often presented within this frame of reference. For a discussion of what Pope Paul VI calls a 'partial and fragmentary' approach to evangelisation, as opposed to an approach embracing 'all its essential elements', see *Evangelii Nuntiandi* #17 and ff.

'Mission' is what God does.

The alternative paradigm construes 'mission' in more expansive terms. 'Mission' is understood as God's action in time which begins within the very life of God, flows forth in creation, and is ongoing across the entire universe. The Church's role in this conception is to be the community of Jesus' disciples who are intentionally at the service of God's mission in time as this mission has been revealed firstly in the Old Testament, and most definitively in the mission of Jesus as depicted in the Gospels. The central motif in this view is Jesus' proclamation of, and witness to, the coming of the Kingdom of God. The Kingdom embodies a preferred future for all of creation. The mission of Jesus, carried on by faith communities, is to put in place conditions for human existence consistent with the Kingdom present in time, by giving specific meaning and witness to what the 'coming of God's Kingdom' looks like in particular contexts. In this paradigm of mission meaning-making becomes an integral part of Christian leadership.[9]

In Jesus' teaching, the Kingdom of God has both a temporal and an eschatological dimension. It can never be fully realised within time, and so presents a continuous challenge to the human imagination. Jesus' life and mission set the trajectory for any authentic Christian understanding of what 'making the Kingdom of God present in time' means. As human contexts change, it invites us to continually think about what the 'preferred future' which God has in mind for creation might be. Jesus' teaching also spells out clearly the values which guide decisions that need to be taken to move society and culture in 'Kingdom directions'. Rather than focussing the mission in the first instance on the Church, this paradigm suggests that *God's mission has a Church*. The Church is a community of disciples, and also an institution, at the service of God's mission, and therefore at the service of those who make God's Kingdom come in all the sets of relationships which constitute human life.

The Kingdom and the Church are integrally interrelated. As Pope John Paul II clarifies:

> ... *one may not separate the kingdom from the Church. It is true that the Church is not an end unto herself, since she is ordered toward the Kingdom of God of which she is the seed, sign and instrument. Yet, while remaining distinct from Christ and the kingdom, the Church is indissolubly united to both. Christ endowed the Church, his body, with the fullness of the benefits and means of salvation.*[10]

---

9   For a discussion pertaining to the two paradigms above see Stephen Bevans & Roger Schroeder *Constants in Context* (Maryknoll, N.Y: Orbis, 2004), 396–398 et al, and also Stephen Bevans 'The Mission has a Church: the Mission has Ministers: Thinking Missiologically about Ministry and the Shortage of Priests' *Compass* Vol 43, No 3, 2009, 314.
10   Pope John Paul II in *Redemptoris Missio* (1990) #18.

Nevertheless, God's action occurs both within and beyond the Church. As a consequence, in fulfilling its mission, the Church has to be sensitive to the many ways in which God is at work in the world, and the ways in which the Church community can be at the service of God's action. The Church is of its nature a sacrament of the Kingdom.[11] It both points to the Kingdom and makes it present. Being at the service of mission commits the Church community to discernment and dialogue both within the community and with the wider world. In this understanding, 'mission' has multiple dimensions. It addresses the *quality of life within the faith community* and *the condition of life for all of God's creation*. This is one reason why the Church sees Catholic education as integral to its mission. The Catholic school links the Church with the wider world in a variety of ways.

MISSION IN CATHOLIC SCHOOL SYSTEMS: GENERIC AND CONTEXTUAL UNDERSTANDINGS

Some Catholic educational leaders see mission in *generic* terms, others see it in *contextual* terms. Both of these understandings have a pedigree in Catholic teaching. They can usefully be thought of as 'ideal types' rather than clear-cut descriptions of life 'on the ground'. As such they serve to throw important leadership issues into clearer relief.

Mission: generic understanding

In the generic perspective, all Catholic schools have essentially the same mission. This is usually understood as helping the students to 'integrate faith, life and culture' as set down in *The Catholic School* (1977)[12] and repeated in all subsequent documents on Catholic schooling from the Congregation for Catholic Education. This understanding often results in mission becoming a taken-for-granted aspect of Catholic schooling and, partly in consequence, important questions remain unanswered. For instance: What do we mean by 'integrate'? What assumptions sit behind this meaning? Are they valid? What do we mean by 'culture'? What understanding of 'faith' is embodied in this generic construction of mission?

The generic construction often carries within it a large number of unstated pre-suppositions that are rarely acknowledged, let alone critically explored.[13] When mission is given taken-for-granted status, the thinking of

---

11   For an historically influential discussion of Church as sacrament see Avery Dulles S.J. *Models of the Church* (Dublin: Gill and Macmillan, 1976), 58–70.
12   Congregation for Catholic Education 1977 *The Catholic School* #41.
13   Vatican documents on Catholic education use the term 'culture' with a variety of meanings and it is left to the reader to determine which is which. This is not uncommon in other Church

school leaders focuses on operational and strategic concerns. As we will argue later, this opens the way for the rapid secularisation of the Catholic school or school system.

The generic understanding of mission is often employed by Catholic school system authorities to set priorities for schools. The school then develops its mission directions with respect to these. System leaders devise various processes, often referred to as 'system processes', to monitor outcomes and make interventions with respect to an agenda that is centrally-directed but locally-adopted and implemented. Career structures are developed to support and reinforce these arrangements. This model is often based on the unstated belief that the system has a mission in which schools participate.

Mission: contextual understanding

A second approach construes mission in contextual terms. The mission of the school in this perspective is formulated as a response to needs that arise within a specific educational community, living in a particular environment, at a particular time. Mission thinking requires knowledge of the community and the needs of members, which implies the need for dialogue with them. It also requires some understanding of the social, cultural and ecclesial environments, the times in which people live, and how they understand and relate to these. The aim of 'integrating faith, life and culture' takes on a localised meaning. Criteria based on shared values have to be devised to guide discernment so that decisions can be made and priorities assigned. The result is that mission is often articulated in terms of 'directions to be pursued'. These are then accepted by all participants as aligned to the aspirations and needs of a community, and thus underpinning the mutual commitments that bind the community together. Because the process of articulating the mission of the school *is dialogical, it is also educational.* As such it becomes an exercise in community-building.[14]

The role of a central office in this model is to facilitate the work of school leaders in *community-building* by helping the individual school communities identify the shared values that underpin group life and the shared aspirations that enable the group to set common goals, thus to negotiate the commitments

---

documents as Catholic anthropologist Gerard Arbuckle has pointed out. See Gerald Arbuckle *Culture, Inculturation & Theologians: A Post-Modern Critique* (Collegeville Minnesota: Liturgical Press, 2010), 139ff. See also the discussion in Jim and Therese D'Orsa *Catholic Curriculum: a Mission to the Heart of Young People* (Mulgrave: Garratt Publishing, 2012), 88–100.
14   A helpful discussion on the nature of community can be found in Evelyn and James Whitehead *Community of Faith: Strategies for Developing Christian Communities* (Minneapolis: The Winston Seabury Press, 1982), 49–60. The Whiteheads argue that a community is a group of people held together by shared values, common goals and mutual commitments. The values shared by members of a Catholic school community may be sourced in faith, in culture or in both.

needed to meet those goals. A second aspect of the role is to work with the community to explore how it will *hold itself accountable* for meeting its commitments. The central office also plays a third role, that of *critical friend* seeking to lift the level of local aspiration so as to set challenging goals. This aspect of the role often needs to be prophetic, involving advocacy for the marginalised whose voice may otherwise not be heard.

The mission agenda in the contextualised model is locally-directed and centrally-supported. Mission is advanced by ongoing central office–local school dialogue. A contextual approach to mission acknowledges that mission has to be continually re-formulated as contexts change.

Mission in a liminal era

Leadership today requires a level and quality of thinking that is often new, and always demanding. This is because, as societies become more complex and interconnected, many once taken-for-granted 'truths' simply no longer hold. As a consequence, people are losing confidence in the meaning-systems that once anchored their lives. While this is certainly true of religion, increasingly it is true of culture as well. It is no simple matter to lead others when the meaning systems by which they make sense of their lives are contested or in transition. We are rapidly losing contact with many certainties once taken for granted, and find it hard to live with the uncertainties of the post-modern world.

The Second Vatican Council brought the Catholic Church into a new relationship with the modern world just as the modern world was yielding ground to the post-modern. The gap between faith and post-modern culture has been widened by the abuse scandals that have seriously undermined the confidence of Catholics in the Church as institution, and in its institutional leaders. Within the context of this prevailing climate, the Catholic school rather than the Catholic parish, remains, as has been the case for some time, the major point of contact between the institution and many of the faithful, and with this situation come new responsibilities.

Leadership in Catholic schools and systems now mirrors the situation in many other service agencies. Leadership is becoming more diverse and diffuse as it is shared across various levels of operation. Expectations about the technical competence required of school leaders in operational and strategic thinking have risen sharply as a result. However, there seem to have been no equivalent demands for technical competence in mission thinking.

The leadership of Catholic organisations today is also complex because of the different ways in which people understand what it means to be 'Catholic'.

'BEING CATHOLIC'—THREE PARADIGMS

In our experience of working with school communities, and of accessing a variety of literature related to Catholic education, the term 'Catholic' is today used in three principal ways.

'Catholic' as marker of institutional identity

Common usage interprets 'Catholic' as *a marker of institutional identity*. The hierarchy and clergy, as authoritative voices within the Catholic community, rightly seek to preserve this identity. 'Catholic' used in this sense operates across a spectrum of meanings. Interpreted in a quite narrow way, the institutional usage can be compared to that of a franchise in which strict conditions are applied as to who can claim the name 'Catholic'. On the other hand, used in a quite broad way, it can refer to all the officially sanctioned actions of Catholics. The meaning which the term 'Catholic' has for the formal bodies that make up the institution, such as Catholic schools and Catholic Education offices, seems to lie somewhere between these two limits, as determined by the local bishops.

There is an inherent tension between 'Catholic' understood as 'institution' and Catholic understood as 'community of faith'. In the broader culture people do not trust institutions because they are seen as self-serving. However, in the Church it is the existence of the institution that has provided the conditions needed for communities of faith to come into and remain in existence. It is a question of both/and rather than either/or.

'Catholic' as marker of personal identity

As membership of the Catholic community has become more diverse, the term 'Catholic' is now used as *a marker of personal identity*. Many people today identify themselves as 'Catholic' without much reference to the institution or even to a community. This designation is now used by the majority of parents supporting Catholic schools and, by extension, the young people who attend the schools. The parents' connection to the school community is often their one remaining connection to the institutional Church. The irony in many dioceses is that the loyal support of this group makes the existence of Catholic schools and systems possible. The majority of the group see 'being Catholic' as something that they can opt into, or out of, several times during a life journey without this compromising an underlying commitment to 'the Church' and what they see as the 'values of Jesus' which they wish to nurture in their homes. While institutional Catholics see such a position as untenable, it is the reality with which school and system leaders have to work.

'Catholic' as marker of communal identity

The position the Catholic school holds within the Catholic community, broadly considered, means that it is capable of bridging the gap that often exists between the institution and the individual. Schools attempt to do this by introducing and re-introducing Catholics living in the fragmented post-modern world to the experience of community.

Catholic educational policy in regard to Catholic children is that schools be inclusive rather than exclusive, on the grounds that all have a right to education and that the Gospel should be available to all.[15] While we may not yet know precisely what lies beyond the post-modern period, inclusiveness is most likely to characterise schools in the fourth era of Catholic education. The emerging leadership challenge for school and system leaders lies in knowing how to address the needs of Catholics with quite different understandings of what 'being Catholic' means.

LEADING FOR MISSION

The idea of leadership evokes notions of how leaders manage their interactions with colleagues in order to influence them. They seek to do this in a way that strengthens the organisation by achieving goals that contribute to its mission and to the growth and development of all involved.[16] 'Leading for mission' gives a particular orientation to this definition. It is a form of leadership that seeks to influence colleagues *by highlighting the significance of what they do, in the process of affirming who they are, and so lifting their level of aspiration.* Leading for mission in Catholic educating communities involves engaging colleagues, transforming outlooks, and sustaining the efforts that bring the reign of God into being in a particular place and time.

While school and system leadership share much in common, they also differ in significant ways. Defining the 'preferred future' for a system is quite a different task from determining it for a school. As we have noted above, the relationship between system and school can be construed in multiple ways, and this has important consequences for the culture of the school system.

The mission of a system has regard not only for the schools and their sustainability, but also for the teachers and school leaders who live out their

---

15   E.g. Vatican II's *Declaration on Christian Education* (1965) and the *Congregation for Catholic Education's Catholic Schools on the Threshold of the Third Millennium* (1997). Local bishops and other Catholic educational authorities interpret these documents in terms of the availability of places in Catholic schools. *The Declaration on Christian Education* interprets the Church's responsibility even more widely than the Catholic community, on the basis that education is a human right and should be available to all.

16   This conception of leadership is more fully developed by James Kouzes and Barry Posner in *The Leadership Challenge* (4th ed.) (San Francisco: John Wiley and Sons, 2007).

careers in the context of the school system. System goals, more so than school goals, are tied to those of the institutional Church which sponsors the schools as 'Catholic'; to those of the government which sponsors schools as 'schools'; and to those parents who, as clients, also sponsor Catholic schools. Balancing the multiple, and sometimes contradictory, demands of these sponsoring bodies is challenging enough in stable times, but extremely complex in a liminal era such as exists at the present time. If school leaders have to be meaning-makers, then so too do system leaders. Both groups face a common challenge with regard to how this is best done.

Our contention is that theological reflection, the process of 'doing theology', is essential to meaning-making in a Catholic school system, and so is a key skill in mission thinking. Put simply, 'doing theology' involves taking human experience seriously and interpreting it meaningfully in terms of the wisdom of our culture and that of our faith tradition. It is a skill that needs to be reclaimed by leaders. The methodology of this book seeks 'to model the message' with regard to theological reflection.

STRUCTURE OF THE BOOK

Following this introduction, *Leading for Mission: Integrating Life, Culture and Faith in Catholic Education,* unfolds in five sections. In Part A we explore human experience as a resource in leading for mission, borrowing the concept of social drama from anthropology. Chapter 2 explores the experience of liminality. Chapters 3 and 4 examine the social dramas that unfolded as Catholic leaders negotiated the transition processes associated with earlier eras of Catholic education. The focus here is on the wisdom generated through these experiences. In this respect leading for mission has an impressive Australian heritage.

In Part B the focus is on what the wisdom of our faith tradition has to say about leading for mission. The chapters in this section address core religious constructs in leading for mission. Our experience has been that many Catholic leaders have quite naïve ideas about concepts such as 'culture' and 'mission', and have little sense of the Scriptural foundations on which Christian leadership stands. Chapters 5 and 6 deal with the emergence of leadership heritages in the New Testament, and Chapter 7 looks at key understandings of mission as these have evolved in the official teaching of the Church since Vatican II.

Part C seeks to access the wisdom of our cultural tradition in addressing the challenges of leading for mission by exploring competing conceptions of culture and the process of meaning-making. The section draws heavily on the fields of cultural anthropology and hermeneutics. Chapters 8 and 9 outline two understandings of culture: the one modern and the other post-modern. Chapter 10 introduces readers to hermeneutics and the process by which people customarily make meaning in their lives.

If the aim of Catholic education is to integrate faith, life, and culture, then the question is: how is this being done in our Catholic systems today? Part D explores current practice. Here a number of contributors offer reflections based on particular experiences of leading for mission. In successive chapters Paul Sharkey reports on a major project sponsored by the Catholic University of Leuven and the Victorian Catholic Education Commission which seeks to re-contextualise the mission of the schools as a response to the present challenges of liminality; Br Michael Green presents the interpretation Marist Brothers place on leading for mission in liminal times; Anne Benjamin and Michael Bezzina outline how the Australian Catholic University is preparing school and system leaders to address the contemporary challenges; and Chris Barrett looks at the way in which leadership for mission was managed in the Archdiocese of Sydney under the leadership of Br Kelvin Canavan.

The final section of the book, Part E, draws the conversation to a close by posing these questions:

- What is the 'heart of the matter' when it comes to leading for mission as the Church embarks on the fourth era of Catholic education?
- How do we best respond in leading for mission?

Discussion here focuses on priorities, frameworks and processes. Chapter 15 examines the nature of the evangelisation–secularisation tension at work in the life of all Catholic schools and school systems. Chapter 16 outlines a specific model of theological reflection for use in leading for mission. Chapter 17 draws the themes of the study together, exploring the relationship between mission thinking, strategic thinking, and operational thinking; and concludes by outlining the characteristics of mission thinking.

Part A
CATHOLIC EDUCATION AS SOCIAL DRAMA:
Negotiating liminality

The aim in theological reflection is to bring the wisdom of faith, of culture, and of human experience into 'conversation' in exploring an issue. In the present study the issue is 'leading for mission'.

Mission is a complex idea in Catholic education, one which has undergone major reformulation in Australia as eras have changed. In this section we focus on how this has occurred. In the chapters that follow we explore what can be learned about the way in which those responsible for Catholic education have exercised leadership during two such changes of era. We begin by exploring the concept of liminality as proposed in anthropology (Chapter 2), and then consider two major crises Catholic educators have faced historically (Chapters 3 and 4).

Anthropologists identify liminality as a stage in the process of major cultural change which begins when an important aspect of culture, one that has had taken-for-granted status up to that time, starts to be questioned. Since the taken-for-granted aspects of culture operate outside of awareness, the impending changes first surface as a pervasive sense of unease, a sense that all is not well, which is often felt before it is consciously acknowledged. Once this sense of unease is acknowledged, a crisis arises within the community as various interest groups seek to impose on the emerging situation competing interpretations as to what is happening, and what they see should be happening. Communities have characteristic ways of responding to such crises, some of which resolve them and others of which only deepen them. Anthropologists refer to the set of events that unfold in any major cultural change as a 'social drama'.

In a liminal period, meanings and norms come under scrutiny. The social drama unfolds as various groups strive for influence, thereby creating internal tensions that have to be resolved by some form of redressive action. The narrative of how this drama unfolds becomes part of the mythology of group life, an integral aspect of its culture. Social dramas and the cultural changes that they introduce play a key role in *the renewal of culture*. How major social dramas are handled by a group becomes a defining element in the wisdom of the group. When a community has negotiated major cultural change well, it develops a certain resilience and confidence in facing new challenges.

Our essential argument in applying this anthropological construct to the Catholic Church is that Australian Catholic education has already passed through three major eras, and is on the cusp of a fourth. A social drama has played out each time there has been a change of era and, *each time, the mission of the Catholic school has had to be reformulated*. Thus, exploring the process by which change has occurred is important in any study concerned with leading for mission.

Catholic educators are currently caught up in a further change of era and have much to learn from how earlier social dramas have unfolded. The narrative of these changes is both a *legacy* and a *resource* that we ignore at our peril.

The first era of Catholic education was that of 'schools for Catholics' funded by government and staffed by lay people. An interpretive narrative of the drama which saw the shift from this first era to the second, the era of the religious, is set out in Chapter 3.

Beginning in the late 1950s, and continuing for nearly thirty years, another social drama began to unfold. In this transition period a number of factors converged to bring about a second major change in Catholic education. The 'era of the Catholic lay teacher' had arrived, not as a decision of bishops as in the first era, but as the result of major changes in the Australian Church and in Australian society, and with the help of governments, Commonwealth and State. The mission of the Catholic school had to be reformulated to accommodate these facts. That it was negotiated successfully is a measure of the resilience of Catholic education in this country. An interpretation of these responses is given in Chapter 4.

The process of change did not stop with the 1980s. The post-modern turn began in the mid-1970s and has gained pace in the Western world since that time. This has combined with a new form of globalisation to create an ideational milieu which challenges many of the taken-for-granted assumptions on which religious truth is based. It is a cultural development that impacts on faith development.

The impact of post-modern thought and the advent of a multi-cultural multi-faith Australia have created a new environment for faith, so that Catholic education is now challenged to respond to the demands of living in this environment. What the new era will be called is yet to be determined, but we are caught up in the sense of unease which heralds an impending social drama.

The experience of having successfully negotiated the dramas associated with earlier changes of era encourages us to believe that God's grace and power will be with us in negotiating what lies ahead. There seems little doubt that the mission of the Catholic school will have to be refined to meet the new situation, so leading for mission will take on new meaning and new responsibilities. This is what we want to explore in the chapters ahead. Our immediate aim in Part A is to base this exploration solidly in Australian Catholic experience. What wisdom does this experience offer? That is the question examined in the next three chapters.

2
LEADING FOR MISSION IN A LIMINAL ERA

Educational leaders today function in the confusion of a liminal era. This confusion is the result of the large shift in human consciousness impacted by globalisation and its allied phenomena: secularisation and pluralisation. These are invading all aspects of human life and radically affecting people's understanding about what it means to be human. The situation is not helped by the fact that many Catholic school leaders simply do not understand these mega-phenomena.

One of the essential functions of schooling is the transmission of culture from one generation to the next. Schooling takes on an added degree of complexity when cultures are in a state of flux. Even so, society expects educators to 'read the signs of the times' and respond in a way that best serves the interests of their students. In our present situation of liminality, this means that educators can easily become the victims of the messianic hopes held by the school's sponsoring bodies and its clientele. At the government level the hope is that schooling can somehow promote economic growth and redress youth unemployment; at the Church level it is that Catholic schools should somehow redress the falling numbers attending Sunday Mass; at the parent level it is that students will acquire values and attitudes that often run counter to the ones they experience in their own homes. In such circumstances leadership is bound to be very demanding. In contrast to stable times when mission is more clearly a given, in a liminal period effective school leadership requires sound thinking about the school's mission. Commitment to quality mission thinking is the *sine qua non* of the kind of leadership the times demand.

THE EXPERIENCE OF LIMINALITY

To speak of a 'liminal era' is to invoke the language of anthropology. The word 'liminal' was famously introduced by British anthropologist, Victor

Turner, to describe the situation of young men during initiation rituals.[17] Turner describes tribal rituals during which a young man enters a 'liminal' stage in which he is no longer a child, neither is he an adult. The young men involved live in an 'in-between state', standing on the threshold of adult life.[18] While there may be excitement at moving forward, there is also sadness at what is being left behind, so *grieving is part of the ritual*.

The concept is also employed by Catholic cultural anthropologist, Gerald Arbuckle to describe a range of 'threshold experiences' that are part and parcel of the 'social drama' which accompanies major cultural change as this is experienced by individuals, organisations or whole peoples. Thus he writes:

> *In the ... liminality phase, a culture feels both attracted by the security of the past and the call to face the future. It is a period of sometimes anxious reflection, a search into mythological roots to obtain a sense of identity and self-worth. This can lead to outbursts of localized, excessive nationalism or delusions of grandeur, a widespread repression or denial of the realities of loss. This is a risky time because the temptation is for the culture or organization to cling tenaciously to what has been lost and simply refuse to face the future; the group can initiate a spectacular project that is totally out of touch with reality.*[19]

The experience of liminality marks a stressful stage in the 'social drama' brought about by cultural change. While there is a certain level of excitement at the call of the future, there is also the sense of loss at what is being left behind. If an incapacity to deal with loss generates tensions, *it also releases the creative energy needed to bring about change*. Liminal periods are times for decision. This is because they are filled with an anxiety which is experienced as a crisis of meaning, and this demands decision because the stresses involved are such that people cannot live with them for long periods.

As globalisation has advanced, both religious and cultural leaders have found themselves caught up in a 'threshold experience'. Few seem clear about what a globalised world will look like, but all know beyond doubt that they are being projected, willingly or not, into that world. People grieve for a simpler age now lost. They know there can be no return to that age, but lack rituals that enable their grief to be expressed symbolically. Because

---

17 Victor Turner *The Ritual Process: Structure and Anti-Structure* was first published in 1969, and is now regarded as a classic in the field. For a discussion of Turner's analysis of ritual see Gerald Arbuckle *Culture, Inculturation and the Theologians: A Post-Modern Critique* (Collegeville, Minnesota: Liturgical Press, 2010), 90ff.
18 This usage is employed in psychoanalytic theory to describe the twilight state between being awake and dreaming. People here are said to be in a 'liminal state'—on the threshold of a dream.
19 Gerald Arbuckle *Refounding the Church* (Homebush NSW: St Paul's Publications, 1993), 183.

of this, necessary change is postponed or subverted. We see this pattern of alternate excitement and grief in schools, in the Church and in society, as older values and practices lose their salience, and new cultural and religious trends emerge. The anxiety that is associated with a liminal era generates the need to respond creatively or, alternatively, to retreat.

A liminal era presents a particular challenge for those entrusted with the education of the young since, by the nature of their work, they have to be forward-looking. Educators today are preparing young people to live in a world that lies largely outside their imagination and possibly their comprehension as well. Realising this, governments now seek to exercise more and more control over the education process as if they, rather than educators, have the imagination and foresight to know what is needed. In many respects schooling is being 'teacher-proofed' as a consequence of government policies.

Educators have to manoeuvre around this obstruction and monitor the competing currents of thought that are now shaping the emerging globalised world. Furthermore, they are charged with the creative task of discerning the implications—intellectual, social and religious—that the situation has for the immediate tasks of leading school communities and framing the education of young people. How school and system leaders engage with these tasks shapes in large measure how they understand the mission of their school or system.

COMMON RESPONSES TO LEADING IN A LIMINAL ERA

In summary then, in a liminal era people are caught in a kind of no-man's-land, an in-between state, living between 'what was' and 'what will be', uncertain about how to move, excited but also grieving. Leaders respond to this situation in four characteristic ways.[20]

Denial

The first approach is simply to ignore what is happening and the need to make sense of it, by adopting a 'business as usual' approach and so maintaining what has been. Another form of the denial response is to launch a 'grand project' to deflect attention away from the realities of the present situation. This strategy is a favourite of governments. The three remaining approaches accept the need for change but make sense of the situation and respond to it within different sets of beliefs.

---

20 The discussion which follows acknowledges the inspiration provided in Chapter 7 'Denial, Grieving and Leadership' in Arbuckle, 1993, 180–200.

Traditionalist

People taking a traditionalist stance make sense of the situation of liminality by 'canonising the past'. 'What was' provides the key criteria in determining 'what will be'. In this approach tradition is valued, but the conception of it is essentially static and therefore inadequate. While it is essential to conserve the essence of a community's tradition if the community is to survive, the traditionalist approach often allows for the preservation of *only one version of a tradition*. The leader's understanding of the tradition becomes interpreted as 'the tradition'. Obviously, this approach is problematic when dealing with a living tradition, or with a plural tradition. The traditionalist approach suppresses any need to grieve for what is lost through change, because change is so highly controlled that little seems actually to be lost.

Critical

The critical approach adopts an iconoclastic stance to the tradition. The present is seen as owing little to the past, and the future even less still. A leader operating from a critical perspective interprets a liminal era as *one in which a point of discontinuity has been reached,* one in which 'what was' no longer provides the model for 'what is' or 'what needs to be'. The leader is therefore free to choose his or her own course in a tradition-free space. However, the problem is that colleagues are also free to choose their own course in this space, so the exercise of leadership comes to hinge on how power is used and how power-bases are constructed.

Human history provides many examples of this dynamic at work. The prophetic tradition in the Bible, essentially a voice from the margins, is steeped in the critical approach, its strength deriving from the fact that the words of the true prophet were legitimised as 'a word from the Lord'. The post-modern perspective is another example of the critical approach. It critiques the use of power in society but, unlike the prophetic tradition, does so without offering solutions that enable movement beyond the experience of liminality; rather, *it asserts that liminality is a permanent state of affairs.*

Transformative

A fourth approach makes sense of the liminal situation by holding that there can be continuity between the past and the future because people past and present share a common narrative. However, as contexts change, new values—or new perspectives on perennial values—emerge, and older ones are subsumed into them. Change, therefore, needs to occur as part of a consciously designed process in which action and reflection interact. The tradition—cultural or religious—is valued as a 'living tradition', one in which the narrative is continuously reinterpreted. The transformative approach allows change to occur in the depth dimensions of the culture. This leads, in turn, to major reshaping at the surface level. 'How things are done around here' can undergo significant change as creative responses are made to the emergence of new needs. However, the past is not forgotten; it is seen as an earlier chapter in an ongoing story that values, includes and makes sense of the group's collective experience without being confined to a single interpretation of that experience. Understanding the tradition as 'living' is transformative because it permits grieving over loss, while legitimating change. Rituals of loss are seen as important aspects of the transformation process.

In almost any community today, consciously or sub-consciously, people hold one or other of these four positions, sometimes oscillating between them. In an educational community this produces tension and a good deal of confusion, and it is this that makes the leadership of schools and school systems increasingly demanding.

The dilemma for educational leaders is that there is some substance in all four positions. There are situations in which denial is a wise response, generally however only as a delaying tactic while greater readiness is established. The traditionalist position makes sense of life in terms of protecting *enduring values*. The transformative perspective sees *communal life as lived within an ongoing narrative* in which outlooks and attitudes evolve as contexts change and the narrative unfolds. It is an experience of loss and gain. The critical perspective highlights the way in which *culture marginalises some people at the expense of others* and focuses on the injustice of this situation without necessarily being able to suggest a remedy. Difficulties arise, however, because people holding these positions have, quite legitimately, different expectations of what a school or a school system can achieve.

LIMINALITY AND THE CATHOLIC SCHOOL: NEGOTIATING CHANGE

If the situation is confusing at the cultural level, it is no less so at the ecclesial level, since the factors which shape people's thinking about cultural issues also impact on their thinking about religion and religious faith, and the place these occupy in their personal and collective lives. An older Catholic culture, as a 'Catholic plan for living', has substantially collapsed as the context in which Catholics live has changed. As a result, Catholics now hold the equivalent of the four responses identified above—denial, traditionalist, critical, and transformative—about this situation. While these outlooks represent a legitimate pluralism within the faith community, such pluralism is experienced as something new in many communities, and there are few forums in which these differences in perspective can be addressed through meaningful dialogue. There seems even less scope for dealing with the grief that accompanies what people experience as real change. This adds to the current crisis within the Catholic culture.

Negotiating liminality

The experience of liminality is certainly not new to Catholic education in Australia. Catholic educational leaders faced and negotiated major crises in the late 1960s in NSW, and nation-wide in the early 1970s. There is a good deal to be learned from how these crises were handled. These are interesting periods in the narrative of Catholic school and system leadership in this country. In many senses the way in which they were negotiated has provided the pattern for the evolution of the two system cultures that have characterised Catholic school education in this country: the models adopted by Sydney and Melbourne. These are used with various adaptations elsewhere.

While Catholic leaders similarly face liminality today, the cause and scope of the contemporary situation are quite different from earlier experiences. Church leaders today are presented with the fact that Catholics in significant numbers are now ceasing to 'practise', and this raises doubts about the grasp which the school's clientele has on Christian faith. The sociological changes behind this are little understood, neither are the global factors cited previously. However, both have significant consequences for the leadership of Catholic schools and the place of these schools within the Australian ecclesial context.

As a result of sociological and religious changes, the current reality is that, for an increasing number of families, the Catholic school represents their only point of contact with the Church. It is in this context that *a new Catholic culture is being forged,* and no one seems to have control of the process by which this is happening. In the 1970s it was congregational leaders who were asking the question: 'Will life return to what it was, or has it changed for ever?' Today it is bishops and other leaders within the Church who are posing a similar question. How this question is answered has huge significance for the future of the Church. As yet, there seems little consensus about what the answer might be. bishops clearly place differing interpretations on the situation and address it in different ways. Church leaders, clerical and lay, seem divided across the spectrum of responses outlined above. While some may be in denial, others make responses along either traditionalist or transformative lines. Many lay Catholics clearly take a critical stance.

MISSION AND THE CRISIS OF LIMINALITY

In a liminal era, 'mission', and its correlate 'Catholic identity', move from the background to the foreground as people wrestle with uncertainty, the excitement of new options, and the experience of loss.

Recontextualising mission

Catholic school leaders find themselves confronting three major questions:

- How should we now construe the mission of our Catholic school and Catholic school system in this situation?
- How should we understand the relationship of the schools and the systems to the wider Catholic faith community?
- What does school and system leadership demand of us in the present situation?

These questions raise complex issues which need to be answered with new urgency in this liminal era.

Addressing the crisis of meaning

The culture of the Catholic school is being shaped not only by the uncertainty which characterises its ecclesial context, but also by the uncertainty generated by changing educational demands that flow from developments in Australian society and culture. Our contention is that both Church and school leaders face a *crisis of meaning* that makes it imperative to acquire a new vantage point from which to view the situation. Such a vantage point, if discovered, would give them the capacity to re-imagine the mission of their respective institutions and re-shape it. Leadership in a liminal situation becomes a ministry of meaning-making that requires imagination. However, since imagination is shaped by culture, this can occur *only if culture is seen as a potential ally rather than a potential enemy*. In the Australian context this means Church leaders must take Australian culture seriously and come to grips with its current dynamics. The process involves getting in touch with the human experience of people and the aspirations this experience engenders.

LEADERSHIP AS A MINISTRY OF MEANING-MAKING

If leaders are to be effective in negotiating the dilemmas posed by a liminal era, they have to be able to make sense of it for themselves and then for those they lead. An important skill in this task is discerning the *imaginal horizon* within which colleagues customarily function, and challenging them to move beyond this horizon. In normal times, culture is an asset in this regard, but in a liminal era it can become a liability because it constrains what people see as options and so puts limits on what they hope for.

Culture limits what we see as options but, because we take culture for granted, we do not realise this is occurring. Australian culture and Church culture both function in this way. Challenging the imaginal boundaries imposed by these cultures becomes important in opening up the paths to new solutions and new possibilities. Leaders create the spaces in which school cultures can develop and renew themselves. The task is not an easy one and requires leaders to make this journey of imagination themselves before inviting others to set out for the new lands that have been encountered. Catholic school and system leadership is a journey made in faith—that is its essential challenge.

In a liminal era meaning-making becomes part and parcel of the mission and ministry of system leadership. Like all forms of ministry, this has a requisite skill-set. A primary skill is the ability to read contexts and to understand the dynamics that are driving change in both the religious and cultural arenas, particularly as these dynamics impact on schooling. Secondly, it involves understanding the role and function of narrative, ritual and symbolism both in helping followers move beyond the taken-for-granted and the familiar, and helping them grieve for what has been left behind. Mission thinking, understood in terms of meaning-making, therefore reaches beyond the cognitive to address both the affective and evaluative dimensions of life.

PRIORITIES IN LEADING FOR MISSION

PRIORITY 2.1   Understanding Context

In leading for mission, it is necessary to understand the cultural and faith contexts in which the school or school system functions, the dynamics at work in those contexts, and the ways in which the dynamics challenge the taken-for-granted assumptions on which the Catholic school or system stands.

PRIORITY 2.2   Understanding People

In leading for mission, leaders must be aware of the way in which their people customarily respond to the changing contexts, and promote opportunities for dialogue, so that people holding legitimately different perspectives can move towards a workable consensus.

Continuing the Conversation

- Drawing on your own experience, name some of the once taken-for-granted aspects of 'being Catholic' that have ceased to exist. Which aspects do you see as currently in the process of disappearing? Have your reactions to these changes been primarily positive or negative? In your judgement, what is the characteristic response of your colleagues to these changes: denial, traditional, critical or transformative? What has been the characteristic response of your leaders? Has the response been a general one or is it selective, changing from issue to issue?
- What opportunities for dialogue exist, or need to be created, in your school or school system, so that a working consensus can be developed that permits effective responses to changes within the context?

3

FIRST TRANSITION ERA: FROM 'SCHOOLS FOR CATHOLICS' TO 'CATHOLIC SCHOOLS'

Many Catholics today think that lay educators leading Catholic schools is a relatively recent phenomenon. This is not the case. Lay Catholics led and staffed schools for Catholic children for almost half a century before the era of the religious commenced. The narrative of Catholic education has, in fact, passed through three principal eras and, we argue, is on the cusp of a fourth. A central thesis of this study is that, as eras change, so too does the mission of the school. During transition periods mission thinking becomes a priority. In studying them it is possible for us to see how changes in aspiration shape mission and drive change. Such study of transition eras is important in exploring what 'leading for mission' demands as a new transition era unfolds.

MISSION EXPANDS IN TRANSITION ERAS

The focus of this chapter is on the first of these transition eras, one that saw 'schools for Catholics', which operated from within the educational arrangements for all children prevailing in society at that time, replaced by what today we understand by 'Catholic schools'. In 1879, in a joint pastoral letter, the NSW bishops denounced public education as unsuitable for Catholic children, and provoked a reaction that brought denominational schooling to a close in NSW.[21] Their actions initiated a second era in Catholic education which ran from then until the late 1960s, during which religious congregations took over the control and development of Catholic education. A third era began in the 1970s and ran almost to the present. It has been an era in which lay people have again constituted the bulk of the teaching

---

21   Patrick O'Farrell *The Catholic Church and Community: An Australian History*, Revised ed. (Kensington: New South Wales University Press, 1985), 184–189. While support for government-funded schools for Catholics had been withdrawn earlier in the smaller colonies, the bishops there had not made such a public issue of the matter.

force in Catholic schools and have moved into senior leadership positions. This arrangement was made possible by the reintroduction of government funding. It has seen the major responsibility for the control and development of Catholic schooling pass to powerful Catholic educational bureaucracies operating within legal and statutory frameworks set by public policy.

It would seem, however, that this third era is beginning to give way to a fourth, one in which school and system leaders must consider the shift in human consciousness brought about by what has become known as the post-modern critique, launched by scholars in the late 1970s. This, coupled with the consequences of the new globalisation and advancing religious and cultural pluralism has, since the 1990s, been impacting on all societies across the planet. In the emerging fourth era, school leaders must turn their attention to the issues of knowledge-construction and meaning-making as societies track past post-modernism to whatever lies beyond, and as cultures are reshaped. These changes in society and culture make their impact on the Catholic community, and shape the aspirations parents have for their children's education, and so for what they expect schools will do. As in all transitional periods, changing aspirations reshape mission. The situation requires Christian leaders to use the resources of human experience, faith and culture in being proactive, rather than reactive, as they meet the challenges which changing aspirations pose for the mission of the Catholic school.

In each of the three eras of Catholic education noted above, the way in which both the mission of the schools and leadership for mission were understood evolved as circumstances changed. The processes by which the transition was made from one era to another constitute what is known in anthropology as a 'social drama'.[22] How leaders negotiate this social drama determines *the human cost of change*. In the story of Catholic education in Australia, the Catholic community negotiated the change from 'schools for Catholics' to 'Catholic schools run by religious congregations' successfully, in the sense that the understanding of Catholic education shared within the community was strengthened. However, as the narrative reveals, there were significant human costs. In this chapter we wish to acknowledge a social drama that has been largely written out of the history books.

Anthropologists, such as Gerard Arbuckle, hold that social dramas unfold according to a pattern, and it is important in studying a culture to understand this pattern.[23] The way to do this is to explore how it plays out

---

22 Gerald Arbuckle *Culture, Inculturation and Theologians: a Post-modern Critique* (Collegeville: Liturgical Press, 2010), 90–96. Arbuckle is drawing on the work of Victor Turner e.g. *From Ritual to Theatre: The Human Seriousness of Play* (New York: Performing Arts Journal Publications, 1982), 92.
23 Drawing on Turner, Arbuckle analyses social drama into four stages: (i) 'breach', where

in particular transitions, and to discern what it tells us about what is possible and not possible in bringing about change. Foundational eras are important in this regard, because at these times values and principles *cannot be taken for granted* but are fought over, forged and eventually owned to such an extent that later generations take them as givens, quite oblivious to how things came to be the way they are.

LEADING FOR MISSION: THE FOUNDATION ERA

The first broad chapter in the narrative of Catholic education is the era from 1806,[24] when the first school for Catholics is known to have been operating, to approximately 1890, by which time the Australian bishops had established nation-wide a system of schools independent of government support. In this first era, fundamental principles were established and directions set. It is also the era that Catholic educators know least about. The efforts of many hundreds of Catholic lay people working under arduous conditions to educate young Catholics have been largely written out of the story of Catholic education. So too have those of the priests whose missionary commitment laid the foundation on which the religious could build, consolidating Catholic education and giving it an identity during the second era. The social dramas associated with the establishment of Catholic schooling and the transition from 'schools for Catholics' to 'Catholic schools' set important directions in the mission thinking of Catholic educators, much of which is taken for granted today. In exploring the era of 'schools for Catholics' we are retracing the mythic roots of Catholic education which we forget at our peril.

Schooling at the time of settlement

Living in the twenty-first century, it is hard to imagine what life was like for Catholics in the late eighteenth and early nineteenth centuries. Ireland was still operating under the Penal Laws which had applied for nearly three centuries, closing many positions in public life to Catholics. In the late eighteenth century, the English legal system was harsh. Over one

---

the prevailing social relationships and arrangements break down. This generates (ii) 'crisis'. The chaos, senselessness and meaninglessness of crisis gives way to (iii) 'redressive action', which is a complex stage involving separation and liminality after which people move back into relationship with the broader society—a situation which may see either (iv), a reintegration with society, or a deeper separation or 'schism'.

24 This school opened its doors somewhere between 1803 and 1806. Its existence is known from a despatch of Governor King, 12 August 1806, cited in Ronald Fogarty *Catholic Education in Australia 1806–1950* (Melbourne: Melbourne University Press, 1959), Volume 1, 17. The teacher's identity is not known.

hundred and fifty offences carried the death penalty. Most of these related to protecting the rights of property owners from infringements, many of which would be considered as minor today. The rapid expansion of the population, and the migration from rural villages to the cities, created mass poverty and increased crime as poor people in both Britain and Ireland sought to survive. For the English authorities, the Irish were seditious Catholic barbarians who refused to be 'civilised' according to English standards. Transportation to the Americas became an alternative to hanging, and the means to relieve pressure in overcrowded English prisons. When the American Revolution stopped transportation to the west, Australia became the alternative destination. The First Fleet, which arrived in Sydney to establish a penal colony in 1788, came ill-prepared for both the task and the harsh environment, and in consequence the early settlers struggled for almost a decade just to survive.

Education was not a priority for the colonial leaders, nor did it feature in the colonial budget for the first thirty years of the colony's life. 'Schools' were opened, but operated privately. The Colonial Office had no experience of setting up a society from scratch, and so had not anticipated that provision had to be made for the education of the children of serving administrators or of those born to the convict women, many of whom were sexually abused by their jailers.[25] The notion of compulsory education did not exist at the time. The first schools in the colony of NSW were established in 1792 for the children of officers and for orphans.[26]

Catholics and Catholic schools in early Australia

For the first thirty years, the Australian colonies had no permanent serving priest. Richard Johnson, Anglican chaplain to the First Fleet, was the first clergyman to arrive in Australia. He was followed in 1798 by a group of Non-conformist Protestant ministers forced to abandon their mission in Tahiti. Following the 1798 rebellion in Ireland, two Catholic priests were transported to the colony with other rebels. One, Fr Dixon, was eventually accredited as Catholic chaplain for a short time under tight supervision, before being repatriated.[27] As chaplain, it is probable that he would have

---

25 Frs Conolly and Therry were the first two official Catholic chaplains approved by both ecclesiastical and government authorities, and funded by the British government following the political furore over the deportation of Fr Jeremiah O'Flynn (see below). They arrived in 1820 on a transport ship which became subject to a judicial enquiry. Therry testified to this enquiry about the appalling way in which sailors prostituted the women convicts. Patrick O'Farrell, 18.
26 Fogarty, 5.
27 The first recorded public Mass was celebrated in Australia in 1803, fifteen years after the First Fleet arrived. Permission to celebrate Mass was withdrawn following the 1804 Castle Hill rebellion. It was not until 1820, 32 years after settlement, that the Catholic Church was officially established in Australia with the arrival of Frs Conolly and Therry as official chaplains.

been expected to set up a school. If he did so, this would have been the second school for Catholic children, the first having been established about the same time.²⁸

Attitudes to schooling in early Australia

At the turn of the nineteenth century the assumption of successive Governors was that education was the province of the clergy. This had been a tradition in England dating back several centuries. Education was seen by both Catholic and Protestant clergy as an essential element in the mission of the churches. Early colonial policy was that the administration sponsored schools, but the clergy managed them, preferably with associated costs being shared. At the time, there was no concept of public education as we know it today. The value of schooling was judged in moral terms: its mission was to civilise the young and so bring order into society. This carried little weight with the poor. However, given the reputation of the Australian colony as a moral 'cesspool', such a mission was badly needed to affirm the human dignity of the poor.²⁹

Under prevailing British policy, Richard Johnson, as Anglican chaplain to the First Fleet, became educational leader in the colony. The first problem that he and the Non-conformist clergy faced in meeting their educational responsibilities was that there were no funds. Governor King sought and received assistance from Protestant mission societies in England to set up an Orphan School in 1800. He supplemented this assistance by taxes (levied illegally) on goods landed in the colony. His successor, William Bligh, was the first Governor to make explicit provision to fund schools, thirty years after settlement began.

Role of Catholic chaplains

The colonial administration sought to have an English Catholic chaplain sent to the colony, but none was available from the hard-pressed English Catholic Church. So in 1815 the Catholics of the colony petitioned Rome for assistance. Authorities there, rather carelessly, accredited the Gaelic-speaking Jeremiah O'Flynn as chaplain to the colony without conferring with the British Colonial Office. Lacking diplomatic credentials, and unlikely to be given them by the British, the eccentric O'Flynn decided to

---

28 Fogarty, 17. The evidence as to who was responsible for, and who taught in these schools, is inconclusive.
29 In 1832, Dr Ullathorne, the first Vicar General of Australia, commented: 'We have taken a vast portion of God's earth and made it a cesspool; we have poured down scum upon scum and dregs upon dregs of the offscourings of mankind and we are building up with them a nation of crime, to be a curse and a plague', quoted in O'Farrell, 1.

come to Australia and bluff his way into the colony as Catholic chaplain. On his arrival in 1817, Governor Macquarie afforded him recognition pending the arrival of his 'credentials' from England. When these did not arrive, O'Flynn went into hiding, but was discovered and deported. O'Flynn's adventure accomplished three things: it reinforced fears held by colonial administrators about Irish Catholic priests; it generated a sense of persecution among Catholics; and the incident was exploited politically in England to embarrass the government which no doubt expressed its anger to the Governor of NSW. The result, however, was that both England and Rome acted to resolve the matter. Two Irish chaplains, Frs Conolly and Therry, were sent to Australia in 1820. By this stage the Protestant churches were providing what general schooling was available and were supported by the government in doing so.

It was Fr Therry who was to make the greater mark on Australian Catholicism. John Therry was dedicated, willful and entrepreneurial, but ill-equipped for the role he was thrust into in both temperament and lack of education.[30] He fought with everyone who did not see things his way: ecclesiastical superiors, peers and government officials. He brought to Australia the seething resentment the Irish had as victims of English oppression, and interpreted all setbacks in his dealing with government as further examples of English persecution. His lack of diplomacy divided and isolated the Catholic community. In his tussles with Protestant clergy, Therry cast himself as the underdog, and Catholics as the victims. His confrontational approach quickly alienated the administration and English clergy of all persuasions, and set the scene for the sectarian strife that was to hamper Catholics for the next half century. However, among some sections of the Catholic population, particularly the Irish, Therry had a solid support base, and was regarded as a hero because he stood up for them against the government.[31]

Government-funded schools for Catholics

When Therry arrived in 1820, the Catholic population on the mainland where he ministered was a diverse group. The bulk were ex-convicts, a large proportion of whom were Irish and, never having been educated themselves, had little interest in educating their children. There was also a

---

[30] Therry was ordained before he completed his theological studies. His finances were often chaotic, but he went on to amass a personal fortune in property and cattle which he left to the Church. After a tumultuous early career in Sydney, and later as Vicar General in Tasmania, he died as Parish Priest of Balmain in 1864.

[31] O'Farrell, 18–31 et al. For a sympathetic treatment of Therry's role in the foundations of the Australian Church see John McSweeney *A Meddling Priest: John Joseph Therry* (Strathfield, St Paul's Publications, 2000).

smaller group of political exiles for whom education was important. The only available schools were run by Protestants, and Catholic parents who wanted schooling for their children sent them to these schools. Therry, fresh from Ireland, interpreted this situation as proselytising and quickly set about establishing 'schools for Catholics' under the patronage of the colonial administration. These were run by lay people. The first was headed by George Morley at Parramatta, and the second by Thomas Byrne in Sydney.

The growth of schools for Catholics in subsequent years was spectacular as the following table suggests.

YEAR	NSW	VIC	QLD	TAS	SA	WA	TOTAL
1833	10	–	–	1	–	–	11
1848	31	6	2	4	2	3	48
1858	64	89	4	5	6	6	174
1865	98	94	4	4	6	6	212

FIGURE 3.1 Schools for Catholics 1833–1865[32]

In the main, schools of this era were staffed by lay people and supported financially by the government of the day.[33] The schools were largely one-teacher enterprises[34] which catered for students between the ages of seven and ten. Few stayed at school longer than two years. There was usually a mix of Catholics and students from other denominations in the classes which were often large. Attendance was problematic as many parents saw little value in education. More often than not, teaching lacked organisation due to a dearth of resources, particularly text books, and poor facilities; students were often forced to play in the adjoining streets during breaks. Many teachers had little in the way of formal training and there was no way of obtaining it in the colony. More often than not, teachers learned on-the-job. Their salaries were generally so low that teaching was regarded as the province of the dedicated, or as a profession of the desperate.

Birth of public education

While Australia was a long way from England and Ireland, it was influenced by educational developments in those countries, in particular by attempts to establish systems of general education. The argument for general education was that, in a functioning democracy, citizens should be able to read and

---

32 Compiled from tables in Fogarty Volume 1, 38, 54 and 74.
33 Arrangements varied in the different colonies. In some, teachers were paid on the basis of student numbers; in others, fees were charged to complement government salaries.
34 In some cases the schools were run by married couples operating as a team.

write. The problem faced in Ireland, as in Australia, was how to provide a general education for a population that was divided across religious lines and had little interest in education.

Since the churches were responsible for the schools, the clergy had to come to agreement about how such a system would work without privileging any one denomination. Various proposals were explored in Australia without success. The denominations regularly changed positions. In assessing proposals, sometimes the Catholics sided with the Non-conformists and sometimes with the Anglicans, so that no consensus emerged, to the frustration of the administration. These struggles over 'the Education Question' took place as the Catholic Church's hierarchy was being established. This added to the tensions.

Since Australia was an English colony, both Rome and Britain deemed it necessary that Catholic leaders be acceptable to the English Governors. By 1830, tensions among the Catholic chaplains, and between them and the government, made it necessary to have some form of ecclesiastical authority in the colony. A young British Benedictine, William Ullathorne, was sent as Vicar General to NSW in 1833 and was followed by Australia's first Bishop, another Benedictine, Bede Polding, two years later.[35] Among his missionary initiatives, Ullathorne sought to recruit priests and school teachers.[36] Polding was to head the Church in Australia for the next forty years, first as Bishop and then as Archbishop. To him fell the task of steering a fledgling Church, whose members were among the poorest in the colony, into the mainstream of Australian life. He had to do this in the face of vicious sectarianism, the advent of liberalism, English-Irish resentment among his fellow bishops, and rivalry among his priests between those who were diocesan and those who were members of religious orders.

Polding saw himself as a missionary bishop, and in this role was forced— by inclination and circumstance—to determine and defend what was essential in Catholic education. As leader, Polding was a poor administrator, but a great meaning-maker. In the heat of a major battle over public policy in education, he formulated and defended a concept of Catholic education that still has relevance today.

---

35 Prior to Polding's appointment, the Church in the colony was under the jurisdiction of the Vicar Apostolic of the Cape, Madagascar and Mauritius, Edward Slater. O'Farrell, 18.
36 One such recruit was a well educated Catholic layman, William Augustine Duncan MA (Edinburgh) who, for a time, functioned as a school teacher in NSW and also founded the first Catholic newspaper *The Australasian Chronicle* in 1839. See *the Australian Dictionary of Biography*, and also O'Farrell, 66–67.

Formulating an understanding of Catholic education

While a number of models for public education were proposed in the colonies, the way in which the Irish national system was considered illustrates best what the key issues were. Under this system, school subjects were divided into secular and denominational.[37] Students from the different denominations shared a common Bible reading, but separated for denominational instruction. Following its adoption in Ireland, the Australian bishops were initially willing to accept this position as the least bad option. However, as Polding wrestled with the issues that the adoption of this scheme would raise, he began to discern clearly the *essential elements of a Catholic education*.

The outcome of this discernment is found in Polding's sentiments collated by Fogarty from various sources as follows:

Education, in the Catholic view, was a unity: it was not a 'thing of mechanism' that could be put together bit by bit, a morsel of religious instruction here and of secular instruction there, like 'separate parcels with as little reciprocal action as have two books in a library'. On the contrary, Christian education was a 'thing of life' with mutual influence and interpenetration between the parts. Not only the subjects taught, but the teacher, and his faith, the rules and practices of the school day, all combined to produce the result that the Church understood to be education. For this reason Catholics asked for schools wherein ... 'every kind of instruction imparted to them (the children) should be interpenetrated by Catholic doctrine, by Catholic feeling and practice': where, in short, the environment itself was Catholic.[38]

This was the vision that informed the decisions of the Australian Catholic hierarchy in the period 1844–79 in their negotiations about education, whether with colonial authorities or later with representative governments.[39] Although the matter was resolved at the level of principle and vision, there were a number of issues that compromised its implementation. The first was the lack of trained Catholic teachers. The second was the apathy of Catholics towards education. The third derived from the fact that a number of bishops were still in the throes of establishing their own authority, and operated quite autocratically.

---

37 History was not taught as a secular subject since it was regarded as denominational.
38 E.g. Testimony to the Select Committee in Education of 1844, Polding's pastoral letter of 1859, and that from the 1862 Provincial Synod. Other bishops communicated similar sentiments e.g. Bishop Geoghegan of Adelaide in his pastoral letter of 1860. Fogarty, 187–8.
39 Polding himself founded the Sisters of the Good Samaritan in 1857 in pursuit of his vision. Whilst the congregation grew slowly, and the needs for Catholic education were vast, the Sisters epitomised much of Polding's vision in the way in which they pursued their educational apostolate in the harsh colonial environment. See O'Farrell, 174–5.

Beyond this, the major problem was that the *bishops had not established 'Catholic education' as a brand in the imagination of the Catholic community*. There were few models of a Catholic school that fully implemented Polding's vision because of the need to continually compromise in order to retain government funding. For ordinary Catholics, the schools their children attended remained essentially similar to other public schools. The difference was that they were attended mostly by Catholics and the teachers were Catholic. As Fogarty notes of the Catholic denominational schools of this era:

> ...*Notwithstanding all that had been said and written by the bishops on the subject, the laity had only vague notions of what Catholic education was. For most of the ordinary people it was purely an abstraction: there was nothing concrete, no coherent system of Catholic schools, no organized body of religious teachers, no tangible evidence, as there is today, of a special type of education known as Catholic education. In general, all schools were government schools: the government helped build them, the government equipped them with books and the government paid the teachers' salaries...*

> ...*Catholics schools, either through custom or regulation, were not generally called 'Catholic schools' ... the term 'Catholic school' tended to fall into disuse, with the result that no popular concept of Catholic education had ever developed.*[40]

The result was that parents failed to discriminate between the schools, due largely to the apathy they felt for things educational.

As the debate dragged on, the crisis heightened. Principles were being overtaken by practice. In the 1840s, the management of schools passed successively from Church representatives to a variety of lay boards and councils whose initial brief was the supervision of how funds were spent. However, other responsibilities soon followed, eventually extending to certification of teachers, premises, text books and standards. As the educational bureaucracy expanded, the level of regulation increased. While Catholics were represented on the boards and councils, they were in the minority. In the tense atmosphere of the time, implementation of regulations was often stage-managed to the disadvantage of Catholics and other denominations. Sometimes this reflected the stance of the authorities, at other times the bias of particular inspectors. From a Catholic perspective, life in denominational schools was becoming uncertain, even arbitrary. The sustainability of schools for Catholics was rendered problematic by the constant need to find Catholic teachers. In addition, the growing acceptance of the public schools by Protestant denominations meant that they closed many of their denominational schools.

---

40 Fogarty, 209–210.

A stage was reached where the continuation of the denominational school system was seen by Protestants as mainly favouring the Catholics. Given the sectarian tensions of the time, such a situation was intolerable.

The bishops, on the other hand, refused to agree to any school system that involved Bible reading, and argued that if education was to be secular, then it should be just that, secular, and not involve any denominational influence. Bible reading, even from the Catholic Douay version, was seen as disguised Protestantism. This impasse was never resolved, and so public policy developed in a way that excluded from education all reference to religion, thus accelerating Australia's development as a post-Christian nation.[41]

Across the 1870s, one by one the smaller colonies reduced or withdrew funding for denominational schools; and where this did not occur, regulation was used to systematically reduce the number of denominational schools. As Figure 3.1 above makes clear, what happened in the smaller states was relatively unimportant compared to what happened in NSW and Victoria where the bulk of the schools for Catholics were located. The governments in these states were not in a financial position to accommodate the substantial number of students in Catholic schools should they close through lack of funding. A stalemate ensued. However, to anyone with eyes to see, the writing was on the wall for the denominational schools.

'CATHOLIC WITHOUT COMPROMISE'

In 1866, the bishops and clergy of NSW set out nine tenets on which Catholic education should rest.[42] When the NSW government passed its proposed Bill ignoring several of these tenets, the bishops recast them, identifying four non-negotiables and four desirables. In their view, if the government was to support denominational schools for Catholics, then it needed to acknowledge as a matter of public policy the following essentials:

1. the right of the Church to establish a school for Catholics in areas where the numbers of Catholic students warranted this
2. the right of the clergy, as managers of the school, to appoint and dismiss teachers

---

41 The proponents of secular education in the late nineteenth century were not secularists in the sense we use that term today. Many of them were clergy whose intention was that education should be open to human enquiry and not weighted down by dogmatism, as was perceived to be practiced in some religious denominations, Catholics in particular.
42 Resolutions of the Roman Catholic Clergy of the Archdiocese of Sydney, forwarded to parliament, 16 July 1866, cited in Fogarty, 492.

3. that where Catholic and non-Catholic students attended the same school, Catholics not receive religious instruction from non-Catholics or in the creed of any other denomination and that text-books objectionable to Catholics not be used
4. that aid needed to be granted to Catholic authorities to train Catholic teachers.[43]

The bishops did not regard these requirements as being specific to Catholics, but advocated that equivalent conditions apply to all denominations. Needless to say, public policy makers were not prepared to give the bishops or priests the powers they sought because no other denomination was making comparable demands. Furthermore, the third of these demands was problematic because, in the existing schools for Catholics, non-Catholic students were not being accorded this right in regard to their own faith.

A new chapter opens: the first Catholic school system

While the battle over the 'Education Question' was approaching its denouement in NSW, another development was taking place in the small colony of South Australia: the first Catholic education system was being established in Adelaide under Fr Julian Tenison Woods. The first Bishop of Adelaide, Bishop Murphy, had planned to have a Catholic School from the beginning. Hence, on his arrival in 1844, he had brought to Adelaide William and Anne James—teachers from the Rocks in Sydney—whose task it was to establish the first school. The passing of the Education Act in 1852 saw the four schools, which were said to be Catholic and which had received some government support, placed in the hands of a Central Board, composed of representatives from the major denominations who provided education in the colony (however, this did not include a Catholic member). The Act prescribed the number of students required for a school to be supported, as well as the courses to be followed, and required the daily reading of Scripture without sectarian influence or any denominational catechism being added. The poor state of the Church in South Australia saw the Bishop accept these conditions in order to have the teachers paid.

The second Bishop of Adelaide, Patrick Geoghegan (1859–64) came from Victoria where he had been embroiled in the education debate. He was appalled at the state of the Catholic schools and immediately made Catholic education a major issue. His pastoral letter of 1860, which drew heavily from Archbishop Polding's of 1859, concluded with the following

---

43 For the full wording of these re-cast demands of the NSW bishops see Fogarty, 493.

challenge: 'Wherever there is a Pastor and a Flock, we implore you to make a commencement of a Catholic School. Let each do what he can.' Between this and the arrival of the Bishop Sheil in 1866, approximately fourteen such schools were in operation. All, with the exception of the Jesuit College at Sevenhill, were in the hands of lay teachers. Financial support consisted of the sixpence-a-week fee, the School Fund set up by the Bishop from Propagation of the Faith allocations, and diverse fundraising activities such as the raffling of one of the Bishop's carriages.[44]

The arrival of Bishop Sheil saw the appointment of Fr Julian Tenison Woods as the Director of Catholic Education and his move from the parish of Penola to Adelaide. The system which he immediately began to establish was greatly enhanced, and indeed sustained, by the Josephite congregation which he and Mary MacKillop had established in Penola in 1866, and whose sisters began work in Adelaide in 1867. Under Woods' system the Josephite Sisters began to take over existing schools and to establish new schools, including those in a number of rural areas. In 1869, the Sisters opened their first 'free school'.[45] Within a relatively short time, two thirds of Catholic children in South Australia were attending Josephite schools. Before the local Bishop John Sheil left for the First Vatican Council (1869–70), he appointed Fr Woods Director General of Catholic Education. In this capacity the energetic Englishman supervised the roll-out of the Josephite free school system.

What became known as the Sheil-Woods model had a number of unique features:

- planning was centrally controlled
- schools were staffed mainly by religious Sisters
- the Sisters gave preference to starting schools in rural areas
- local schools were the responsibility of local boards which, among other things, were responsible for fund-raising in local communities
- standards were centrally monitored
- the system was heavily promoted in the Catholic press so that a sense developed that Catholic education was unique.

The model caught the public imagination, and the Sisters of St Joseph expanded quickly as a result.

Woods set up the school system without much reference to local Irish clergy who resented this fact. The latter found it hard to imagine a system

---

44 Margaret Press *From Our Broken Toil: South Australian Catholics 1836 to 1905* (Adelaide: Catholic Archdiocese, 1986), 131–45 and also 146–177.
45 Fogarty, 233.

of Catholic schools surviving independent of government assistance. Furthermore, the development challenged their right to appoint teachers in their parish schools. While the Bishop was away there was little the clergy could do about the changes Woods had introduced, but when he returned they complained loudly. In the face of the hostility the model had generated among the local clergy, the Bishop deemed it wise for Woods to resign and vacate the diocese. However, the precedent for a system of Catholic schools had been set, and while Sheil walked away from it because of internal politics, other bishops soon took it up: firstly, Quinn in Brisbane; and later Vaughan, who was to succeed Polding as the Archbishop of Sydney.

Archbishop Vaughan: founding father of Catholic schooling

Vaughan was initially sceptical of the Sheil-Woods model but, once convinced of its worth, became its principal advocate. Beginning in the mid-1860s, Catholic education entered its first liminal period. The growing aspiration among the Australian bishops was to make the shift from *denominational schools for Catholics* to *Catholic schools run mainly by religious*.

Reading the signs of the times, Vaughan saw that the public mood had shifted against denominational education. In 1872, the Victorian government had suddenly withdrawn funding for denominational schools, catching Bishop Goold unawares.[46] Given the apathy among Sydney Catholics on education matters, Vaughan was not going to be similarly caught out. He and his fellow bishops in NSW decided to issue a series of pastoral letters, all authored by Vaughan. In these the bishops condemned the public schools. In the first pastoral issued in 1879 they claimed that national schools were

> ...*seedplots of future immorality, infidelity, and lawlessness, being calculated to debase the standard of human excellence, and to corrupt the political, social and individual life of future citizens*...'[47]

The press in all colonies had a field day with such hyperbolic language, but it caught the attention of Catholics, so much so, that Catholic enrolments in Sydney's major public schools dropped by up to twenty percent within a week. The inevitable blow fell later that year when the NSW government withdrew support for all denominational schools. The bishops were then forced to implement a new concept of Catholic education, one in which Catholic schools could be Catholic without compromise. The question was

---
46 Archbishop James Alipius Goold (1812–1886) was the first Catholic bishop of Melbourne.
47 Quoted in O'Farrell, 184.

whether or not such an arrangement could survive. If it was to survive, then it would have to be funded by the Catholic people. The coming of the religious would play a major role in making this possible.

In adopting the new strategy, Vaughan and his fellow bishops believed that state funding would soon be restored. Their grounds for optimism lay in the manifest injustice of Catholics being forced to pay taxes to support a school system that the Church held to be unsatisfactory, because it did not recognise the fundamental human rights and moral responsibilities of parents to educate their children as they believed appropriate. In this they were wrong.

In the three years between the *Education Act 1880* and his final departure from Sydney in 1883, Vaughan, despite poor health, proved a tireless advocate for Catholic education.[48] This advocacy among the Catholic community was not without result. In the year he left Sydney 12 500 of the 15 200 Catholic children in his diocese were in Catholic schools. Two-thirds of the schools were being run by religious, and forty-five new Catholic schools had been opened replacing denominational schools that had to be closed.

For Vaughan the role of *the religious as teacher* was integral to his understanding of Catholic education. As Fogarty concludes, the coming of the religious which was initially seen as an economic necessity soon came to be seen as a moral necessity.[49] The presence of religious was perceived to create the Catholic environment that gave the schools the unique identity that the bishops had long held to be the distinguishing feature of Catholic schools. A new era had dawned.

RECLAIMING THE FOUNDING MYTHOLOGY OF CATHOLIC EDUCATION

We have focused on the founding mythology of Catholic education largely because the participation of hundreds of lay people in this chapter of the narrative was subsequently erased from collective memory. The commonly held mythology of Catholic education was that the religious replaced a rather incompetent group of lay people, and the Catholic community rejoiced. This underestimates the contribution made by the Catholic educators of the first era—both priests and lay teachers. It also discounts the very trying conditions under which they made it.

---

48   Vaughan suffered from a heart condition. His trip to England was to recruit more religious for the Australian mission. He died of a heart attack while in Liverpool. His Irish successor, Archbishop Moran, refused to repatriate his body to Australia. This did not occur until 1946 when Vaughan was reburied in the crypt of St Mary's Cathedral, Sydney.
49   Fogarty, 259–260.

Once the bishops took their stand, many of these teachers were forced, as a matter of necessity, to transfer to the 'immoral' secular system that the bishops condemned; others went willingly.[50] While 'schools for Catholics' had always struggled to get good Catholic teachers, the project was not without its obvious successes. In some rural areas as late as 1890 these Catholic teachers were so highly regarded by the local Catholic community that no Catholic school was established in the area during their tenure as head teacher of the local public school. Lay Catholic educators never disappeared entirely from Catholic schools as they developed across the second era, but their place in the schools was always secondary to that of the religious.

Buried within the founding narrative is a *deeper mythology* that needs to be reclaimed as it defines important fundamentals of Catholic education, many of which have contemporary relevance:

- The early Catholic educational enterprise had a fundamental mission orientation. In this it reflected the commitment of its leader, Polding, who more than any other leader, forged its essential meaning.
- Catholic leaders recognised very early that what made Catholic education unique was the environment in which learning took place. Creating this was the work of the teachers, some of whom were very proficient at it.
- Catholic life in this era was characterised by an impulse for a separate identity. While Vaughan sought to shape the ecclesial environment as 'Australian', his Irish colleagues chose another path: to replicate the Irish Church in Australia. They operated from a cultural perspective that was so taken-for-granted that it could not be questioned. However, it seems clear that both Vaughan and his Irish colleagues favoured a separate identity.
- Catholic leaders sought to preserve the traditional role of the Church in education, a role which was under challenge from liberal democratic thought. Events in Australia were played out against the background of bitter experiences in Europe, which led Church leaders there to question the way the Church–State relationship was being re-shaped in all liberal democracies. Church leaders stood apart from this development, a position they subsequently came to regret as an opportunity missed.
- When the religious arrived in Australia in numbers, and local foundations flourished, the trajectory of Australian Catholic culture had been set.

---

50 O'Farrell notes that in Victoria by 1878 twenty-five per cent of the teachers in public schools were Catholics. O'Farrell, 187.

Catholic schools became integral to the form that Catholic separatism took in Australia for many decades. The early narrative of Catholic schools reminds us that culture and faith are inextricably linked.
- From the outset, and despite the serious sectarian divisiveness of the times, Catholic schooling was inclusive, with children of non-Catholic parents being enrolled. This aspect of the 'schools for Catholics' era comes as a surprise to many.
- The founding myth of Catholic education is that it is directed to the marginalised, in that the Catholic community was itself a marginalised group. When the religious came, they came as missionaries impelled by that vision. Over two thousand priests came from Ireland, many inspired by the same motivation.
- The clergy recognised early that no matter how acute the vision of a bishop with respect to Catholic education might be, that vision could not be realised without committed, trained teachers. The early priests and bishops went to extraordinary lengths to obtain such teachers, even helping married couples come to Australia as assisted migrants. A great attraction of the religious was that at last Catholic schools would have an assured supply of trained teachers.
- The bishops constantly fought to resist the secularisation of schools for Catholics, but their efforts were thwarted by the way in which regulations were interpreted and enforced. Their strategy of compromise ultimately proved self-defeating. They saw the presence of the religious as a way to evangelise schooling. How this would occur was largely left up to the leaders of the religious congregations.

When a community successfully negotiates the social drama associated with major changes, something is lost and something is gained, as the mission of the group expands. The aspiration that drove the first transition in Catholic education was twofold: to implement in Catholic schools an environment which, in the eyes of the bishops, was truly Catholic; and secondly, to resist the intrusion of liberal and secular ideas into Catholic schools. As the social drama played out, the bishops' decision fostered Catholic separatism and the creation of what in the next chapter we term, 'the Catholic wall'.

PRIORITIES IN LEADING FOR MISSION

PRIORITY 3.1 Understanding the founding myth

In leading for mission, it is important to know the narrative of the organisation and its founding aspirations, as these set the trajectory for all that follows.

Priority 3.2 Keeping the narrative alive

Because the narrative reflects the action of God's grace in the life of the community, in leading for mission the leader is responsible for keeping the narrative of the community alive.

Continuing the Conversation

How familiar are you with the founding myth of your own school or system? What hopes drove its foundation? What problems had to be overcome in realising these hopes? Given the problems they faced, how did the community rise to the challenge of realising their hopes? What is to be learned from this experience?

In many Catholic schools and systems, it is still possible to access people of the 'foundation generation' in order to relive the founding period. In other cases leaders have commissioned quality research so that this period can be revisited, and the above questions answered. Reconnecting staff to the founding experience is an important exercise in leading for mission.

The following group exercise is useful in exploring the collective memory of the school, and the lived values that drive its development. It is called 'historicising'.

As teachers, leaders and administrators, you are caught up in 'historically decisive events'. An 'historically decisive event' is one that meets the following criteria:

- you were personally involved
- you feel strongly about it
- significant amounts of staff energy were mobilised (most times this energy is used constructively; sometimes it is used destructively).

Using a series of charts to cover the past five years, work backwards year-by-year and have members of the group nominate both the *'historically decisive event'* in which they were involved, and *how they felt about it at the time*. Ask people to list events one at a time.

Two things generally emerge from this exercise. Firstly, in most schools, the staff's collective memory proves to be quite short. Staff have little recollection of what happened five years ago, even when events mobilised great energy. Secondly, the events that mobilise staff energy have very little to do with what happens in the classroom, but tend to be those that *create or sustain the relational environment of the school*.

4

SECOND TRANSITION ERA: CATHOLIC EDUCATION IN THE LATE TWENTIETH CENTURY

In the previous chapter we put the spotlight on the social drama that unfolded in Catholic education when, in the late nineteenth century, the Australian bishops opted for systems of Catholic schools separate from the public systems. This strategic choice was made for sound pastoral reasons in an era when Catholics were generally apathetic towards the benefits of education. The bishops' intention was to build the poorly educated and often marginalised Catholic families into cohesive parish communities. The Catholic schools were to play an instrumental role in achieving this aim which also depended on the religious congregations providing the bulk of the trained teaching force. In implementing this strategy, the bishops successfully appealed to the prevailing Catholic sense of victimhood. They mobilised Catholics by appealing to the mythic roots of Irish Catholicism, nowhere better summed up than in Frederick Faber's hymn, 'Faith of Our Fathers', which provided their pastoral project with its unofficial anthem.[51] It was a bold strategy, not without its costs. As a result, for three-quarters of a century, Catholics came to dwell within a 'Catholic wall' which insulated them from many of the developments underway in the surrounding culture. Their strategy ushered in a second era in Catholic education, the era of the religious.

In this chapter we focus on events that unfolded as this era ended. These created a new social drama that began in the 1960s and was not resolved until the mid-1980s. While the illustrative case study material is drawn from the archdioceses of Sydney and Melbourne, other dioceses have their own particular stories of how they negotiated the second transition era in Catholic education. As in the previous transition era, the mission of Catholic schools was to expand as this transition was negotiated.

---

51   The hymn begins: 'Faith of our fathers living still, in spite of dungeon, fire and sword.'

LIFE WITHIN THE 'CATHOLIC WALL'

Prior to the 1960s, Catholic schools were integral to a Catholic culture built around the parish. This culture reflected the Irish model of Catholicism established by the Australian Catholic hierarchy over the previous century. Following the lead set by Rome, Australian Church leaders in this era had developed a 'hermeneutic of suspicion' in regard to most things 'modern'. Under the impact of this hermeneutic, 'modern' was equated with 'the world' seen as a surrounding culture that was anti-Catholic, hostile to Church teaching, and thus to be rejected.[52] The aim of Catholic separatism was *to build a pastoral wall around Catholics* that would protect them from contamination caused by contact with 'the world'. The Catholic school was to play an integral role in the implementation of this policy, and this determined important emphases in its evolving mission.[53]

Catholic separatism rolled out in several strands. 'Support Catholic schools' became a mantra of the bishops and a marker of Catholic loyalty. As a consequence, the schools took on iconic status, a symbol that Catholics in this country would not bow to the injustice of Protestant and secularist oppression. The religious congregations who arrived from Europe, together with those founded locally, became 'heroes of the faith' in the emerging Catholic culture. The bishops issued a firm prohibition against 'mixed' marriages which were seen as a threat to the integrity of the Catholic community. The social life of Catholics came to centre on the parish. Every parish had a range of Catholic sodalities in which Catholics could meet with, and hopefully marry, other Catholics.[54] Catholic separatism was reinforced by the force of Church law when the Australian bishops promulgated the 'Commandments of the Church' which in the eyes of many Catholics came to have similar moral force to the Ten Commandments.

The religious who staffed Catholic schools in this era lived lives almost totally enclosed within the Catholic wall, and their educational endeavours were to play a major role in sustaining it. While Catholics often lived in a state of uneasy co-existence with the surrounding culture, this began to change in the late 1940s and 1950s when communism made its presence felt in secular society. bishops of the day were fiercely anti-communist, and Catholics were encouraged to actively fight against communists who were seeking to take

---

52 This perspective was not without its historical justification in Europe.
53 While Catholics mixed widely in society at many levels, including the political, the pastoral 'wall' which surrounded them in their Catholic life was extensive and strongly shaped their view of the world at the time.
54 In this era groups such as the Children of Mary, the Legion of Mary, the Holy Name Society, the Catholic Young Men's Society (CYMS) and Young Christian Workers (YCW) all flourished. Parish balls, a variety of sporting clubs, walking groups and drama societies were other common features of adult life within 'the Catholic wall'.

control of the unions. At the forefront of this development was the *Catholic Social Studies Movement*, headed by B.A. Santamaria, which operated under the patronage of Archbishop Mannix.[55] Santamaria was to become an influential player not only in Australian politics, but also in the development of the Catholic Church and, in consequence, Catholic education.

Religious education within the Catholic wall

Catholic separatism had an important impact on the development of religious education. Instruction in the era of the Catholic wall was largely *catechetical*—it assumed *an active faith on the part of students*. This active faith was encouraged through a range of devotions and Catholic practices: rosary during the months of May and October, May altars, opportunities for members of classes to attend confession, school children attending Mass together on Sundays. A robust prayer life featured at the school: morning prayers, angelus at midday, prayer on the hour, and litany to Our Lady at the end of the day were part of Catholic school experience. Secondly, instruction was *dogmatic* on the grounds that Catholics needed to know what Catholics believed. Thirdly, instruction was *apologetic*. Catholics needed to be able to explain and defend their faith, and prove why it was right in the face of other claims.

Religious Instruction was, however, rarely scriptural. Scripture occupied at best a support role. Reading the Bible was still regarded as 'something Protestants do'. Naïve literalism in the understanding of Scripture was the order of the day even among the clergy and educated Catholics.

THE APPROACHING STORM: CATHOLIC LIFE IN THE 1960S

The initial mission of the schools for Catholics had been relatively simple: civilising unlettered children. 'Civilising' was seen as a *moral goal* that included 'passing on the faith'. The educational ideal of this era was that the Catholic school set its students on the path to becoming 'scholars, saints and gentlemen' who would make their mark in Australian society.[56] This was an ideal imported from Ireland, the 'land of saints and scholars'.

---

55   The Movement was successful in this endeavour. It ran into trouble when the anti-communist crusade endeavoured to mobilise Catholic support to take over the Labor party. This led to a split in the Labor party and the creation of the Democratic Labor Party, a process which also split Catholics. Some (but not all) bishops in NSW, in particular, objected to the intrusion of the Church into the political realm in the name of 'Catholic action'. They appealed to Rome which upheld their position. In consequence the Movement was disowned as 'Catholic Action' and re-formed as a right-wing political movement called the National Civic Council. This continued to draw significant financial and moral support from certain bishops, as well as clergy and religious; so much so that, until the 1980s, it was widely regarded as 'the Catholic voice' on many political matters.

56   The ideal presumably included ladies as well!

Catholic education creates life chances

By the late 1950s, the cultural ground on which the Catholic wall was built began to shift as Catholic schooling started to open up pathways to economic prosperity for the embattled Catholic community.[57] The prestige of the schools grew once working class Catholic families came to appreciate the value of education. In consequence, 'creating life chances for students' became integral to the mission of Catholic schooling. The change in attitude was hastened by the creation of new educational opportunities opened up by the Church. Catholic students could win what was termed 'diocesan scholarships' which enabled them to attend special classes that prepared them to sit for, and win, Commonwealth scholarships. This strategy enabled many more students than formerly to complete their secondary education.[58]

The changed social environment of the post-war years improved educational opportunities and, with the lowering of social barriers, combined to undermine the suspicion of the surrounding culture that had helped create the Catholic wall.[59] By the 1960s, Catholics in increasing numbers were taking an active part in public life. The idea of Catholics venturing out beyond their wall to change the world through Catholic Action, only to retreat back behind it, no longer captured the imagination.[60] Many Catholics now living permanently beyond the Catholic wall, encountered the people there on a daily basis, and had come to share their lives and many of their aspirations. They had become acculturated. These Catholics now sought 'to live in the world, but not be of the world'. They defined 'being Catholic' differently.

---

57 Catholics had limited opportunity for social advancement in the pre-war period as they were discriminated against in business. Advancement was possible, however, in the police force and the public service.
58 For example, in Victoria Year 7 students could sit for 'diocesan scholarships'. Successful students then attended in Year 8 a special school that functioned as a 'gifted and talented' class preparing them to sit for the Commonwealth scholarship tests. While called 'diocesan scholarships', it was actually the religious congregations who met all the costs associated with providing these opportunities.
59 Post-war optimism also played a part in the shift in perspective, as did the fact that Catholics and non-Catholics had fought together and had come to count on each other as 'mates' during World War II.
60 From the 1920s the term 'Catholic Action' was used to describe the work of laity in support of the hierarchy. Subsequently the idea broadened to include many different works carried out by lay people in order to create a more just society in workplaces, universities etc. Catholic Action received impetus from the development of Catholic social teaching. The nature and degree of official connection of the various groups with the local hierarchies varied over time and from place to place. For a rich depository of material on Catholic Action in Australia see Helen Praetz *The Church in Springtime: Remembering Catholic Action 1940–65*. Eleven interviews with key people involved in Catholic Action, or those who knew them, 2010. http://repository.mcd.edu.au/896/ Another valuable resource is Bruce Duncan *Crusade or Conspiracy: Catholics and the Anti-communist Struggle in Australia* (Sydney: UNSW Press, 2001), 9–28.

In the 1950s and '60s, most Catholic schools still operated under the taken-for-granted assumptions of Catholic separatism, even as these were becoming increasingly problematic in the new social environment.

Young religious encounter the modern world

As more students stayed on at the secondary schools, the religious congregations began to ensure that their members gained the tertiary qualifications needed to teach at senior secondary level.[61] This brought young religious—whose early training was completed within the Catholic wall—into contact with developments in the modern world, and also with the Catholic Action movement then active in the universities. They came to share Catholic Action's goal of *engaging with 'the world' with the goal of changing it*.[62] Young Catholics were becoming familiar with Catholic social teaching which provided a general blueprint for social change.

'Social transformation' soon became an added dimension in the mission of the Catholic school. The Young Christian Students (YCS) played a key role in this development as students were introduced to the See-Judge-Act method pioneered by the Young Christian Workers under the leadership of Cardinal Cardijn. Under this model, social transformation occurs because students learn to look critically at the situation in which they live and reflect on what the Gospel (or Catholic social teaching) says to the situation in order to make a judgement about what needs to be done to improve it. They then act to bring about improvement.[63] When the younger religious brought this perspective into secondary classes, many young Catholics lost any residual fear of the society and culture that they encountered beyond the Catholic wall. Changing it for the better became a faith project. The Catholic Action movement gave many educated Catholics *the confidence to think for themselves* in addressing issues that arose in their environment.

Thus, even prior to the Second Vatican Council (1962–65), an inherent tension was building in Catholic schooling between the contradictory objectives pursued, as some elements in the Church sought *to engage with the world* while others sought to *sustain Catholic separatism*. It reflected the growing ferment for change throughout the Church.

---

61 In the fifties, relatively few religious had tertiary qualifications. Those who did had generally acquired them before they joined their congregation.
62 This represented an altogether new way of 'being Catholic', and many left their congregations to pursue it as lay people.
63 Judging was often done under the rubric 'How would Jesus handle this situation if he were confronted with it?' A problem with the model was that at the time Catholic appreciation of the New Testament could best be described as naïve literalism. The text was generally taken at face value.

Religious vocations plateau as a new social drama unfolds

As the 1960s wore on, the storm continued to build. The surge in vocations that had characterised religious life in the immediate post-war years began to plateau. The leaders of religious congregations now faced a dilemma because they could only guess as to whether this development would be a temporary or a permanent phenomenon. If the latter, the congregations would be unable to cope with existing demands for personnel, and taking responsibility for new schools would be out of the question. Their only realistic option would be to work co-operatively with the bishops in order to develop an alternative mechanism in establishing new schools. Otherwise, the Church would have to abandon its ambitious goal of providing places for all Catholic students in Catholic schools.[64]

When Catholics made their exodus from behind the Catholic wall into the cultural plains beyond, they found that other Catholics were already there. These were the European migrants who held a different view of what 'being Catholic' meant.[65] When the latter's children began to attend Catholic schools in large numbers in the 1950s and 1960s, the mission of the schools gained an enhanced significance. 'Creating life chances' held a whole new meaning when applied to the sons and daughters of migrants wanting to be 'at home' in Australian culture. Once the migrant population sought a Catholic education for their children, Catholic schools had little option but to take part in the exodus and themselves move out from behind the Catholic wall.

For an increasing number of Catholics it was becoming clearer that the fortress mentality of the pre-war years no longer served the community well. Catholics were becoming active participants in the formation of the national culture. This was no simple task in the 1960s because the national culture was itself caught up in its own social drama. What sociologists refer to as 'the revolution of expressive disorder' had swept across Europe and the United States in the late 1960s, and produced a huge and disorienting cultural shift in Australia, particularly in the 1970s.

From the early 1960s to the early 1970s, the entire Western world experienced a dramatic, highly intense transformation of its cultural values and behavior patterns that started as a form of cultural revolution among a small group of committed radicals and climaxed by changing some of

---

64 Co-operative action was to lead to the creation of regional schools under joint sponsorship. Parishes, dioceses and religious congregations were involved in a variety of governance arrangements.
65 Aspects of the Italian migrants' experience of Australian Catholicism are found in Adrian Pittarello *Soup without Salt: the Australian Catholic Church and the Italian Migrant, a comparative study in the sociology of religion* (Sydney: Centre for Migrant Studies, 1980).

the most profound habits and assumptions of Western society. The catalytic actions of white middle class youth affected everything: politics, arts, education, and religion.[66]

When the Catholic Church brought the long, slow process of redefining its relationship with the modern world to a kind of summation at the Second Vatican Council (1962–5), in Australia the Catholic Wall was on the point of collapse, and a 'perfect storm', was heading its way which would complete the task.

LIFE BEYOND THE WALL: CATHOLIC SCHOOLING IN THE 1960s AND 1970s

By the early 1970s three things had become clearer to those planning Catholic education:

- the numbers of religious vocations were not going to recover; in fact the situation was getting worse. The vocation of the Catholic teacher therefore had to be recognised and its parameters defined.[67]
- since most of the teaching congregations had been founded to educate the poor, religious—in increasing numbers—were leaving school ministry to take up other forms of ministry which they believed were more clearly aligned to the original charism of their particular congregation.[68]
- government funding ensured that lay leadership in Catholic schools could be a permanent feature of the future.

All three trends meant that new relationships had to be formulated at the macro-level between congregations and dioceses, and at the micro-level between lay people and religious working in the schools. New structures had to be put in place for this to happen, and it was becoming increasingly possible to talk about 'the culture of Catholic education'. However, before this conversation could take any definitive shape nationally, significant

---

66 Gerard Arbuckle *Violence, Society and the Church: A Cultural Approach* (Collegeville Minnesota: The Liturgical Press, 2004), 157ff.
67 This theme would be articulated in the document issued by the Vatican Congregation for Catholic Education *Lay Catholics in Schools: Witnesses to Faith* 1982.
68 Religious were both responding to their original charisms, and were also being given an opportunity to move from principalship and the classroom. Given the number of parish primary schools, the number of principals required had outstripped the capacity of the congregations to supply candidates suited to the role. Fr. Martin negotiated with the superiors, and when the congregations had carried out their discernment, they made their positions known to Fr. Martin who conferred with the parish priests. Because of the nature of the congregations, this process of negotiation was Victoria-wide. By the end of the 1970s the process which had occurred over a number of years was fairly well completed. In the view of Anne O'Brien who, from 1973, assisted Fr Martin as Executive Officer to the Director and later as Executive Secretary of the CECV, it had worked very well (correspondence 30 January 2013).

events were to intervene in both NSW and Victoria that would have a lasting effect on how the culture of Catholic school systems would develop.

Wyndham report shapes the direction of change in NSW

The first of these was the implementation of the Wyndham Scheme in NSW. In 1955, the Director of Catholic Education in Sydney, Fr John Slowey, was co-opted to a state government committee chaired by Harold Wyndham and charged with reviewing secondary schooling in the state. The reforms proposed by this committee were given legal force in the *Education Act 1961*. The most far-reaching of these was that secondary schooling should be extended from five to six years, that is to Year 12, by 1967. The proposals also mandated an overhaul of the curriculum and the building of specialist facilities—science laboratories and libraries—so that a broader curriculum could be delivered, particularly in girls' schools.

The difficulty this scheme presented for the Catholic sector in NSW can best be understood by looking at its implications for Catholic girls' schools. In 1961, of the 13 600 girls in NSW Catholic schools, half were in schools that finished at Year 10. Boys moved out of many Catholic primary schools after Year 4 while the girls continued on at the same school until Year 10. Of the 86 Catholic secondary schools attended by girls in NSW, just over a third prepared them for the final school examination. In 1961, only 600 girls state-wide were due to sit for the Leaving Certificate. The low retention rate meant that curriculum offerings were limited, and that learning happened under much less than ideal conditions.

The structural linkage between primary and secondary schooling in the Catholic sector meant that any rationalisation of the secondary school system would require a consequent rationalisation of the primary school system.[69] In other words, the Wyndham Scheme required that *the entire Catholic school system in NSW be rationalised*. As well as this, new facilities had to be built. The rationalisation was scheduled to be completed before the start of the 1966 school year. This requirement placed the future of many Catholic schools under threat.

At the time, dioceses in NSW had little in the way of professional expertise to carry out such a task, little history of co-operation among the congregations (which would be needed if it was to be accomplished), and no financial support on offer from the NSW government.[70] To describe the

---

69 Jim D'Orsa *Monsignor John Slowey: Servant of Education, Facilitator of Change*. (Sydney: Catholic Education Office, 1999), 49.
70 At the time, apart from the Director, Fr. Slowey, the CEO Sydney staff consisted of three: a lay man, Ambrose Roddy—fortunately of extraordinary ability—as well as Frs Hine and Dickenson, who were part-time.

situation as dire would be an understatement.[71] The crisis precipitated by the Wyndham Scheme projected embryonic Catholic Education Offices across NSW into *a hands-on leadership role*. Fear for survival played an important role in this development, as did the extra-ordinary leadership and negotiating ability of Fr Slowey, the Director of Catholic Education in Sydney. People trusted the Director and came to trust the organisation he led, precisely because he was the leader.

The Sydney Plan

The task of rationalising the schools was complex as it meant closing some schools, changing the status of others, rationalising teachers, religious communities, and so on.[72] The final *Sydney Plan* was presented to the Catholic community in 1964. The Catholic Education Office then had the arduous task of convincing an often sceptical Catholic public of the need for rationalisation with its consequent disruption to the education of their children, and the costs they were being asked to incur.[73]

The implementation of the Wyndham Scheme also placed immense financial burdens on the Catholic Church in NSW. In Sydney, Cardinal Gilroy intervened to establish the Catholic Building and Finance Commission, and centralised all school finances. The Commission operated at arm's length from the Catholic Education Office and handled all building projects as well as the planning required to implement the *Sydney Plan*. Once the Wyndham Scheme was in place, responsibility for financial management of the school system reverted to the CEO, augmenting both its authority and its leadership role.[74]

The culture of Catholic education systems in NSW was formed against the background of this crisis. Centralised systems of Catholic education evolved in NSW[75] from within a hermeneutic of trust despite the loss of a degree of local autonomy. Events unfolded differently in Victoria.

---

71   In 1962, in the face of financial crisis, the Catholic schools authorities in Goulburn NSW took extreme action, with the support of the Catholic community. They closed all Catholic schools for a week and sought to enrol the students in the local government schools. Although shortlived, the Goulburn 'strike' as it became known, reverberated throughout the country galvanising the various campaigns for government funding for Catholic schools. O'Farrell, 407.
72   In the 1960s, co-education was not seen as an option in Catholic schools as this had been condemned as 'false and harmful' by Pope Pius XI in his encyclical *Divini Illius Magistri* published in 1929 (#68).
73   This task was made more difficult when the Democratic Labor Party (DLP) opposed the plan, interpreting it as a grab for power by the dioceses.
74   Archbishop James Carroll, the auxiliary Archbishop of Sydney, was heavily involved in the State Aid campaign, necessitated by the schools' financial crisis. In this he acted as the Cardinal's deputy. After preliminary work, the campaign began officially in 1967. See Michael Hogan *The Catholic Campaign for State Aid* (Sydney: Catholic Theological Faculty, 1987), 167–186.
75   The exception was Lismore diocese.

Catholic education in Victoria in the post-Mannix era

In the ten years from 1960, the leadership of Catholic education in Victoria was problematic. In that period Melbourne had three archbishops and three Directors of Catholic Education as it faced the impending storm. In 1963 the long-serving Archbishop of Melbourne, Daniel Mannix, died and was succeeded by Archbishop Justin Simonds. Mannix had always been content for the religious congregations to run Catholic education in Melbourne as a loosely federated group of mini-systems, and saw to it that the Melbourne Catholic Education Office had limited authority to interfere with this arrangement.

On 9 July 1963 an historic meeting of key players in Catholic Education—priests from the Catholic Education Office, superiors of religious orders, parish priests and members of the Diocesan Secondary Schools fund—with Archbishop Simonds in the chair, met to consider the pressing issues of Catholic Education. The meeting resolved to establish an advisory board 'to achieve greater success in the administration of education in the archdiocese'.[76] The Archbishop subsequently acted to put Catholic education on a more cohesive footing by creating the Catholic Education Advisory Committee (CEAC). The CEAC operated through sub-committees: one composed of lay academics which dealt with standards in the schools, and the other—strongly connected to senior officials in the Archbishop's office—dealt with finances. Tensions grew as trust eroded between these two groups. Clergy on the finance sub-committee were not used to having their decisions challenged by lay people. The situation was not helped by Archbishop Simonds' ill health. When Archbishop Knox assumed control of the Melbourne Church in 1967, he inherited a complex situation. Anne O'Brien sums up the situation at the time as follows:

In the latter part of 1968 the academic subcommittee expressed concern about the administration of Catholic education. Neither the role of the Director nor that of the Catholic Education Office had been clearly defined, and the CEO was inappropriately staffed as well as being hopelessly understaffed. Abuses were allowed to go on unchecked in schools; too many people were permitted to make ad hoc decisions on educational matters; decisions were delayed because problems were not faced and nobody seemed to know who should face them. There were no proper lines of communication between the CEO and the cathedral bureaucracy.[77]

---

76 Anne O'Brien *Blazing a Trail: Catholic Education in Victoria 1963–1980* (Ringwood: David Lovell, 1999), 52–53.
77 Ibid, 56.

Denied the professional support needed to operate effectively, Melbourne's first attempt to create a broad-based structure to develop the Catholic school system ended in acrimony. This experience made it clear that the Catholic Education Office needed a policy-making Board and more professional expertise to adequately service schools. The problem was working out a way to fund it.

In 1969, the Archbishop accepted the resignation of Fr John F. Kelly as Director of the Catholic Education Office and appointed Fr Pat Crudden as his successor. However, he quickly lost confidence in Crudden and replaced him. The abrupt manner in which this happened added to the sense of crisis in Melbourne. The events of the 1960s meant that, as the culture of the system was taking shape, it already contained within it a 'hermeneutic of suspicion'.[78] This added to the difficulties faced by Crudden's successor, Fr Frank Martin, who became Director of the Catholic Education Office in 1970.

Fr Frank Martin founding father of the CECV

Fr Martin provided the leadership Melbourne badly needed at the time. His genius and insights lay in both the organisational and political arenas. He led the development of Catholic Education in Victoria as government funding structures were being put in place following the Karmel report to the Commonwealth government (1973). In a very real sense, Fr Frank Martin was the 'founding father' of the Catholic Education Commission of Victoria (CECV).

Late in 1969 a number of professional officers had been appointed to the Catholic Education Office to help deal with the crisis existing in the school system as student numbers continued to rise and the financial situation became more acute.[79] It was through their work that the scale of the problems facing Catholic education in Victoria became clear.[80] By the time that Commonwealth government recurrent funding became available in 1973, easing the financial burden, professionally staffed CEOs were in place in both Sydney and Melbourne. These operated according to quite different remits, which were the products of their very different

---

78 The presence of this hermeneutic is evident in O'Brien's treatment and in Helen Praetz's earlier account of the same period. See Helen Praetz *Building a School System: A Sociological Study of Catholic Education* (Melbourne: Melbourne University Press, 1980).
79 O'Brien, 70.
80 These were set out clearly in Martin's 1971 report *The Future for a School System* which recommended that the focus be on the development of the primary school system, that secondary development be slowed, that religious gradually be phased out of leadership positions in favour of lay principals, and that appropriate conditions of service be put in place for lay staff. The report, while bearing unwelcome news, spelled out the realpolitik of the time. O'Brien, 71–2.

histories.[81] In NSW the CEOs took a much more hands-on approach to leadership than was impossible in Victoria where the system remained quite devolved. Fr Martin held a strong belief that the values of collegiality, co-operation, co-responsibility and subsidiarity espoused by the Second Vatican Council should be lived out in the development of the Catholic school system. His approach helped rebuild morale within the CEO and in establishing a relationship with the congregations as the 1970s unfolded.[82] The educational cultures that developed in NSW and Victoria according to patterns established by Frs Slowey and Martin provided contrasting models that other states could adopt or adapt. In this respect the development of the culture of Catholic education systems in the 1960s and 70s is 'a tale of two cultures'.

A 'perfect storm' arrives

By the mid-1970s the gathering storm had reached its climax as multiple factors converged. Educational leaders across Australia found themselves dealing concurrently with the demands arising from:

- cultural change within the Church as the Catholic wall collapsed creating serious divisions over the future direction of the Church[83]
- cultural change within Australian society as the revolution of expressive disorder impacted on many aspects of life[84]
- demographic shifts in society and in the Church due to migration and the post-war baby boom
- introduction of lay teachers into Catholic schools in both teaching and leadership roles as the numbers of religious continued to decline
- need to ensure adequate arrangements were being put in place for the training of lay teachers for Catholic schools
- changes in theological outlook as a consequence of the Second Vatican Council and its translation into new approaches to religious education[85]

---

81   These two models provided the templates other states could work from in developing their own pattern of administrative structures. For instance, Queensland opted for its own version of the Victorian structure as a consequence of research done in *Project Catholic School* (1979), with Sr. Anne McLay R.S.M. as Director.
82   O'Brien, 66.
83   The most prominent members of the Catholic separatist group in Victoria were Bishop Stewart in Bendigo and B.A. Santamaria in Melbourne. These two agitated against 'modern catechetics' for most of the 1970s.
84   See footnote 15 above.
85   Throughout the 1970s the Melbourne CEO was under attack from Catholic separatists for curriculum materials its staff produced to support religious educators who were attempting to handle the changes in theological emphasis emerging from the Second Vatican Council. Teachers often had a limited grasp of the Council's teachings and little understanding of their implications. The in-servicing of teachers became a major responsibility for CEO staff.

- the advent of recurrent funding from governments, and the need to put structures in place to manage it.

Catholic education was hit by this storm on multiple fronts, creating a crisis of liminality like no other. The fact that it not only survived, but also thrived, speaks volumes for both God's providential care, the resilience of its leadership, and the strength of the cultures emerging in the CEOs. Coupled with these was the willingness of Catholic school teachers, both religious and lay, to engage enthusiastically in a range of personal and communal inservice and renewal programs designed to meet the needs generated by the major movements impacting from society, culture and the Church. bishops, congregational superiors, and Catholic Education Offices all contributed to the substantial range of offerings available to Church personnel during this period.

Religious education beyond the storm

In the 1970s, as a consequence of the shifts indicated above, teachers in Catholic schools found themselves in a new place. Many came to understand their place as akin to that of missionaries who had crossed a cultural boundary. It could no longer be assumed that all, or even most, of the students in any Religious Education class had an active faith. The changed situation raised an important question: If Religious Education is no longer catechesis, then what is it?

When the Church began to espouse the 'integration of faith life and culture' as a major goal of Catholic education,[86] Catholic school teachers, faced with the rapidly changing culture and the new theological outlook of the post-conciliar period, had great difficulty in understanding what this meant. There was confusion about how the new goal related to the previous 'big three' in the mission of a Catholic school: handing on the faith, creating life chances, and bringing about social transformation.[87] What seemed clear to many teachers, given the new context, was that Catholic schools needed to undergo some form of renewal. But at the time neither the schools nor school systems had access to the frameworks and processes necessary for this to happen. So teachers continued to muddle through.

When most Catholics had lived within the Catholic wall, their experience of faith and culture had more or less coincided. However, when they decided *en masse* to live beyond the wall, new markers of religious identity had to be developed. Efforts by the Melbourne CEO staff to help young people create some Catholic landmarks in the new territory drew

---

86   Congregation for Catholic Education *The Catholic School*, 1977, #37.
87   In the 1970s cultural anthropology was still developing as an area of academic study that could be applied in Western settings.

intense fire from within the wall. Partly as a consequence of successive leaders' determination to engage with this issue, the Melbourne CEO became a powerhouse in the development of post-conciliar Religious Education frameworks, and in providing accompanying in-service that tried to engage with the changing culture of the times. The Director of Religious Education, Fr Tom Doyle, who was later to become a long-serving Director of Catholic Education in the Melbourne Archdiocese (1980–2002), led his talented team with enthusiasm and courage in assisting teachers with new thinking, new methodology, and new texts, despite the opposition they encountered.[88] His was a strong sense of the historic significance of being called upon to help Catholic school teachers, at a time of great change, to implement the theological insights and implications of the Second Vatican Council. To this day, those who benefitted from his efforts recall with pleasure the visits to Melbourne of outstanding scholars from overseas, and the stimulation provided by the various conferences and seminars on offer during that period.

THE CATHOLIC LANDSCAPE AFTER THE STORM

The leadership of Catholic schools in the 1970s became increasingly complex and demanding, particularly when their effectiveness and relevance was questioned. The questioning came from two directions. For those still living within what was left of the Catholic wall, Catholic schools seemed very ineffective in their traditional role of 'handing on the faith', given that Mass attendance was dropping. For those residing beyond the wall and encountering first hand the pastoral needs there, Catholic schools did not always seem particularly relevant, but for a different reason. Their questioning centred on the quantum of Church resources devoted to Catholic schooling.

A pervasive sense of unease developed as people came increasingly to suspect that, as the numbers of religious teaching in schools declined, somehow the Catholic identity of the schools was being compromised. The prevailing assumption was that the presence of religious underwrote the Catholic identity of the school. The critiques of Catholic schooling were not confined to Australia, but surfaced in the United States, the U.K. and elsewhere. They drew a belated, but as it transpired a very effective, response from Rome with the publication in 1977 of *The Catholic School* a document containing a robust defense of Catholic schools.[89]

---

88   Fr Doyle succeeded Fr Martin as Director of Religious Instruction in government Schools (1970–73) and from 1973 to 1997 was Director of Religious Education, a portfolio which included Religious Education in both Catholic and government schools.
89   Education proved to be a complex topic at the Second Vatican Council. The original

By the early 1980s questions about school identity were reformulated in terms of questions about the school's 'mission', so that the mission of the school could be more appropriately matched to the needs of the new context in both Church and society.[90] In the new Catholic landscape, neither the mission of the parish nor the mission of the school could be presumed; *both needed to be articulated.* Learning how best to do this became the challenge of the 1980s. This required the development of frameworks and processes. The religious, although declining in numbers and influence in the emerging school systems, played an important role in meeting this need.

Renewal in teaching congregations: 'evangelising the culture'

Once they moved beyond the Catholic wall, the religious congregations quickly assessed the changes underway in society and in the Church. Many had sent some of their most talented members to the great Catholic centres overseas in the early 1970s, so that a decade after the Council, they had access to the expertise needed to engage in the 'renewal' mandated by the Council. In a relatively short time 'renewal' came to be re-interpreted as 'evangelising the culture' of the congregations, and they developed the frameworks and processes needed to achieve this goal.[91]

The principles of renewal outlined by the Council called on the congregations to reclaim the 'charism' of their founders which had often faded from sight as the congregations had become institutionalised. Accordingly, they began reformulating their mission in more prophetic terms, no longer accepting the traditional institutional role assigned them by local churches. This development called into question some of the taken-for-granted assumptions about their involvement in Catholic schooling, and led them to ask: What was the mission of the Catholic school in the post-conciliar context? Should the congregation stay involved in Catholic education and, if so, on what terms?[92]

---

intention was to produce a document on Catholic schooling. However, the Commission appointed to deal with the matter shifted the focus to human rights—the rights to education and to culture—as fundamental to human dignity, and the role the Church had in promoting these through education. In the course of the Council the schema charting discussions went through seven major revisions, and when Pope Paul VI indicated that there was a deadline for Council documents, the Commission dealing with the issue codified its work into a set of principles (*Decree on Christian Education 1965*) with an understanding that Catholic schools would be explored in light of these principles in subsequent years. In point of fact it would take the Vatican twelve years to produce *The Catholic School*.

90   The language of the day did not use the word 'mission'. The discourse of the time spoke of 'apostolic effectiveness' since schools were seen as part of the 'apostolate' of the congregations or dioceses running them.

91   A number of congregations were influenced in the development of 'renewal processes' by American anthropologist E.T. Hall's theory of culture first published in 1959. See E.T. Hall *The Silent Language* (New York: Anchor Books, 1973), 60ff.

92   When Fr Martin learned that the Sisters of St Joseph were proposing to discuss this

The renewal of religious life resulted in many congregations interpreting their charism as *service to the marginalised*. New historical research into the founder's life often separated fact from fiction. Founders were seen as people who taught the faith community 'new ways of living the Gospel'.[93] Religious learned from experience the importance of putting their trust in good processes when discerning what these 'new ways' were.

First generation of school renewal projects

It is perhaps not surprising that, having seen the benefits of 'renewal' in their religious communities, congregational leaders began to look for processes that could foster renewal in their schools. They sent personnel overseas to investigate processes for bringing this about. As a result, a number of approaches to 'school renewal' that had been developed in the United States were trialed in Australia. The CEO Sydney adapted the National Catholic Education Association's *Vision and Values* for use in its primary schools.[94] The Melbourne CEO sponsored the *Colloquium on the Ministry of Teaching* developed by the Jesuit Secondary Education Association (JSEA). Jesuit schools in Australia pioneered the JSEA's new *Curriculum Improvement Process*. These projects constituted the first generation of *Catholic school improvement projects* implemented in Australia. Across the balance of the decade, a second generation of projects was created, specifically tailored to the Australian situation. These aimed to assist school communities to articulate their mission and consolidate their Catholic identity. These projects ran under the general title of 'School Development'.[95] For the time being questions about the Catholic identity of the schools were put to rest.

Negotiating liminality: gain and loss

Negotiating liminality involves the process of gain and loss. As few transitions in Catholic education are ever likely to be as extensive as that which occurred in the period from 1960 to 1980, it is worth dwelling briefly on what was gained and what was lost.

---

question at their provincial chapter in 1970, he felt compelled to ask Archbishop Knox who was opening the chapter, to request them to put a moratorium on any decision to withdraw, so great would have been the impact of such a decision on the parish primary schools. (O'Brien, 71).
93 Phrase used of the work of St. Mary MacKillop by the Australian Catholic bishops' Conference, in their Prayer for the Year of Grace 2012.
94 NCEA *Vision and Values* (Washington, National Catholic Education Association, 1983).
95 Major projects were sponsored by the Christian Brothers in Victoria, by Catholic Education Queensland and by the CEO Melbourne. In the early 1990s the Christian Brothers' model was adopted by the CEO Parramatta and, in adapted form, by the CEO Sydney. Staff of the CEO Melbourne had played an integral role in the development of the model.

As the transition was negotiated, Catholics lost any sense of inferiority or defensiveness in the Australian cultural environment. This was in fact a gain. The transition saw the bishops' role in Catholic education change as its administration became more bureaucratised and professionalised. However, the bishops remained vitally involved in Religious Education and the development or adoption of Religious Education curricula. Some also took a leadership role in the theological and spiritual development of teachers. The transition also saw religious congregations consciously step back from institutional leadership roles and adopt a more prophetic stance with respect to Catholic education. While the clergy remained active pastorally in the schools, and carried a degree of administrative responsibility, they were now reliant on the professional expertise of the CEOs in effecting these responsibilities. The CEOs continued to grow and develop in response to the demands of society, culture and the Church. Finally, having served its purpose, the Catholic wall collapsed. In all of these experiences involving loss, there was accompanying grief that often went unacknowledged. Grief plays a role in all social dramas, and if it is not acknowledged, anger soon follows. This may be suppressed for a time, but then breaks out when it can no longer be contained. Many school and system leaders have had to deal with the problems this anger creates.

The great gain in the transition was that Catholic education became *the major field of ministry for lay Catholics*. Catholic education emerged with robust leadership structures enabling a new class of leader to respond, within Catholic education, to the demands of a lifelong vocation.

As this transition period drew to a close, new approaches to consolidating the Catholic identity of schools and clarifying their mission were created. Once the religious congregations opened their teacher training facilities to lay people, the supply of teachers needed to sustain the schools and their leadership seemed assured. The renewed flow of government funding also meant that the future appeared financially secure. It was a time for optimism.

PRIORITIES IN LEADING FOR MISSION

PRIORITY 4.1   Re-contextualising mission
In leading for mission, it is necessary to recontextualise mission as contexts change.

PRIORITY 4.2   Acknowledging and managing grief
Since change can often leave good people feeling marginalised, in leading for mission leaders have to make a space for grief, acknowledging that change has a very human face.

Continuing the Conversation

- In the era of the religious, the mission of a Catholic school was thought of in generic terms. Catholic schools handed on the faith, created life chances, and prepared young people to bring about social transformation starting with the life of the school. These goals are still vitally relevant. How are they being interpreted in the context of your school? How effective is the school in pursuing these goals? Are there now new generic areas that the mission of the school has to embrace?
- In a transition era there is gain, loss and grief. Think back on a major change that has occurred in your school or CEO. Recall the people involved in the change and their reactions to it. Who were the victims of change? Did the process of change allow for grieving? What were the consequences for the implementation of the change?

Part B
RESOURCES IN LEADING FOR MISSION:
Wisdom of our faith tradition

Leading for mission has its roots not only in Australian Catholic experience, but also in the longer Christian faith tradition. In this section we examine something of what the wisdom of our faith tradition has to add to what has already been explored. It is necessarily selective. As we have worked with Catholic school leaders in graduate programs, it has become obvious that many have only limited access to what their faith tradition has to offer in regard to leading within a faith community. Most of their understanding of leadership derives from their culture and its various leadership commentators, some of whose insights are, undeniably, of great value.

Any exploration into the Biblical foundations of leadership is demanding. What currently seems unavailable is a treatment of the scriptural foundations of Christian leadership that matches in depth the work done on mission by theologians such as Stephen Bevans, or biblical scholars such as Donald Senior, Caroll Stuhlmueller and James Okoye. A helpful approach for beginning to address this lacuna is found in the work of the eminent Catholic Scripture scholar, Raymond Brown.

In his classic work, *The Churches the Apostles Left Behind*[96], Brown provides a useful starting point in exploring the scriptural foundations of leadership. He approaches the New Testament literature by asking how the writers deal with a single question: How will the community survive now that our last contacts with the apostolic generation are passing away?[97] Given

---
96 Raymond Brown *The Churches the Apostles Left Behind* (New York: Paulist Press, 1984).
97 The Apostolic Age is approximately the second one-third of the first century. The

that Christian communities of the first and second centuries had relatively poor communication with each other, and that they confronted different issues, or issues presenting in different ways, it is not surprising that their leaders developed a variety of answers to this question. What they have bequeathed to those who lead in later generations are *traditions of Church leadership*. Generalising about leadership in Scripture, as often happens when people hold a naïve understanding of the nature and purpose of the texts is not helpful; neither does it do the texts justice.

The New Testament writers were caught up in a major social drama. They had to deal with the crisis caused by the death of those regarded as the definitive teachers. The construction of a Christian knowledge base, the education of new members, and the formation and catechesis of the children of existing members, became major issues in leading for mission in the early Church. It is against this background that Brown suggests that various scriptural 'heritages' on leadership arose. Leading for mission in this era became *synonymous with meaning-making*. The genius of the authors of the four Gospels was to adopt narrative theology as a literary form to achieve this goal. In all four Gospels the story of Jesus is told in a meaningful way against the background of the human experiences of the communities that the writers led or were endeavouring to instruct. Proclaiming the Good News of Jesus *in a way that was meaningful to their hearers* came to define the educational mission of the early faith communities. Catholic educators today live within that creative tradition, so it is important to understand it *at its sources*.

Chapter 5 sets the scene in exploring the scriptural tradition of leadership and, in the process, covers the earliest of the New Testament scriptural traditions, the Pauline heritage. It is from this early source that the ideal of servant leadership emerges.

Chapter 6 takes the exploration further explaining the leadership issues that arose and the heritages that were formed from Luke–Acts, Matthew and John. These introduce a range of new concepts in Christian leadership such as the role of the Spirit or Paraclete in the mission of the Church, the qualities of leaders, the role the leader's vision plays, and the inclusive nature of the Christian community. Brown explores these heritages in terms of their strengths and limitations, the way they continue to play out in contemporary Church life, and the ambiguities to which they give rise even today.

The Christian tradition about leading for mission continued to develop beyond the sub-apostolic era and has taken different forms in different

---

apostolic generation was comprised of those who had had direct contact with Jesus and his disciples. See discussion in Raymond Brown, 15.

eras.[98] In a liminal era, such as the present, the mission of the Church tends to undergo significant clarification and expansion as sectors within the Church endeavour to respond to the needs of their times. In Chapter 7 we examine the development of mission as a concept in the Catholic faith tradition. Since mission is also used as a cultural construct, and the two meanings—religious and cultural—overlap to some extent, understanding the religious construct is clearly important. How leaders understand leading for mission depends on how they understand Christian leadership and how they understand mission. In this section we seek to explore these two matters in order to open up an imaginal horizon within which leading for mission can be better understood.

---

[98] Noted Protestant missiologist David Bosch outlines changes in the paradigm of Christian mission in his seminal study *Transforming Mission: Paradigm Shifts in Theology of Mission* (Maryknoll NY: Orbis, 1991). Stephen Bevans and Roger Schroeder in a comparable study trace the development of Christian mission through six eras in *Constants in Context: A Theology of Mission for Today* (Maryknoll NY: Orbis, 2004).

5
NEW TESTAMENT LEADERSHIP HERITAGES EMERGE: THE SUFFERING SERVANT

In dealing with the New Testament literature, it is helpful to divide the era in which it was sourced, and subsequently written, into three parts. The first period, in which the material was sourced, but not yet written, corresponds to the life of Jesus. The second, known as the apostolic period, extends from Jesus' death to approximately 70 AD when the temple in Jerusalem was destroyed, a political, social and cultural catastrophe leading to major changes to Jewish religious practice and identity. This is the time during which all the apostles and Paul disappear from the Christian story. The final period, sometimes called the sub-apostolic period, is the one in which the bulk of the New Testament literature was written. The exception, on which there is near-universal agreement among scripture scholars, is the genuine letters of Paul which belong to the second period. The sub-apostolic period extends out into the early second century AD. In this period those who knew Paul and the original disciples of Jesus began to disappear from the scene, and with them the teaching authority they carried because of this association. It was the period in which Christian religious identity became distinguished from Jewish religious identity, and the 'Church' began to take on an institutional form. It was also the era in which the first and second generation of members who had been born into the Christian community, rather than joining it voluntarily, came to maturity.

All of these contextual issues were alive in the communities for which the New Testament authors wrote, and sit behind their concerns and interests. The era was characterised by what today we would clearly identify as leadership issues, and therefore it is in this era that the trajectory of Christian leadership was set. This was not done in a cohesive manner, however, but on a community by community basis as issues surfaced. The leaders in this period faced the challenge of making sense of what was happening. The New Testament literature is testimony to their efforts as *meaning-makers in a liminal era.* New patterns, many of which we now take as givens, were forged in this time of radical uncertainty.

EMERGENCE OF LEADERSHIP HERITAGES

In terms of the scope of the present study, we are obviously limited in the justice we can do to the New Testament sources of Christian leadership. In this chapter we provide an introduction to major themes, and we also consider the heritage of Paul which was largely defined in the apostolic era. In the next chapter we explore developments in the sub-apostolic period in which new challenges arose and had to be addressed. The focus moves to the trajectory of leadership that then emerges, as leaders wrestled with new mission contexts and pastoral circumstances. Their efforts, in confusing and often painful situations, gave rise to a number of leadership heritages. Our treatment focuses on those found in the Gospel of Matthew, Luke–Acts and lastly the Johannine corpus (Gospel and Letters).

With Raymond Brown as guide

Our guide in this endeavour is noted scripture scholar Raymond Brown. In 1984 he published his classic work, *The Churches the Apostles Left Behind,* which we regard as a seminal reference in dealing with leadership for mission.[99] In his treatment Brown contends that the New Testament literature was composed by authors, mostly anonymous, who lived in post-resurrection and post-Pentecost Christian communities. They were leaders in their communities and shared an immediate concern, namely, the future of those communities. Each author sought to address real issues in specific contexts. They did this in the light of a confronting question: *how will my community survive the passing of the generation who knew Jesus' immediate disciples, and the authority that this generation carried?*

Brown argues that, in answering this question, the writers laid the foundations of New Testament heritages that contain different nuances in the understandings they include as to what it means to be 'a church'. He traces seven of these heritages in his study. Our contention is that, implicit in these same sources, there are equally nuanced understandings which can be accessed about what leadership and leadership for mission involve for Christians today. It is these we wish to explore in the balance of this chapter and in the next, working at the leadership issues with the assistance of Brown's treatment of the ecclesiologies of the New Testament communities.

---

[99] Raymond Brown *The Churches the Apostles Left Behind* (New York: Paulist Press, 1984).

Liminality in the New Testament sources

New Testament leaders of the sub-apostolic era sensed they were moving into what we have earlier described as a 'liminal era', a disorienting in-between time, when something that had once been taken for granted—apostolic authority—could no longer be assumed. This presented a challenge—in some instances: crisis—which had to be negotiated. The leaders also saw that the way in which leadership was exercised in their Christian communities was important to the well-being of their communities, both as this presented in the immediate life of the communities themselves, and as it would help them survive into the future. The writers exercised leadership through meaning-making. In doing so they called on the resources of both their cultural and faith traditions.

Leadership heritages in the New Testament

Brown further suggests that the New Testament writings can be grouped in terms of the particular apostolic traditions that underpin them, and from which they draw their authority. Thus, it is possible to talk of leadership in the Pauline tradition, the Johannine tradition, the Petrine tradition, and so on. Since the concerns of the communities differed from place to place, and since communications were difficult, the traditions developed with a degree of independence from one another. From the beginning then, by dint of circumstance, *the Christian tradition on leadership developed as a plural tradition.* When it comes to Christian leadership, from the outset it has never been the case that 'one size fits all'.

There are many commentators on leadership in the New Testament. However, these often tend to project modern-day leadership theories into the texts, rather than examining how the leadership situations are dealt with in the texts themselves.

When we speak of the 'Christian community' in this context we are not speaking of a universal Church, but of local communities existing in widely differing contexts, and largely isolated from one another. It is not surprising, in the circumstances, that the leaders of these communities arrived at different understandings about what it means to be a Christian community (ecclesiology) and what leading the community to achieve its mission (missiology) entails. Brown's interest is in the first of these issues; ours lies in the second.

Another factor also comes into play. The Gospel writers lived in communities that existed in a specific cultural milieu *which they took for granted*, and so the way they construed leadership and mission was unconsciously shaped by the opportunities and constraints imposed by that milieu. Faith and culture were therefore intertwined in the way the writers attempted to make sense of the situations that they confronted. This introduced both strengths, and limitations, to the thinking that stands behind the texts. Since both culture and faith are present in the texts, these need to be approached critically.

The sub-apostolic period as a liminal era

Very little could be taken for granted in the sub-apostolic period as the culture of Christian communities began to take shape. Community leaders of that era faced six significant challenges, all of which find resonances in the experience of Catholic educational leaders today.

- Pastoral issues. They were dealing not only with the problems of creating new Christian communities, but of caring for the established communities and dealing with the problems that arose within these as they became more organised and confronted new challenges.
- Authority issues. The authority of the leaders was based on the fact that they had known the disciples who knew Jesus personally. As this foundation to this authority began to erode, they were led to question how a Christian community could remain authentic in proclaiming the message and continuing the mission of Jesus.
- Christian identity. The leaders were continually faced with identity issues forced on them by 'conservative' members of the movement who wished to retain essential features of their Jewish identity and impose these on new members.
- Interpreting the Good News for people of other cultures. As the movement spread to Rome, Greek towns and Hellenised parts of Palestine, Jesus' message had to be re-interpreted in terms of the questions presenting in new cultural contexts.
- Developing a shared corporate Christian identity. In the sub-apostolic period leadership became important in uniting followers who were organised into house churches on a fairly ad hoc basis. The concept of 'the Church' as distinct from 'the churches' began to emerge.
- Passing the Good News on to a younger generation. The sixth challenge derives from the fact that, whereas the original followers of Jesus were adults, by the sub-apostolic period, a new challenge had to be faced within the communities: How do we pass on our faith in Jesus to our children?

The scriptural basis of leadership in the New Testament was formulated against this background, one that shares many features with the situation faced by leaders in our faith communities today: uncertainties about authority and identity, dealing with a multiplicity of cultures, organisational issues, and connecting with young people.

Leaders in the sub-apostolic era, separated as they were by culture and geography, made a number of different responses to the issues outlined above. In doing so they reflected different leadership stances, all of which must be recognised as having some legitimacy, but none of which can be regarded as being definitive for all times and places. Thus, even from the earliest times, *there has been not one model of Christian leadership, but a number.*

In reviewing the various heritages that set the trajectory of leadership for mission we ask three questions:

- What was the context in which the heritage emerged?
- What model of leadership does the heritage encompass?
- What specific leadership practices does the heritage embody?

LEADERSHIP IN THE APOSTOLIC ERA: THE CHALLENGE OF MEANING-MAKING

In the apostolic period a central question in Christian meaning-making for leaders dealing with those Jews who were attracted to the message of Jesus was: What sense of a dead Messiah can we possibly make for these people? Those followers of Jesus, who had themselves experienced him as risen, had to resolve this question in a way that made sense for their fellow Jews. They had to be meaning-makers.

How to explain a dead Messiah?

The genius they showed in doing so created the possibility of a *Christian identity open to all the nations*. This was an extraordinary feat of imagination for people brought up within the Jewish religious tradition. It set the new imaginal horizon within which Christianity would emerge and spread. It proved an example of 'leadership for mission' on the grand scale. They had to make sense of something any Jew would have found most unexpected and devastating, a catastrophe whose meaning lay outside the comprehension of most viz. that the person they held to be the promised Messiah had died very publicly and ignominiously. This was the fact of the matter for most Jews, and so for them it was also the end of the matter in considering Jesus as Messiah because, in their understanding, the concepts of Messiah and death were mutually exclusive. The Messiah rescued Jews from death; he did not join them in death. While Jesus' disciples had experienced him as risen, this was not the experience of their fellow Jews. How then to negotiate the dilemma this created? The Christian orientation to leadership emerges from the way in which this issue was eventually resolved, and the notion of 'servant leadership' was born.

If asked where the idea of servant leadership arose in the Christian tradition, many people would nominate the passage in the Gospel of Mark where James and John come to Jesus seeking special positions in what they think will be 'the new administration'. Jesus is recorded as dealing with their ambition fairly directly. He calls the group together and reminds them:

You know that among the Gentiles those whom they recognize as their rulers lord it over them, and their great ones are tyrants over them. But it is not so among you; but whoever wishes to become great among you must be your servant and whoever wishes to be first among you must be slave of all. For the Son of Man came not to be served but to serve, and to give his life a ransom for many (Mk 10: 42–45).

Others might cite the incident in the Gospel of John when, at the last supper, Jesus conveys the same message symbolically by washing the feet of his disciples, himself taking on the role usually carried out by a servant, and being subject to objections from Peter for doing so (Jn 13:1–20).

What is clear from the New Testament texts is that, in Jesus' lifetime, his disciples found it difficult to come to terms with who he was and to form any convincing idea of what he was about. So when trouble surfaced on the last ill-fated journey to Jerusalem, they fled back to Galilee in fear of their lives, leaving Jesus to his fate. Scarcely promising leadership material! For them, Jesus' suffering and death, despite, as they recalled later, his many warnings of this possibility, came as a total shock. This is made clear from the Emmaus story recounted in Luke's Gospel (Lk 24:13–32).

The major difficulty for Jesus' first disciples in understanding who he was arose from the fact that they were all Jewish by culture. One of the functions of culture is to limit what people think is possible. Culture of its nature is conservative, and as a consequence, life is lived within imaginal limits, making it possible for people in a society to live together. Transformational leaders tend to extend these limits. They are frequently regarded as disruptive for so doing, and for posing a threat to the power of members of the dominant group, who usually have the most to lose when cultural change occurs. This was as true in Jesus' time as it is today.

The disciples' Jewish culture imposed an imaginal horizon beyond which they found it very difficult to move their thinking. While they clearly came to think of Jesus as the Messiah in his lifetime, their construction of 'Messiah' was that of their culture, and they seemed incapable of moving beyond this construction. In Jewish culture the Messiah was a figure of 'the end of days' who would rule over a world characterised by justice for the needy, and endless peace. The Biblical ideal of right relationships would characterise the world as inaugurated by the Messiah. In this world Israel was to hold a place among the nations that would reflect the power and glory of God. These themes are spelt out specifically in Psalm 72.

In this Jewish construction, the Messiah would live forever, and so the disciples simply ignored Jesus' predictions of his suffering and death. In their understanding, and that of their contemporaries, *a suffering or dead Messiah was a contradiction in terms.*

Re-interpreting the scriptural tradition

Jesus' death, particularly one so ignominious—with show trial, public ridicule, flogging and then crucifixion—must have been devastating, coming so soon after his triumphant entry into Jerusalem, an event which, to the mind of the disciples, would have been construed as 'making it in the big time', and proof that Jesus really did measure up to their conception of the Messiah.

On the other hand, the logical conclusion of Jesus' death to the mind of a devout Jew was that Jesus could not have been the Messiah. Yet the disciples' faith in Jesus told them this could not be right. They were traumatised, and the experience posed questions for them such as:

- How did our beliefs about the Messiah turn out to be so wrong?
- In the light of what has happened, is our scriptural tradition mistaken?

Overtones of their consternation are found in the Gospel account of the Emmaus story where the risen Jesus is recorded as saying:

> *Oh, how foolish you are, and how slow of heart to believe all that the prophets had declared! Was it not necessary that the Messiah should suffer these things and then enter into his glory?*

The text continues:

> *Then beginning with Moses and all the prophets, he interpreted to them the things about himself in all the scriptures.* (Lk 24:25–27)

Reading between the lines here, it is clear that the apostles, confirmed in their faith by the experience of the risen Jesus present among them, eventually went back to the sources in their religious and cultural tradition (Moses and the prophets) in order to make sense of the situation with which they were now confronted. There they found the key to their misunderstanding in the Book of Isaiah, in a set of poems called *The Songs of God's Servant.*

Early Heritage: Paul

Paul is the only member of the apostolic generation to whose writings we have direct access. In his *Letter to the Philippians* he records the words of a poem or song that is believed by scripture scholars to be one of the earliest recorded credos of the Christian community.[100] This reads:

> …Christ Jesus,
> who, though he was in the form of God,
>   did not regard equality with God
>   as something to be exploited,
> but emptied himself,
>   taking the form of a slave,
>   being born in human likeness.
> And being found in human form,
>   he humbled himself
>   and became obedient to the point of death—
>   even death on a cross.
> Therefore, God also highly exalted him
>   and gave him the name
>   that is above every name,
> so that at the name of Jesus
>   every knee should bend,
>   in heaven and on earth and under the earth,
> and every tongue should confess
>   that Jesus Christ is Lord,
>   to the glory of God the Father. (Phil 2:6–11).

This early profession of faith in Jesus contains five direct references to the *Songs of God's Servant* in Isaiah, indicating the importance these had for early Christians in re-interpreting their Jewish cultural tradition, particularly its understanding of God's Messiah. With this re-interpretation of their religious tradition, Jesus' death and their experience of him as risen, took on new significance. When set in the context of these poems, the idea of a suffering Messiah became meaningful and provided a framework within which Jesus' life could be better understood. The development, in time, also paved the way for an understanding of what leadership should mean in a Christian community. Jesus, rather than Israel, is God's servant as presented in the poems.[101]

---

100 For an extended treatment of servant leadership in the New Testament see Efrain Agosto *Servant Leadership: Jesus & Paul* (St Louis: Chalice Press, 2005).
101 The Servant Songs were originally written at the time of the Babylonian exile and are thought to refer to Israel as 'God's suffering servant'. The poems are attributed to Deutero-

It is important therefore to examine the *Songs of God's Servant* because of the pivotal role these play in the evolution of the Christian conception of who Jesus is, and of the way in which leadership came to be understood.

The Songs of God's Servant

There are four *Servant Songs* in Isaiah. The first three are found in Isaiah 42:1–4, Isaiah 49:1–7 and Isaiah 50:4–9. There is then a more sombre piece that runs from Isaiah 52:13 to 53:12. It is the latter that became the most important in the Christian interpretation of Jesus' suffering and death. Here we read of God's Suffering Servant:

> *…he had no form or majesty that we should look at him,*
> *nothing in his appearance that we should desire him.*
> *He was despised and rejected by others;*
> *a man of suffering, acquainted with infirmity;*
> *and as one from whom others hide their faces*
> *he was despised, and we held him of no account.*

Such words must have seemed like an apt description of the disciples' own experience in the immediate aftermath of Jesus' death. The passage continues:

> *Surely he has borne our infirmities*
> *and carried our diseases;*
> *yet we accounted him stricken*
> *struck down by God and afflicted.*
> *But he was wounded for our transgressions,*
> *crushed for our iniquities;*
> *upon him was the punishment that made us whole,*
> *and by his bruises we were healed.*
> *All we like sheep had gone astray;*
> *we have all turned to our own way,*
> *and the Lord laid on him*
> *the iniquity of us all.*
>
> *He was oppressed and he was afflicted,*
> *yet he did not open his mouth;*
> *like a lamb that is led to the slaughter,*
> *and like a sheep that before its shearers is silent,*
> *so he did not open his mouth.*

Isaiah. They are situated within prophesies about the return home of Israel's social elite which had been trapped in exile in Babylon for several generations. The prophecy was realised with the rise of the Medes under Cyrus and the defeat of the Babylonians.

> *By a perversion of justice he was taken away.*
> *Who could have imagined his future?*
> ...
> *The righteous one, my servant, shall make many righteous,*
> *and he shall bear their iniquities.*
> *Therefore, I will allot him a portion with the great,*
> *and he shall divide the spoil with the strong;*
> *because he poured out himself to death,*
> *and was numbered with the transgressors;*
> *yet he bore the sin of many,*
> *and made intercession for the transgressors.*

The passage sets out the basic tenets of what, by Paul's time, had become the Christology celebrated in *Philippians*.

The early Jewish Christians had to wrestle with the realisation that their conception of the Messiah, something they had learned at their mother's knee so to speak, had to be reformulated. As this conception was linked to the highest aspiration of their people, accepting a suffering Messiah represented *deep cultural change*. Such a change was simply beyond the capacity of most Jews to grasp. If embraced, however, it meant life was lived within a new cultural and religious horizon. The apostle's innovative interpretation of Isaiah set the stage for this to happen. What we have here is a legitimate Christological re-reading of an Old Testament passage. In the light of the event of Jesus Christ, the past is being re-read. We too, individually and collectively, must re-read the past in the same way, that is in the light of Jesus' life, death and resurrection.

Exercise of power within the community of Israel

In traditional societies, of which Jewish society in Jesus' time was an example, leadership, power and authority were linked to social hierarchy and exercised in terms of command and control. In Jesus' social context the operation of this social hierarchy was synonymous with forms of oppression, and led to a sense of powerlessness among ordinary people. A well-recognised gap had opened up between the 'mighty' and the 'lowly', which accounts in large part for Luke's consistent condemnation of the rich. The collective aspirations of ordinary people were formed against this background, hence the importance of the Messiah and the prophetic voice in the life of Israel. *Both sustained the hopes of ordinary people.* In Israel, neither the king nor the priest ever had the final say, and they recognised this 'God's word' could come at any time through the prophets. The King often dealt with this possibility by setting up his own group of compliant 'prophets'.

The community knew that it must always remain open to 'a word from the Lord'. Prophets were charismatic characters, often highly imaginative, who were called by God to bear God's word to the rulers and to the people, sometimes with understandable reluctance! Unlike other traditional societies around them, the power and authority of the king or the priest in Israel was never absolute. It was always conditional on God's word. The writer of *Luke* will later develop this understanding of God at work in the life of the community in terms of 'the Spirit', to whose action the community and its leaders must always remain open. For John, this theme is spelled out more specifically in the role of 'the Paraclete'.

God's power in the Hebrew Scriptures is seen as all-pervasive. God has the capacity (resources) to do what God wants while respecting human freedom. Whether God exercises this power depends on God's will or purpose. The way God exercises power provides the model for those who exercise power in the community. After the Exile, during a time of community re-building, God's will was understood as keeping the law as recorded in the Torah. In this circumstance, law and its interpretation in everyday life came to legitimate power and authority within the community.

In the environment of Jesus' time, righteousness was always a public virtue and was defined as 'keeping the Law'. However, it was those in power who interpreted the law and so they could define public virtue on their own terms and to their own advantage. The situation was clearly self-serving. Jesus' savage critique of this truncated understanding of God's purpose, with its cosy benefits for those in power, was seen as subversive—which it clearly was! The fact that those in power did not see Jesus as a prophetic figure illustrates just how corrupting unrestricted organisational power can be.

The *Servant Songs* posed an alternative conception of power and its use, proposing that God's purpose needs to be seen in more expansive terms. People do not always do what is right; they break and destroy relationships. Righteousness is interpreted in terms of living in right relationships and of rebuilding them when they become fractured. It involves reconciliation, healing, and the nurturing of new relationships. This applies not only to people's relationship with God, but also to their relationships with their fellow humans and, ultimately, their relationship with all of creation.

God's Servant brings about peace and justice, not as a matter of command and control, but through the restoration of right relationships, beginning with the human relationship with God. In this understanding, right relationships are restored through service, not through force. This is the key insight in servant leadership. God's purpose is to reconcile, to heal, to nurture relationships and to rebuild them when they are fractured. Jesus' message and ministry pointed to this goal.

The Christian community, from a very early period, began to see itself as in the service of the world, continuing the mission of Jesus, confident that this was the new and expanded direction God's purpose required, and for which God empowered them, just as God had empowered Jesus. The power at work in their efforts was eventually personalised as their understanding of God's Spirit at work in the world grew.

SERVANT LEADERSHIP AS ESCHATOLOGICAL AND CULTURAL IDEAL

The argument we are making is that servant leadership emerged as *the foundation for all Christian leadership* as an early and meaningful ideal. Although, over time, changes in context have often resulted in its being set aside in favour of other forms of leadership, this does not change its status as a *foundational ideal*. It is also an 'eschatological ideal' —one which reaches its final realisation only in God's Kingdom beyond time, but to which we must always aspire here within time.

In recent decades servant leadership has also been famously proposed by Robert Greenleaf as a *cultural* ideal on the basis that, when pursued in the workplace, servant leadership produces the best results for both employers and employees.[102] Surprisingly, it seems that for many Catholic educators, Greenleaf's impressive contribution in the domain of culture is their first introduction to servant leadership. It is regrettable that the Biblical foundations of servant leadership are not as well known to Catholic school leaders as they might be. Starting from Deutero-Isaiah, exemplified in the life and death of Jesus, and running through the early Christian communities and Paul to the present day, there is a thread of religious wisdom extraordinary in its spiritual power. It is a wisdom both fundamentally human and at the same time, for the believing Christian, divine. The challenge for those of us who are Catholic educational leaders is to ensure that, drawing on the wisdom of both faith and culture, we are able to imitate the extraordinary, and very surprising, way that Jesus chose to pursue his mission – as servant of others.

---

102 Robert Greenleaf 'Servant Leadership' in Larry Spears (ed) *Insights on Leadership* (New York: John Wiley & Sons, 1998). See also Robert Greenleaf *Servant Leadership: A Journey into the Nature of Legitimate Power and Greatness* (New York: Paulist Press, 1977).

PRIORITIES IN LEADING FOR MISSION

PRIORITY 5.1 Meaning-making is an essential element in leading for mission in a liminal era

From sub-apostolic times the role of the leader in a faith community has been to help followers to negotiate the meaning of their experience by calling on the resources of their religious and cultural traditions, and so come to see the significance of what they do in daily life.

PRIORITY 5.2 The service of others is integral to all Christian leadership

In the earliest Christian traditions, Christian leadership is construed in terms of Jesus' own example of service to the community. It was through this motif that his immediate disciples made sense of his life and death, and of their own experience of his resurrection.

Continuing the Conversation

Give some thought to the following questions:

- How do you as leader help those you lead make sense of what they do as teachers, advisors, administrators?
- How do those who lead you help you to give significance to what you do?
- Have you ever met someone who models servant leadership? Recall the circumstances of this meeting.
- What skills and attitudes does this person employ that enable you to make this judgement?
- How do servant leaders go about developing and sustaining organisational arrangements that empower people and enable them to grow in their roles?

6
LEADERSHIP HERITAGES IN LUKE-ACTS, MATTHEW AND JOHN

In reading the New Testament it is difficult not to project back onto the texts our own contemporary experience of 'being Christian'. Unless we work at becoming aware of the original human contexts that shaped the texts, and in which they had meaning for those to whom they were immediately directed, we run the risk of reading them solely through lenses which provide us with less insight than we might have. Furthermore, these lenses can seriously distort the beauty and the power, and also the cultural limitations, of the original texts. It is important, therefore, to try to grasp something of the context of the New Testament texts. Doing so places those who strive to provide Christian leadership in our time in a better position to ascertain how they may continue to engage their communities in the meaning-making processes in which leaders in these early communities successfully engaged. As well as grasping the context, it is also important to ponder why these texts came to be included in the canon of Christian Scriptures. One of the reasons that this occurred was because these texts spoke then, and indeed they continue to speak, so authentically not only to the faith carried within the Christian communities, but also to their human condition as well.

A most remarkable thing about the early Christian movement was that it could build the strength that it did across Asia Minor and other parts of the Roman Empire by the end of the sub-apostolic period. This was an era in which travel and communication were precarious and difficult, so that Christian groups could actually exist in large towns quite independently of one another. Furthermore, the result of encountering the Gospel through the work of different itinerant preachers produced a situation that led to rivalries and divisions within communities. It was also an era in which there was not yet a clear delineation about what 'being Christian' vis-à-vis 'being Jewish' meant. This had to be worked out. The Christian leadership tradition developed in a context in which meaning was at a premium, and meaning-making was a key responsibility for leaders. With this background in mind we continue the exploration of leadership traditions in the New Testament, again with Raymond Brown as guide. In reviewing a selection of three of these traditions, we look at the setting in which each heritage emerged, the model of leadership implicit in the heritage, and the leadership practices associated with this model.

LEADERSHIP TRADITION IN LUKE–ACTS

The writer of Luke–Acts is thought to have created his account in the 80s or possibly later, that is at least a decade and a half after the deaths of Peter and Paul, and nearly a half century after the death of Jesus. The account is unique in its re-telling of the story of Jesus found in Mark's Gospel, but adding the stories of Peter and Paul. The common theme in both Luke's Gospel and Acts is the action of the Holy Spirit, understood as God's presence, power and guidance.

Context: Luke–Acts as narrative theology

Luke–Acts is structured as a theological narrative. The significance of the narrative lies in its theological trajectory which moves from what God has done in Jesus, to what God has done in Peter and Paul, and then to what God continues to do in the Christian communities. The action of God's Spirit provides the basis for identity among Christians who are part of an ongoing and identity-defining narrative of which God is the author. Thus the Christian leader not only needs to know the narrative of the community, but also to discern God's action in its communal life. The leader must also be able to see herself/himself and the community as participants in the unfolding of the narrative.

Paul is a significant figure in the narrative of Luke–Acts because he exemplifies its missionary thrust. In proclaiming the good news of Jesus to the gentiles, Paul is portrayed as having a role parallel to that of Peter in presenting the message and mission of Jesus to the Jews. Acts balances these two characters, giving each almost equal space. Paul's significance is that he has been commissioned by the risen Christ, so linking the story of the early Christian communities to Jesus' story.[103]

In Luke–Acts the mission of 'the church'[104] and its evangelising activity are construed mainly in local terms. Paul, for instance, carries out his missionary work, not as a freelance agent, but as the agent of a particular Christian community. This gives him credibility with other Christian communities.

---

103 The writer of Luke–Acts uses 'church' in relation to local churches.
104 The institutionalisation of the Church was embryonic at this stage.

Luke–Acts makes it clear that the powerful presence of God's Spirit sits behind the early successes of the first evangelisers.[105] However, the writer does not identify the Spirit specifically as a person; rather the Spirit is God's powerful presence in history. The narrative theology in Luke–Acts tells the story of a new creative act of God underpinning the missionary thrust of the Christian movement, one that will be ongoing in human history, empowering the efforts of local Christian communities. The narrative strategy found in Luke–Acts implies that taking the message of Jesus beyond the Jewish roots of the early communities is continuous with both the story of Jesus and that of Israel. All reflect the ongoing and purposeful action of God's Spirit. While this may give leaders cause for optimism that present difficulties can be overcome, it does not remove the need for effort and skill in resolving them.

Leadership Model in Luke–Acts

Luke–Acts situates membership of the Christian community *within a compelling narrative of mission* that links past and present, and projects into the future. Continuing the mission of Jesus provides the basis for Christian identity, whether personal, communal or corporate. The leader is the holder of the narrative, and carries responsibility to discern the action of God's Spirit in the life of the community as it continues the mission of Jesus. The narrative therefore has a dynamic quality as God is continually at work empowering, transforming and sustaining the life of the faith community.

As meaning-maker, the writer of Luke–Acts realised that, with Christians moving away from their initial moorings in Judaism, it was important to know that their movement had a distinguished narrative. He uses two approaches to do this. Firstly, he situates his narrative in continuity with that of Israel, Jesus, Peter and Paul.[106] Secondly, he sets the narrative down in terms that make sense to people living in a new cultural context. For the writer of Luke–Acts God's plan might have begun in Israel, but it leads to Rome, and the empire is its destiny. As Brown notes of this strategy:

> To have had a significant past helps to give confidence about the future; and Luke supplied Christianity with a history that gave it that confidence. If the Paul of Acts says that he is 'a citizen of no mean city', the Christians who read Acts came away with a pride that they were adherents to no mean religion. [107]

---
105 See for instance Acts 1:5, 2:38, 8:29, 10:38, 15:28, 16:6, 19:21
106 Luke's infancy narratives contain characters representative of the Old Testament, for example Simeon and Anna, who are presented to Jesus, indicating continuity between the old and the new dispensations.
107 Brown, 69.

The leadership model in Luke–Acts is premised on the belief that God acts through local faith communities—God's actions are reflected in the way faith communities come to understand the Gospel and live out its demands. Within this belief the Spirit plays a decisive role—empowering, guiding and transforming. Discernment of God at work in the life and witness of the community lies at the heart of leadership. This element in the leadership model in Luke–Acts has found ready witness in the lives of great Christian leaders, prophetic figures, founders of religious orders and lay movements throughout the history of Christianity.

Luke–Acts also draws attention to the *limits of narrative* as a tool in leadership. The portrait of Christian life it presents can be criticised as triumphalistic. In the narrative, all setbacks are portrayed as temporary, since God's Spirit will ensure all works out for the best. The Christian movement is presented in ideal terms, constantly growing numerically and spreading geographically. The portrait does not admit of serious failure, and so provides little guidance in dealing with it.[108] Consequent Church history illustrates a similar willingness to ignore failure, to explain it away, or to manipulate the narrative in order to avoid facing its consequences. Luke–Acts suggests that the Spirit will always come to the rescue of the Church in moments of crisis. In Brown's judgement this borders on suggesting that the Church always and in all circumstances has a claim on God.[109] Such a *deus ex machina* exaggeration is unlikely to overcome the effects of poor leadership.

Specific leadership issues raised by Luke–Acts

Luke–Acts raises issues about the skills of leadership in a Christian community. For instance, it highlights the importance and positive value of narrative in building a sense of corporate identity, and giving significance to what people do as members of a community. Christian leaders need to recognise that God is active in the life of a Christian community, and they must be able to discern God's power, presence and guidance. Discernment, which requires time for reflection and prayer, operates at two levels. Firstly there is the *historical* level, knowing how God has acted in the past, what people's experience of living out the Gospel in this context has been, and what forms it has taken. Secondly, at the *missional* level the question is: given the trajectory of the community's narrative, what is it called and empowered to be in the present? There were no easy answers to these questions in the sub-apostolic period.

---

108 Luke–Acts is now widely recognised as narrative theology. It is not, therefore, necessarily a reliable historical source in certain respects, since factual history is not its purpose. However, it held such status in Scripture scholarship well into the 20th century. Historical and other details in Luke–Acts need to be compared with other sources available to the scholar, for example, the genuine letters of Paul.
109 Brown, 70–72.

Leaders also need to recognise that the narrative of the community is never finally told. It is carried in the hearts of members past and present and is constantly added to, re-interpreted, and subject to further insight. As a basis for identity it is dynamic, which means the leader has the constant challenge of keeping the story alive.[110]

Leadership of a Christian community requires that a balance be struck between the need for openness to the future implied in the action of the Spirit, and the need for closure implied in most institutional planning processes. The touchstone here seems to be that God transforms through the power of human aspiration, that is, through what people hope for, and thus one of the tasks of leadership is to raise the level of aspiration at the local level. In this sense Christian leadership is *essentially transformative*.

LEADERSHIP TRADITION IN THE GOSPEL OF MATTHEW

The author of the Gospel of Matthew, like that of the Gospel of John, has interwoven the circumstances of his post-resurrection and post-Pentecost community into the account of Jesus' public ministry. In Matthew, for example, the Pharisees play a prominent role because of their importance as the Jewish leaders in the re-founding of Judaism after the destruction of the temple in 70 AD. At this stage the dynastic leadership, the priestly group previously centred on the temple, had either died or disappeared. The Gospel makes it clear that, during his life, Jesus dealt mainly with his own Jewish people, not with gentiles. This historical reality is then combined with the memory that, post-resurrection, Jesus' followers came to realise the universal significance of who he was and what he taught, and so their mission was to 'all the nations'.

The eminent scripture scholar, Francis Moloney, presents a fascinating observation in regard to the strength of the mission command in the Gospel of Matthew. He suggests consideration of the likelihood that one of the motivations driving the writer was that his Christian community was reluctant to move out into mission. Referring to the 'woes' addressed to the Pharisees in Matt 23, he reflects:

> ...*Remember that the Pharisees are not listening to their condemnation; they are not reading or hearing this Gospel ... but Matthean Christians are. Maybe there are many in the community who wish to return to the old and secure ways that they have lost by 'crossing the road' from the Synagogue*

---

110 School communities often have certain members who take on a role as 'keepers of the story' and as such should be acknowledged and celebrated. In other Catholic service organisations Mission Directors may have this role.

to the Christian community? Maybe they are the ones to whom the 'woes' are addressed in Matt 23? For that reason (among others) does the Gospel close with a massive missionary mandate (Matt 28: 16-20).[111]

Context of Matthew: pluralism in the faith community

The broad consensus among scholars is that Matthew was a reflective Jewish Christian who was probably a former scribe. This gives him an educational background similar to Paul. His construction of the infancy narratives, and the lacing of his narrative of Jesus' ministry with Old Testament quotations, indicates that he had access to a Jewish school where these texts would have been available and could be systematically studied. The Gospel of Matthew is thought to be addressed to an ethnically mixed community, possibly based in Antioch, originally a Jewish community now open to gentiles. The author is struck by the fact that it is the gentiles, and not the Jews, who are accepting the Kingdom proclaimed by Jesus. In the infancy narratives the Magi are characters representing gentiles—they come spontaneously to find Jesus, but cannot, in the Gospel writer's view, succeed, unless the Jewish Scriptures are explained to them. The second set of characters in the drama are Jewish leaders who have access to the Scriptures, but fail to interpret them and seek to destroy Jesus, so the hope of the Kingdom is taken away from them.

The Gospel of Matthew seeks to make sense of the situation in which Christians are being reported to the Roman authorities by their fellow Jews, and persecuted as trouble-makers. Some have lost heart and defaulted. The author's community is beset by problems. Matthew, however, deals with divisions within the community by leaving judgement to God. In his view *patience, mercy and forgiveness are needed to maintain the fabric of community life* (see Matt 18:21–35).

Finally, Matthew's community has a strong sense of organisation and authority modelled on the newly emerging rabbinical authority.

Leadership model in Matthew

In Matthew's Gospel, all power in the Church comes from Jesus and must be exercised according to his standards. Jesus' 'standards' are presented in Matthew as five 'sermons': Sermon on the Mount (Chs 5–7), Sermon on Mission (Ch 10), Sermon on Parables (Ch 13), Sermon on Church Life (Ch 18) and the Eschatological Sermon (Chs 24–25). In Matthew's view,

---

[111] Francis Moloney, correspondence with the authors in regard to the material in this chapter, 27 January, 2013.

leadership within the Church has to keep two things in balance: *respect for the rules of the community and its authority, and the need to deal with pastoral issues in a nuanced manner*, so reflecting Jesus' attitudes in interpreting the Law and exercising authority.

In this leadership heritage, which is the dominant one in the Western Church, the survival of the community depends on members recognising that Jesus remains present to them through his teaching, and through their willingness to live by the moral precepts embedded in that teaching—the Good News of God's Kingdom. This requires the community to have structure and an authoritative voice. The 'church' becomes the place where Jesus' teaching is preserved and lived. Since the Kingdom of God is central to Jesus' message, those leading the community must be concerned with how the Kingdom of God is made present in its life. More than the other Gospel writers, Matthew seems to have anticipated the difficulties that would arise in a church that was structured and had authority. Chapter 18, the Sermon on Church Life, is clearly directed to those who act with authority and have pastoral responsibilities.

Jesus used the metaphor of God's Kingdom to encapsulate both his message and his mission. His choice of image inevitably raised the issues of prestige and power, both of which Matthew sees as temptations (cf. Mt 4:5–10). As was discussed previously, Jesus' teaching about the Kingdom of God centres on the notion of 'righteousness'. Leaders, like all Christians, are called upon to live in right relationship with God, their fellow human beings and all of creation. Since leadership is a form of relationship, the righteousness demanded of leaders is interpreted in terms of service, both in building up the life of the community and in healing its divisions.

Matthew highlights the need for leaders to understand their pastoral obligations towards the misled and marginalised members of the community. He presents Jesus as the model in his concern for 'lost sinners'. This expectation of leaders is demanding, but nevertheless remains a requirement of Christian leadership. For Matthew, authority is neither Christian nor un-Christian; it is the way in which it is exercised that is the issue.

Specific leadership issues raised in Matthew

In dealing with the exercise of leadership, Matthew emphasises the place of law and authority, but his approach is nuanced. The key leadership insight of his Gospel is that *all authority comes from Jesus, and so must be exercised according to his standards.*

In Matthew's judgement, if the Church is to survive beyond sub-apostolic times, it must do so as a society among other societies, which means that issues of power and authority in leadership have to be addressed. This has to be done on Jesus' terms, not by borrowing practices from other societies that are incompatible with Jesus' teaching and example. As Brown observes in commenting on the treatment of authority found in Matthew:

The order in chapter 18 proclaims that the power to forgive indefinitely is a greater Christian possession than the power to excommunicate. Lest it be accused of laxness, the church is often very careful about forgiving. Yet, the number of people who have turned away from the church because they found it too forgiving is infinitesimal; the number who have turned away because they found it unforgiving is legion. For this reason, Matthew's pastoral judgement on those in the church who refuse forgiveness is the very harsh conclusion of the parable. In their case the Matthean Jesus has defined the unforgiveable sin: it is to be unforgiving.[112]

Matthew and his community have lived with what he sees as the counter-example provided by the leadership of the Pharisees. He feared that, given the many elements of Jewish religious culture accepted as givens in the life of the mixed Christian community, in time it too would adopt the pharisaic model of leadership. Chapter 18 addresses this matter and is crucial in understanding the exercise of leadership in a Christian community.

In Matthew's view, if the Christian community is to survive, it must avoid accepting the upside-down values of the surrounding society. In this, Matthew is repeating a central theme of the Old Testament. His stance towards the surrounding culture is critical, not condemnatory—as is often the case in Luke–Acts—since not all the culture's values are upside-down. In other words, Christian leaders need to deal with the surrounding culture critically, not naively.

Matthew highlights this theme by talking about the 'lost sheep' and the different set of values involved in caring for the 'one that was lost'. Here we are dealing with an 'eschatological ideal' similar to that of servant leadership. Jesus deals with the 'lost' by speaking of the unrelenting nature of God's forgiveness. The message is simple: if this is how God treats people, it provides the standard by which they must treat each other.

In Western theology Chapter 18 is regularly quoted in the context of 'binding and loosing', and so affirming the place of authority in the Church. However, its considerations of authority are sandwiched between sections that deal with care for one's brothers and sisters, so putting these two aspects of leadership in context. Authority in a faith community has to be co-opted into the service of the community members—lost or found! This insight poses a major challenge for school leaders in managing the complex relational environment of the Catholic school.

---
112 Brown, 145.

LEADERSHIP TRADITION IN THE GOSPEL OF JOHN

The Johannine heritage is set out in the Fourth Gospel and in the three Letters of John which are thought to have been written within a decade of the Gospel. The Letters, while not written by the same author as the Gospel, claim the same authority. The Fourth Gospel is quite complex in its origins, and this shapes the way both Jesus and the Christian way of life are portrayed. Christology, the study of Christ and the significance of the Incarnation, can be 'low', emphasising the human dimensions of Jesus' life (as found for example in the Gospel of Mark) or 'high', emphasising the divine dimension of Jesus as Son of God. The Fourth Gospel is a primary theological source for high Christologies.

Context of the Johannine tradition: polemic within and without

John's Gospel is thought to have been written for a community made up of Hellenistic Jewish Christians who had been responsible for missionary activity in Samaria. This group and their converts had split off from the Jewish Christians in Jerusalem. The Johannine community then split from the synagogue over the community's high Christology, and later became divided within itself over the very same issue. This latter split provides the background to the three Johannine letters.

The Fourth Gospel was written near the turn of the first century AD. This places it some time after a decisive confrontation with fellow Jews in the local synagogues had resulted in the followers of Jesus being banned from attendance, denounced to the Romans as trouble-makers, and in some cases persecuted. The story of this confrontation between the community and the synagogue is captured in John Chapter 9: the story about a man born blind. In this episode the story of the community and its struggles is presented through the lens of a parallel narrative about Jesus and his own struggles. John uses this literary device a number of times in the course of his Gospel.

Commenting on the struggle between the community and the synagogue Brown observes:

The struggle with the synagogue and the resultant polemic atmosphere are very important in understanding what is present in John but also what is absent. The synagogue leaders apparently thought that the Johannine confession of Jesus as God denied the basic faith of Israel:

> 'The Lord our God is one'. In response the evangelist defended the divinity of Jesus so massively that the Fourth Gospel scarcely allows for human

> *limitation ... the entire presentation protects Jesus from whatever could be a challenge to divinity ... the evangelist does not stress that humanity (of Jesus), since it was never queried by the synagogue polemicists.*[113]

The bitterness this caused within the community is reflected in the use of 'the Jews' within the Fourth Gospel as being synonymous with 'the bad guys'! However, for the writer of the Gospel of John 'the Jews' are not simply the Jews as an ethnic group. They are people who have made a Christological and theological decision against Jesus and what he claims to be doing (c.f. John 15:18–16:4).[114]

An important element in the experience of the early faith communities was the growing realisation of Jesus as Son of God. While this is present in the Synoptics, as a consequence of the extended and bitter polemic with the synagogue leaders, John presents Jesus as Lord, and the pre-existent Son of God. The Fourth Gospel interprets Jesus' coming as opening up the possibility of new life—enabling Christians to enter into God's life by becoming followers of Jesus. 'God's Kingdom' is then seen as linking the Kingdom made present in history (the goal of mission) with its fulfilment beyond history in the fullness of God's life.

Leadership model in the Fourth Gospel

For the writer of John, Jesus is the animating principle of the Christian movement. He conveys this understanding using the metaphor of the vine giving life to the branches. The core of Christian life is a personal ongoing relationship to the life-giver who has come down from God. This relationship provides the foundation on which Christian discipleship is built. *Discipleship is the first requirement of leaders.*

In John, discipleship is a motif personalised in 'the beloved disciple'.[115] The leadership of this 'beloved disciple' is continually contrasted with that of Peter, the designated leader of the apostles. For instance, at the last supper the beloved disciple is the intermediary between Jesus and Peter; the beloved disciple arranges for Peter to gain access to Jesus' trial; the beloved disciple does not abandon Jesus when the others do; Jesus adopts

---

[113] Raymond Brown, 105–6. Jesus' divinity is the focus for example in Jn 6:5–6; 6:70–71; 11:41–42; 12:27; 18:6.

[114] For an extended treatment of the terminology 'the Jews' see Raymond Brown's final book, edited, updated, introduced and concluded by Francis Moloney *An Introduction to the Gospel of John* (New York: Doubleday, 2003), 158, 159, 167–69 et al. This book was unpublished at the time of Brown's death.

[115] 'The beloved disciple' is used as a symbol in the Fourth Gospel. It is thought by scholars such as Brown that the symbol draws on the memory of a real historical person who had been a leader in the community but who has now died. This person is seen by the writer as the exemplar of Christian discipleship.

the beloved disciple as his brother in naming the disciple as son of Mary from the cross; the beloved disciple believes without seeing Jesus when he and Peter encounter the empty tomb; the beloved disciple is the one who recognises the risen Christ, when the seven disciples go fishing. He is the one who, unlike Mary Magdalene and Thomas, does not see Jesus after the resurrection, yet he believes. All those who, like him, do not see and yet believe are blessed (John 20:29). They also become beloved disciples.

The point that the writer is making is that love (expressed through relationship) has brought the disciple closer to Christ than Peter's designated leadership position in the early Church. Commenting on this, Brown notes:

While a real person, the Beloved Disciple functions in the Gospel as the embodiment of Johannine idealism: All Christians are disciples and among them greatness is determined by the loving relationship to Jesus, not by function or office.[116]

However, it would be incorrect to assume on the basis of this that the Beloved Disciple has no office or function. He is the one whose 'office' is that of witness, this office lying side by side with that of Peter's 'office' of shepherd. This is a vitally important issue for disciples endeavouring to continue Jesus' mission in today's demanding context, in which authentic witness is so obviously at the heart of mission in all its forms.

In the Johannine construction the leader is aware of the sources in Christian life. The synoptic Gospels and Paul paint Jesus as instituting the sacraments of baptism and eucharist.[117] However, there is an anomaly in this presentation—after his death, Jesus commands his disciples to do things that he never did while he was alive! Jesus, pre-resurrection, heals and preaches, but the Church, post-resurrection, baptises and celebrates the eucharist. If the Church is carrying on the mission of Jesus, why is there this difference? John addresses this question in two ways.

The sacramental references in John are made in terms of what Jesus normally did in his lifetime (cf. the eucharistic discourse following the feeding of the five thousand in Jn 6:27; and Jesus' instruction to Nicodemus in Jn 3:3). The writer stresses that Jesus *continues* to give the enlightenment of faith and the food of eternal life through the signs of baptism and eucharist. In the *Fourth Gospel* Jesus does not simply institute sacramental rituals—Jesus is the life-giver who remains active in and through these two sacraments. They therefore lie at the core of the Church's activity, sustaining the faith life of Christians, and so are essential if the community is to realise its mission.

Leadership in the Johannine view carries an authority justified by *an active personal relationship with Jesus,* mediated through the sacraments and

---

116 Raymond Brown, 93.
117 Cf. Matt 28:19, Luke 22:19, I Cor. 11:23–25.

through knowledge and love of the community, as modelled in the service provided by the beloved disciple. This model is, however, incomplete, as the subsequent history of the Johannine community illustrates. Leaders in this model carry only personal authority, and so there is no real basis for resolving competing claims to authority. The inability to resolve tensions led to the eventual break up of the community.

Specific leadership issues raised by the fourth Gospel

An important feature of the Johannine writings is *their positive regard for the place of women in the Church*. While other New Testament writings reflect the cultural biases of the age with respect to women, in chapters 4, 11, and 12 John's Gospel contains full-scale narratives in which women are the key characters, and make parallel testimonies to the male disciples.[118] These have no counterparts in the synoptic tradition. In these accounts the Samaritan woman and Martha and Mary are presented as characters of absolutely equal importance to the blind man and Lazarus. Since love of Jesus and care of the community are the criteria of discipleship, the models presented in the Fourth Gospel amply illustrate that, as disciples, women can be just as strong as men.

Secondly, the mission emphasis in John differs from that of the synoptics. The mission of the community has moved from proclaiming the Kingdom as preached by Jesus to proclaiming Jesus as God's only Son, the Kingdom incarnate, and the only source of divine life for humankind. This life is nourished by the sacraments.

In John's Gospel an individual relationship to Jesus is the necessary criterion of leadership within the Church. The consequence for Christian leadership is that it *must strive to bring people into some personal contact with Jesus* so that they can experience, in their own way, what made people follow him in the first place. This is a necessary condition if leadership is to be sustainable. The particular mission of the Christian leader is to assist followers to develop their own relationship with Jesus, and so join with the faith community in the journey of discipleship. Of course, this assumes that the leader has already begun the journey and is conscious of the need to journey together with the community!

---

118 For example, Mary's confession in Jn 11:27 parallels that placed on Peter's lips in Matt 16:16–17. See Brown, 94.

LEADERSHIP IN THE NEW TESTAMENT SOURCES

The aim in this and the preceding chapter has been to trace the sources of Christian leadership by identifying the ideals of leadership that are present in a selection of New Testament sources. We have looked at four of the heritages that emerged. Each responds to the issues that arose in particular contexts as leaders struggled to make sense of a new situation. Taken by itself, each heritage is incomplete. The writings of Paul set the trajectory by introducing the notion of the leader as meaning-maker, and the ideal of servant leadership; Luke–Acts points to the role narrative plays in leadership and in shaping the vision of the leader. It also highlights the need for leaders to discern the presence of God's action in the life of the community. The Gospel of Matthew affirms the necessity for structure and authority in the faith community, but qualifies this by cautioning about the standards that must apply to the way these function in the life of the community. Structure and authority are at the service of the faith community, not the other way around. The Johannine writings speak to the need for leaders to have an inner life sourced in the sacraments, and set out the task of the leader as inducting others into the journey of discipleship.

Sitting behind all these conceptions is a Jewish ideal, that of righteousness. This is however, now reinterpreted in the light of Jesus' message and mission. In using and elucidating the metaphor of 'God's Kingdom', Jesus redefines what living in right relationship with God, with other human beings, and with the natural order, means in the context of his time. The Gospel writers all attempt to make sense of this teaching in their own contexts. In doing so they set down some important principles, both in terms of how leadership is to be understood and how it is to be practised. Later generations of Christians will build on these insights, and a tradition will emerge as understandings about 'living in right relationship' deepen in new contexts, along with understandings of how relationships are to be restored once they are broken. With this deepening understanding, and as societies become more complex, two developments occur: the concept of mission expands and a body of Catholic social teaching begins to take shape. These two developments converge in contemporary thinking, and it is this convergence that leaders need to understand if they are to make sense of their current contexts. It is to this theme that we now turn.

PRIORITIES IN LEADING FOR MISSION: LUKE–ACTS

PRIORITY 6.1 Discerning God at work in the life of the community is a significant element in leading for mission.

An important task in Christian leadership is discerning God at work in the narrative of the community so that members see themselves, not as observers of, but as participants in, an ever-evolving story. Each Christian community lives out the Gospel in a particular way. Each is part of the total Gospel story. It is the witness of many communities that makes the Kingdom of God present in time—no one of them does it all! Making present the Kingdom of God as contexts change is a challenge to human imagination and creativity.

Continuing the Conversation

- Can you identify the particular witness to the Gospel that is alive in the narrative of your school community or school system?
- How is this witness celebrated and kept alive in the life of the school?

PRIORITIES IN LEADING FOR MISSION: MATTHEW

PRIORITY 6.2 Authority of itself is neither Christian nor un-Christian; it is how it is exercised that makes it one or the other.

In leading for mission in a Catholic school or system, authority has to be co-opted in the service of community members—both those who are 'lost' and those who are 'found'.

Continuing the Conversation

- Read through Chapter 18 of Matthew seeing it not as an unrelated series of incidents but as a considered reflection on 'leading according to Jesus' standards' by a leader who is observing people struggling to lead by those standards in the emerging Church community.
- Chapter 18 sets out an eschatological ideal—that is, something fully realised only beyond time but which we are bound to struggle with in our daily lives. Map the essential features of this struggle for you
  - in the classroom
  - in leading your team/peers.

PRIORITIES IN LEADING FOR MISSION: THE JOHANNINE HERITAGE

PRIORITY 6.3 Authenticity in leading for mission means entering the path of Christian discipleship and encouraging others to do the same.

Authentic Catholic leaders must have an inner life, nourished by the sacraments, which underpins their care for the communities they lead. In leading for mission, they recognise the importance of this and encourage and provide opportunities for colleagues to develop an inner life so that leadership becomes sustainable in the community.

Continuing the Conversation

- Are you able to articulate the understanding of Christian discipleship alive in your school or system? How would you express this?
- In what ways do school leaders with whom you are familiar seek to develop and sustain their inner lives?
- In what ways does your school/school system seek to develop the inner-life of potential leaders? Is this form of leadership development seen as a corporate or an individual responsibility? What responsibility does the school/school system accept in this area?

7
MISSION AS INTEGRATING AGENT IN CATHOLIC EDUCATION

In order to address issues resulting from liminality, it is first of all necessary to make sense of them, and then to respond appropriately. To be effective a response has to be meaningful. However, in a liminal era meaning is problematic and so responses can easily falter. In such circumstances, mission thinking which grounds educators in their core purpose, becomes a high priority. Mission and identity, inseparable aspects of any institution, move to centre-stage at such times.

Mission is a valued construct in the Catholic tradition and, as we indicated earlier, has undergone important developments in the post-Vatican II period. It is a transforming idea which takes communities beyond themselves. It is also an integrative idea in that it provides a 'home' within which Catholics of many different backgrounds and leanings can dwell and work effectively together, so as to bring about God's dream for humanity, which Jesus called the Kingdom of God. In this chapter we explore why this is the case.

Mission thinking—how we make sense of things and direct our responses as contexts change—is clearly dependent on the meaning we give to the concept of 'mission'. In the balance of this chapter we look at mission as a religious construct.

MISSION AS A RELIGIOUS CONSTRUCT

The word 'mission' has a rich history. Christian reflection on the term and its meaning has developed as people have tried to make sense of mission experience. Over time, what constitutes mission experience has evolved, and with this the conceptual framework within which it is understood. This enhanced framework in its turn expands what Christians construe as mission experience. As a consequence of the way the construct of 'mission' has developed in the past fifty years, often quite narrow understandings have morphed into a more comprehensive, and still evolving, understanding. We begin by tracing this development.

Etymology of the term 'mission'

The word 'mission' entered common discourse via Portuguese in the fifteenth century when traders began sending ships down the west coast of Africa seeking a more secure route for transporting gold, rather than the long and hazardous journey across the Sahara to ports in North Africa. Captains of ships on these routes were said to be 'sent on a mission', and the bases they established along the coast were known as 'mission posts'. A century later, Ignatius of Loyola co-opted this usage for a religious purpose, sending early Jesuits 'on a mission' to foreign lands. 'Mission' entered Church discourse via this route. Rather belatedly, St. Paul became known as a 'missionary' rather than an 'evangeliser'.[119] So integral did the term 'mission' become to Church activity after the sixteenth century that its secular origins were soon lost.[120]

Christian missionaries were integral to European colonisation of the globe, that is, to the colonisation of the Americas from the sixteenth century, and of Asia, Africa and Oceania in the eighteenth and nineteenth centuries. In both these European expansions, Christian mission proved a mixed blessing for indigenous peoples.[121] The association of the Church with exploitative colonial powers remains a negative legacy held in the memories of peoples, offset to some extent by the sincere efforts and positive contributions of missionaries themselves. Many missionaries lived in solidarity with native peoples, and defended them against exploitation. Others recorded anthropological data about customs and languages that has proved essential in maintaining indigenous cultures and preventing irretrievable loss.[122] This kind of activity was in addition to the more clearly expected tasks such as proclaiming the Gospel, establishing the Church, catechising, building schools, and caring for the sick and needy.

'Mission', in the Christian religious construction of these times, was thought of mainly as 'proclaiming the Gospel' and 'planting the Church' in foreign lands. Organisationally, the Catholic mission experience was different from that of mainstream Protestant churches.

---

119 Christians subsequently became so familiar with Paul's 'missionary journeys' that most think the word has been in currency since New Testament times.
120 The original, cultural, meaning was reclaimed in the late 20th century when 'mission' entered the lexicon of organisational theory as meaning 'fundamental purpose'.
121 The close ties between the Church and the colonisers is evidenced by the fact that the first chair of missiology (then understood as the study of Christian mission for the purpose of preparing people to engage in cross-cultural mission) was funded not by a Church agency, but by the Prussian Department of External Colonies.
122 In recent times the Australian Sisters of St Joseph have been responsible for creating resources for teaching in the Tetun language of the East Timorese. Tetun was made the official language of the East Timorese liturgy during the Indonesian invasion. This was an important development in re-affirming East Timorese culture in the face of attempts by the occupying forces to destroy it.

For Catholics, missionary effort was organised through religious congregations and in due course coordinated, and to a degree funded, centrally from Rome[123]. In the Protestant experience missionaries were commissioned by mission societies and local churches who then took responsibility for supporting them in the field, a tradition that still continues.'

Early Catholic mission theology

Catholic theology of mission developed in response to the Catholic *experience* of mission. From the outset, it drew on the experience of those 'in the field' who were primarily engaged in preaching the Gospel, teaching, catechising, and building the Church community in various ways, that is missionaries in the traditional sense. Initially mission theology did not draw on other experiences which were subsequently to influence an expanded understanding of mission, and hence of mission theology, for example, Catholic social involvement which occurred through the agency of the various Catholic Action movements. For several centuries prior to the mid-twentieth century, the missionaries in the field were almost exclusively members of religious congregations, while the role of Catholic lay people was construed in passive terms—providing financial and spiritual support for 'the missions'.

Catholics enculturated under this paradigm of mission tended to think of 'missionaries' as members of the Church's 'foreign affairs' department, and 'missions' as places where 'the missionaries' worked. 'Mission' was therefore regarded as *the province of Church professionals*. Since there was little place in such a schema for ordinary Catholics, nor for diocesan clergy, 'mission theology' became a backwater in theological education. Another reason for the marginalisation of mission in terms of Church life was that mission was seen as occurring only 'over there', 'in the islands', or somewhere a long way from home.[124] It had little to do with what was happening in the local congregations of the sending church. It was thus an optional extra that the Church engaged in only after it had met its own needs—parishes, schools, hospitals, and welfare. A division therefore arose between 'pastoral theology' and 'mission theology'. The study of the former prepared diocesan priests for ministry in parishes, while that of the latter prepared religious for ministry overseas.

---

123 *Propaganda Fide* was a Vatican Congregation or Department founded in 1622 by Pope Gregory XV for this purpose.
124 For a personal experience of the depth of this understanding in the Australian Catholic psyche, see Noel Connolly 'Mission Mother of the Church and of Theology' in *Compass* Vol 40, No 1, Autumn 2006, 1–7.

After decades of groundswell, with the Second Vatican Council (1962–5), a new mission theology began to emerge, one which recognised the importance of a more active role for lay people in the Church, and the need for the Church to become more effective in shaping the complex web of relationships that had come to define human life in the modern era. Prior to the Council, Church leaders had given serious thought to what 'living in right relationship' might mean in the context of the industrial age. From the late nineteenth century this resulted in the identification of important Catholic social values and the development of the extensive and widely admired corpus of Catholic social teaching. As indicated above, the Catholic Action movement sought to promote these values in the public square where the debates that shape public policy take place. This development added a new dimension to what 'making the Kingdom of God present in time' was understood to embrace, and with this the Catholic understanding of mission. With the passing of time, the theology of mission contained in the Church's magisterial documentation began to reflect a richer, more integrated mission theology. The major contours of this development are set out below.

Mission as a construct with interpretive power

Terms which have interpretive power, tend to expand in meaning over time. 'Mission' is one such term. In due course the Catholic missionary endeavour established local churches in almost every nation on earth. The direct consequence of this has been that *the missionary experience has greatly expanded and now takes many forms.* In our time these include preserving the cultures of minority peoples; being advocates for marginalised peoples in their fight against injustice and oppression[125]; assisting indigenous people to protect their physical environment which is integral to preserving their culture; becoming partners in various forms of inter-religious dialogue made possible by first-hand encounters with people of other faiths; working with non-government organisations to bring about reconciliation in countries torn apart by civil strife; promoting the human dignity of refugees; co-operating with other agencies including the United Nations to respect human dignity through education; supporting development projects in poorer countries, and so on.

All these activities are now carried out by Catholic organisations set up to address a particular form of mission, and are staffed largely by lay people and by members of religious congregations with specialist knowledge and skills. The Catholic mission experience has evolved

---

125 This theme is well taken up in the award-winning film *The Mission* (1986).

from a position which concentrated predominantly on 'proclaiming the Gospel' and 'planting the Church' to one that incorporates many of the new forms outlined above. The old distinction between 'pastoral work' and 'mission work' has been replaced by a more holistic notion of mission, one that includes three broad facets:

- the care and welfare of the faith community (mission ad intra—mission within, that is, directed to the faith community)
- outreach as the faith community seeks to engage those who have not yet heard the word of God, and also to be of service to the world (mission ad extra - mission directed beyond the faith community)
- building relationships between churches, cultures and peoples, (mission inter-gentes—mission between communities).[126]

This way of categorising mission has been productive both in terms of how the concept is understood and the way in which it is lived out. Former distinctions like 'old churches' and 'new churches' have given way to an understanding of the global Church as a *communion*: a community of communities. However, without outreach, that is meeting the needs of the world, allowing the world to set the agenda as it were, mission ad intra is the poorer, since there is a tendency for communities to become unmindful of why Jesus engaged in mission and why he instructed and sent his disciples out on mission.

The distinction between 'pastoral theology' and 'mission theology' is no longer either helpful or logical, since pastoral work is now understood as part of the local Church's mission to the faith community in order that the community may become, albeit with human limitations, a manifestation of God's reign or kingdom, and a community committed to making the Kingdom present. Furthermore, this work is aimed to ensure that local faith communities are capable themselves of being communities-for-mission. 'Foreign mission' has now given way to 'cross-cultural mission'. In a global context, cross-cultural mission can include someone operating in a cross-cultural context in their home country, or alternatively, joining a local church community in another country. For example, a cleric or lay person from Africa or India may work on behalf of the Gospel in Australia, or vice versa. The change that has occurred at the level of mission thinking within the Church is summed up in the following diagram:

---

[126] For a discussion of mission inter gentes in the Asian context see Jonathan Tan 'Mission Inter Gentes: Towards a New Paradigm in the Mission Theology of the Federation of Asian bishops' Conferences' (FABC), 2004.

www.jonathantan.org/essays/Missio%20Inter%20Gentes.pdf Downloaded 3 Feb, 2013.

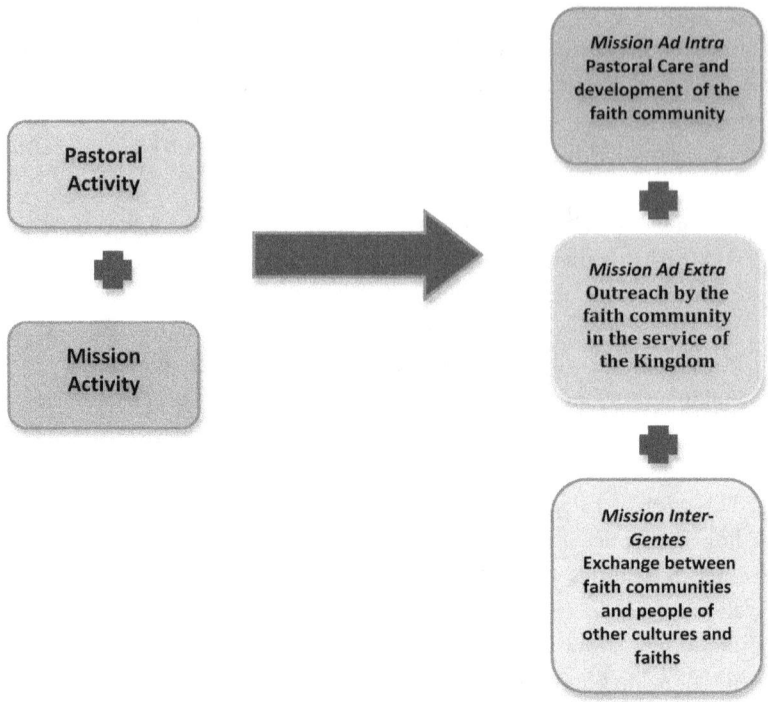

FIGURE 7.1 Changes in the way Catholics construe mission 1960–2012

As the mission experience has expanded, so too has the conceptual framework within which the Church has come to understand this experience. The consequence of these two developments has been that the range of people understood to be involved in 'mission' has increased, which in turn expands the experience of mission, and so on. We now look at this inter-relationship.

RECENT DEVELOPMENTS IN CATHOLIC MISSION THEOLOGY

It is no exaggeration to say that one consequence of the Second Vatican Council (1962–5) was to begin the relocation of mission theology from the theological backwaters to centre-stage in Catholic theology, a process which, however, still has some way to go in practice.

'Mission' in the theology of Vatican II

At the Second Vatican Council the assembled bishops approved two constitutions on the Church, both of which may be construed as missionary character. *Gaudium et Spes (Pastoral Constitution on the Church in the Modern*

World) deals with the Church's relationship with the world and with cultures. *Lumen Gentium (Dogmatic Constitution on the Church)* addresses the nature of the Church, and in so doing draws heavily on Jesus' teaching about the Kingdom of God as found in the synoptic Gospels.[127] It thus reclaims a core element in Jesus' message that had receded in the preceding centuries when the Church had become identified with the Kingdom in the understanding of many Catholics. In the *Decree on the Missionary Activity of the Church (Ad Gentes)* the Council fathers made the important declaration that 'the Church on earth is by its very nature missionary' (*Ad Gentes* #2) implying that, because it is of the nature of the Church, mission is a universal responsibility of all Catholics and should no longer be regarded as the preserve of specialists. It went further in locating mission in the very life of God. The full passage reads:

The Church on earth is by its very nature missionary since, according to the plan of the Father, it has its origin in the mission of the Son and Holy Spirit. This plan flows from 'fountain-like love', the love of God the Father.[128]

In the light of this central insight reminding Catholics of the nature and origin of Christian mission, all substantive theologies of mission take on a Trinitarian character. Those who share the life of God through baptism into the faith community share responsibility for the mission of the community which is to be at the service of Trinitarian mission. What this statement means in practice has taken a good deal of time to unpack, and even today tensions remain about its meaning.

Finally, a short document, *Nostra Aetate,* dealing with the relationship of the Church with religions other than Christian, was to prove one of the most significant of the Council's achievements in regard to mission in the decades following when, under the impact of globalisation, many societies were to become multi-cultural and multi-faith.

Post Vatican II developments

The official Catholic understanding and expression of 'mission' took another major step forward in 1974 when Pope Paul VI called a general synod of bishops at which the theme was evangelisation in the modern world. Discussions here centred on 'the mission of the Church'.[129] These were wide-ranging embracing many points of view, and the assembled bishops asked the Pope to draw the themes together after the synod. This

---

127 For example *Lumen Gentium* Chapter 2 in Austin Flannery (ed.) *Vatican Council II: Constitution, Decrees, Declarations* (Northport: Costello Publishing Company, 1996), 444.
128 *Ad Gentes* 2 in Flannery, 444.
129 This is the meaning of the term 'evangelisation'—the Church's mission is to evangelise, that is to make present God's kingdom or reign in all human relationships.

he did, publishing in the following year (1975) a magisterial document entitled *Evangelii Nuntiandi (On Evangelisation in the Modern World)*. In it Paul VI adopts a quite comprehensive understanding of 'mission'. He begins by invoking Jesus' teaching about the Kingdom of God and equating *Christian mission with those activities that contribute to making the Kingdom present in time*.[130] Paul VI had a particular eye to what 'living in right relationships' meant in the world of the 1970s, a world characterised by rapid cultural change, one which saw the emergence of the post-colonial era in many newly created developing countries. He included the struggle for justice and liberation, the need for socio-economic development, and the evangelisation of cultures, as constituent elements of Christian mission insofar as they contribute to the coming of God's Kingdom. This opened up a new way of thinking about mission and new ways in which lay people in particular could be 'missionary'. In a world rapidly globalising, many of the forms of mission, once solely the concern of missionaries in mission lands, became a concern for all local churches as people mixed and communicated more effectively. In this country the local Catholic school became the principal vehicle by which several of these concerns were, and continue to be, brought to awareness in the Catholic community, and initiatives appropriate within an educational environment were mounted to address them.

Mission as 'God's mission'

As Protestant churches pursued Christian mission within a different organisational framework, it is perhaps not surprising that developments in their understanding of mission followed a somewhat different path from that taken by Catholics. However, in due course, their approach has had an important impact on Catholic thinking. In Catholic thinking, mission has tended to be understood as *what the Church does*. It is therefore something over which Church leaders have responsibility, and over which they exercise control. There is a pedigree in this approach that reaches back to St Paul.[131] As a theological paradigm offering a comprehensive explanation of mission, this understanding may be expressed as '*God's Church has a mission*'. In this perspective the Old Testament is not viewed as having much relevance for mission theology, since mission comes into being only with Jesus and the establishment of the Church.

---

130 Notwithstanding the fact that additional areas have since come into focus, such as interreligious dialogue, *Evangelii Nuntiandi* continues to be regarded even today as a primer on the meaning of mission.

131 Paul presented himself to a new group as someone commissioned by an existing faith community to preach the Good News to them.

Protestants came to hold a somewhat different view. In the 1930s, influential theologian, Karl Barth, began to articulate a new insight. He reacted to what he saw as the excessive optimism and over-reliance on human initiative emanating from the 1910 Edinburgh World Mission Congress. This most important gathering had set the ambitious goal of converting the world to Christianity by the end of the century. Barth reminded his fellow Protestants that 'mission' is primarily God's work, and only secondarily that of the faith community.

For Barth and scholars whom he influenced, the incarnation of Jesus is a definitive step in the realisation of God's ongoing mission. However, it builds on earlier steps, and leads to the creation of the Church as a new instrument of God's mission. Mission is not therefore something that comes into effect with the creation of the Church. In this theological perspective *'God's mission has a Church'* is a better explanatory paradigm.[132] It acknowledges that the whole Bible provides a witness to the unfolding of God's mission or purpose in human history, one which has been ongoing since the moment of creation. These two perspectives on mission, the one emanating from Catholic mission theology and the other from Protestant mission theology, came together in the fundamental insight of Vatican II expressed in *Ad Gentes* #2 referred to above.

Jesus' message of the Kingdom and his witness to its inauguration in time through his own ministry provides the key to understanding what participating in God's mission entails for his followers today. His commitment to this understanding led ultimately to his death. It is his mission which the Church is called upon to continue. So, whilst the long-held paradigm that 'God's Church has a mission' is indisputably valid, the primary or fundamental paradigm is that *'God's mission has a Church'*, the Church's role in mission is being at the service of God's mission as proclaimed and witnessed to by Jesus. The role of the Church is to proclaim and to be a sign of and witness to God's Kingdom as revealed in Jesus, a reigning presence of God embracing human relationships with God, other humans, and all of creation. The Church's prime responsibility is to keep before people, living in ever more complex societies, the necessity of working towards the Kingdom of God. It does this by proclaiming and being a witness to the values and relationships on which such efforts must rest in order to be

---

132 For a discussion of the development of Protestant and also Roman Catholic scholarly thinking on *'missio Dei'* see David Bosch *Transforming Mission* (Maryknoll N.Y: Orbis, 1991), 389–391. For a missiological reflection on the implications of this paradigm see Stephen Bevans and Roger Schroeder 'The Mission Has a Church' in *Prophetic Dialogue: Reflections on Christian Mission Today* (Maryknoll N.Y: Orbis, 2011), 9–18. For another treatment, focusing particularly on post-modern culture, see John Sivalon *God's Mission and Post-modern Culture* (Maryknoll N.Y: Orbis, 2012).

authentic. It is, and continues to form, a community which keeps its focus on Jesus who, as Pope John Paul II reminds us, is the Kingdom of God incarnate (*Redemptoris Missio* # 18).

> *The Kingdom of God is not a concept, a doctrine, or a program subject to free interpretation, but is before all else a person with the face and name of Jesus of Nazareth, the image of the invisible God. If the Kingdom is separated from Jesus, it is no longer the Kingdom of God which he revealed...*

The Catholic school participates in and continues Jesus' mission of making present the Kingdom of God within the parameters imposed by its nature as a learning community embedded in a particular cultural context.

God's mission can be achieved beyond the Church

The notion of mission as God's mission has some important implications. While the mission of Jesus is carried on specifically and intentionally in and through the Church community, empowered by the Holy Spirit, *God is not confined to acting only through the Church in achieving God's purpose*. The Spirit acts where the Spirit wills. This presents many Christians with something of a dilemma. Whilst it is a central tenet of our faith that Jesus is the definitive revelation of God, we also acknowledge God at work in the universe since creation, and clearly see God at work in and through good people wherever they are to be found. What we know, in the face of this mystery, is that the Spirit is to be found at work in what is best in human aspiration. Since over time this aspiration becomes embodied in culture, God is at work in every culture, and this includes the culture of sub-groups within society such as school communities. As Pope John Paul II reminded the assembled Aboriginal people gathered to welcome him in 'Blatherskite' Park near Alice Springs in 1986:

> *...for thousands of years you have lived in this land and fashioned a culture that endures to this day. And during all this time, the Spirit of God has been with you. Your "Dreaming", which influences your lives so strongly that, no matter what happens, you remain forever people of your culture, is your only way of touching the mystery of God's Spirit in you and in creation. You must keep your striving for God and hold on to it in your lives...*[133]

From both an anthropological perspective, and a theological perspective, this understanding provides a basis for entering into dialogue with peoples of

---

[133] Pope John Paul II Address to Aboriginal Peoples and Torres Strait Islanders, 'Blatherskite' Park, Alice Springs, November 1986.
www.vatican.va/holy_father/john_paul_ii/speeches/1986/november/.

all cultures, confident that points of connection can be made and common projects undertaken. Since religion is integral to many cultures, engaging in dialogue with people of other faiths becomes a necessary expression of Christian mission.

MODALITIES OF MISSION

In the long history of Christian mission the notion of proclaiming the Gospel has always held a central place. So much so, that many people understand the word 'evangelise' only as proclamation, that is preaching, teaching, and catechetical work. In fact, many Catholics associate the word 'evangelise' with negative images of street preachers or intolerant missionaries whom they regard as a source of embarrassment. With the best of intentions, in our experience even Directors of Mission in Catholic institutions will say 'I am not here to evangelise …' What people are reacting to in making such statements is that, in the Australian cultural context, it is not seen as appropriate to impose your views on others uninvited. Yet proclaiming the Gospel is *an essential modality* in mission, one which involves both *word* and *witness*. As Paul VI famously noted, 'modern man (sic) listens more willingly to witnesses than to teachers, and if he does listen to teachers, it is because they are witnesses.' (*Evangelii Nuntiandi* #41). Here the Pope is repeating the substance of advice St. Francis of Assisi is said to have given to his confreres: 'Preach the Gospel always; use words if necessary!'

Dialogue as a mode of mission

In the post-Vatican II period, as Catholic theologians further explored the ramification of 'being missionary', awareness of the importance of 'dialogue' and its role in all forms of mission expanded. In common parlance dialogue is often taken to mean 'listening to and talking things over with people'. The notion implies *a degree of mutuality* based on respect for the other.

In mission theology the word has a more expansive meaning that takes note of the contexts in which this mutual exchange becomes possible. Thus Pope John Paul II speaks of four types of dialogue: the 'dialogue of life' by which people holding different religious views share a common life, for example in a neighbourhood; the 'dialogue of action' in which they work together on common projects such as work for social justice, or education; the 'dialogue of religious activity' by which they come together in prayer; and the 'dialogue of theological exchange' by which they listen respectfully to, and share with each other, the religious insights of their respective faith traditions (*Redemptoris Missio* #57). If dialogue is appropriate in various forms of mission inter-gentes (between peoples) and mission ad extra (beyond the Church community), then it is equally, and fundamentally, important when it comes to mission ad intra (within the Catholic faith community). Here the Catholic school provides an important context in which the forms of dialogue set out above can take place, despite different constructions being held within the school community of what 'being Catholic' means. Context and opportunity would seem to present a serious obligation on school leaders in this matter of dialogue.

In mission theology, dialogue is a second foundational modality in mission. Another way of saying this is that, no matter what form mission takes, if it is to be authentic, mission must involve *both proclamation and dialogue*. This has profound consequences for the way in which the Catholic school operates as a Church agency promoting God's Kingdom in time. It is simply not possible to establish the right relationships envisaged in Jesus' teaching, without some form of authentic dialogue taking place, whether mission is being pursued within or beyond the Church.

As a recognised modality in mission, dialogue is a recent addition in the Church's official teaching, although it is deeply embedded in Jesus' own approach to his mission. It has come into recent prominence because, in seeking to make God's Kingdom a reality, mission experience has expanded to incorporate religious pluralism and the need for dialogue with people of other faiths.[134] It has also come into prominence as studies into the processes of knowledge construction and meaning-making have advanced. Genuine truth seekers are generally aware of the limitations of their own understandings, and deeply aware of the need to enter into respectful conversations with others in the pursuit of truth. In many of the human sciences, knowledge is generated inter-subjectively.

Dialogue as a theological category

The theological basis for inter-faith dialogue comes from the Catholic belief that the Spirit of God works to achieve God's mission both within and outside the Church and is present in a mysterious way *in all that is*

---

[134] Pope Paul VI was the first to identify dialogue officially as integral to the Church's mission. He did this in his encyclical *Ecclesiam Suam* (1964) which was published during the Second Vatican Council. Here the Pope was calling for a dialogue with the modern world which the bishops subsequently adopted as one of the Council's major themes. However, the issue of inter-religious dialogue was not taken up in depth at the level of papal documentation until the pontificate of Pope John Paul II (*Redemptoris Missio* ##55–57). The aspect of Catholic teaching dealing with religious pluralism and other faiths is also discussed in a document entitled *Dialogue and Proclamation* published by the Pontifical Council for Inter-religious Dialogue in 1991. This document serves as a commentary on Pope John Paul II's mission encyclical *Redemptoris Missio* (1990).

good in other religious traditions (*Nostra Aetate* #2). This being the case, it is important to discover and affirm what is good in other religious traditions and to identify the points of contact with the Christian tradition.

Dialogue of life and of action provides a basis for collaboration and mutual support. 'Dialogue of action' can result in surprising forms of collaboration. In Sydney, for example, religious sisters work alongside representatives of the sex industry in pursuing the common goal of overcoming the evils of trafficking Asian women into Australia for the purpose of prostitution.

FORMS OF MISSION

When mission is seen as God's mission, and the Church as intentionally a community at the service of God's mission, then the scope of mission expands. Mission then takes multiple forms and involves people working at various levels as they seek to live out the baptismal commitment to make the Kingdom of God present.

Forms of mission: thy kingdom come

Church teaching recognises the following forms of mission:

Mission to the Faith Community:

parish and diocesan ministries including prayer, liturgy, Catholic schooling, youth ministry, care for the aged etc.

Mission by the Community:

- inviting others to consider Jesus and his invitation to relationship
- advocacy on behalf of those denied their human dignity and human rights
- working for human development
- seeking to protect human life
- advocacy and support for the marginalised of society
- promoting the search for peace, justice and the integrity of creation
- seeking to protect natural environments from unsustainable exploitation
- a range of endeavours which, in one way or another, seek to evangelise the cultures within which people live their lives[135]

---

135 In *Evangelii Nuntiandi* #20 Paul VI writes 'what matters is to evangelise man's cultures (not in a purely decorative way, as it were, by applying a thin veneer, but in a vital way, in depth and right to the very roots)… always taking the person as one's starting point and always coming back to relationships of people among themselves and with God'.

Mission between Communities

- inter-religious dialogue
- promotion of national or inter-community reconciliation
- building relationships between churches, cultures and peoples

The growing number of forms of mission in our day reflects the range of experiences people now have in making the Kingdom of God present in local contexts, and a widening understanding of 'call' among a previously passive laity. As the concept of mission has expanded, so too has the meaning that people can give to what they do. It is a timely development in a liminal age.

If the Gospel becomes meaningful to the cultural insider only when it is lived, it generally becomes meaningful to an outsider *only when this lived witness is explained.* Here the passage 1 Peter 3:15 is often cited: 'Always be ready to make your defence to anyone who demands from you an account of the hope that is in you'. Clearly, it is very difficult to explain witness in the absence of any context for dialogue. This applies to mission in all its forms.

After several centuries of rather passively thinking of mission as 'what specialists do', it will take time for Catholics to understand and respond to the challenges implicit in the wider understanding of the Church's mission embodied in contemporary mission theology. In this respect the Church's magisterial teaching seems currently well ahead of Church practice. In our experience, however, many staff in Catholic schools find interpreting their work in terms of contributing to God's mission—to 'God's dream for humankind'[136]—quite liberating. This is particularly true of those who, for various reasons, are distant from the institutional Church and regard themselves as Catholic 'outsiders'. In practice, this realisation has often become a first step in changing their stance towards the Church, enabling them to 'befriend' their Catholic tradition because it is seen from a new perspective.

---

136 For an imaginative and inspiring treatment of the Kingdom of God in these terms see James and Evelyn Whitehead *Community of Faith* (Minneapolis: The Winston Seabury Press, 1982), 104–107.

PRIORITIES IN LEADING FOR MISSION

Priority 7.1 In leading for mission, it is important to be aware of the scope and challenge which making the Kingdom present in time represents for the school community, or for the school system.

Continuing the Conversation

The relationship between the forms and modalities of mission can be mapped using the Mission Matrix below. This provides a simple way of mapping some of the major ways in which a faith community, such as a school or school system, engages in the mission of the Church. It is important for a leader to ensure that each staff member has the opportunity to be aware of how their particular work contributes to making present God's reign or kingdom in the school community.

	FUNDAMENTAL MODES OF MISSION		
	PROCLAMATION		DIALOGUE
	BY WITNESS	BY WORD	
Prayer & Worship			
Pastoral Ministry & Sacraments			
Liberation–Personal and Communal			
Reconciliation–Peoples & Cultures			
Justice & Peace			
Care for the Earth			
Inculturation ( )			
Inter-religious Dialogue			
Evangelisation of cultures			
(Forms yet to be articulated)			

(Rows labelled: FORMS OF MISSION)

FIGURE 7.2 Mission Matrix

For each form of mission it is possible to ask:

- How do we currently engage in this form of mission and how to we explain our reasons for engaging in it? (proclamation by word and witness).
- Who are, or should be, our dialogue partners in this form of mission, and what form does, or should, this dialogue take?

The Mission *Matrix* enables a group such as a Catholic school or system of schools to ask important questions about the way in which it engages in the mission of the Church and, by extension, how it seeks to make the Kingdom of God present in its immediate context.

For instance, in addressing social justice issues, the group might reflect on these questions:

- What message does the school promote about social justice (proclamation by word) in its curriculum, in its pedagogy, in the type of learning environment it seeks to create, in its organisation, and in its relationship with parents and with the local community?
- What specific witness (proclamation by witness) does the school seek to provide to complement its social justice message within the community, in its outreach activities?
- Who are the school's dialogue partners in the promotion of social justice and at what levels does this dialogue take place—life, action, reflection and prayer, exchange?

Other forms of mission down the left-hand side of the matrix can be analysed in a similar way.

Part C
RESOURCES IN LEADING FOR MISSION:
Wisdom of our cultural traditon

As we noted at the outset of this study, the aim in theological reflection is to bring together, in dialogue, the wisdom of faith, of culture and of human experience in exploring an issue. Our focus is leading for mission in Catholic schools and systems at the dawn of a new era in Catholic education. What wisdom does our cultural tradition offer leaders in understanding and negotiating the changes which are giving birth to this new era? This is the question that focuses Part C.

The leadership literature sourced in our culture is vast, and the topic can be approached from a number of perspectives. For example, James Kouzes and Barry Posner adopt an empirical approach in determining the qualities and exemplary practices of effective leaders. Stephen Covey adopts psychological and sociological insights in formulating the habits of effective leaders. James McGregor Burns uses an historical approach in outlining the moral basis of leadership, and the way leaders mobilise and use power in relating to colleagues and in achieving goals. Robert Greenleaf approaches the topic from the perspective of organisational theory in outlining his concept of servant leadership which closely parallels the biblical concept outlined in Chapter 5. All of these authors write from a similar cultural location. They are white, male, urban academics from the United States, and write as though these shared characteristics have nothing to do with what they write or how they write. They offer their insights as a form of *universal knowledge*, even when its major source is their own culture with its taken for granted assumptions.

We encounter the similar phenomenon when reading through the New Testament sources. All the New Testament authors take their cultural background as a given, and this shapes how they interpret the world and how they express their thought.

The impressive feature of culture is that it operates out of awareness in providing us with a primary frame of reference within which we make sense of life. In a school or school system committed to helping students integrate faith, culture and human experience, and a Church that is committed to evangelising cultures, it is important for leaders to be clear about what they mean when they talk about 'culture'. Culture is a term with great interpretive power and like all such terms, its meaning stretches with usage.

The study of culture is the province of anthropology. With the assistance of anthropology we address culture within two competing paradigms – the modern and the post-modern. In Chapter 8 we examine the modern understanding of culture and its ties with the classicist notion. The limitations in the modern concept gave rise to a new post-modern way of construing culture, one based on the notion that cultures are constructed around the ways in which groups deal with difference. In the post-modern conception, what distinguishes one culture from another is the way in which power is used to maintain a balance in society between groups seeking competing goods. The post-modern model of culture, discussed in Chapter 9, places *pluralism and the negotiation of difference* at the core of culture. Catholic teaching on culture has yet to seriously connect with this influential development in anthropology.

The modern and post-modern notions of culture provide important analytical tools in clarifying what we mean when we say that the aim of the Catholic school is to help students 'integrate faith, life and culture' in making sense of their lives, or that a major aim of the Church's mission is to 'evangelise culture'. However, gaining such clarification leaves the job half done if we remain unclear about *how people make sense of their lives*. We have noted several times that in a liminal era meaning is at a premium as older taken-for-granted cultural assumptions begin to break down, and new frameworks of meaning have to be developed. Obviously meaning-making by leaders becomes a key priority. It is therefore important that leaders have *clear ideas as to how it is that people makes sense of their lives*. This is the field of hermeneutics. In Chapter 10 we explore the model of meaning-making used in moderate hermeneutics. In doing so we draw on the work of mission anthropologist Paul Hiebert, and philosophers Hans-Georg Gadamer and Paul Ricoeur.

The overall intention in Part C is to provide leaders with conceptual tools to make sense of a situation in which Catholic schools are educating the first and second generations of students growing up in a post-modern cultural environment that, in many of its assumptions, is disconnected from the modern environment in which their parents were raised.

Facing the Catholic community is the mission question which will come to define the era: *How do we help young people, many of whom experience life as being adrift on the post-modern sea, understand that the Kingdom of God can be present there as well as in every other cultural environment?* In addressing this challenge meaning-making and mission coincide.

8
WHAT LEADERS NEED TO KNOW ABOUT CULTURE: THE MODERN CONSTRUCTION

To talk about 'culture' is to open up Pandora's Box. People refer to the 'culture of the school', 'the culture of a school system', 'Australian culture', 'Catholic culture', 'a culture of learning', and so on. If your football team is not doing well, it is now quite fashionable to say, 'There is something wrong with the team's culture'. How can the one word cover all these situations and remain meaningful? This is the issue we have to address first. There is no shortage of definitions of 'culture', so when discussion turns to 'the relationship between the Gospel and culture' and from there to 'evangelising culture', it is important to be clear about what it is that we are talking about. As the examples above illustrate, common usage provides poor guidance.

WHAT IS CULTURE?

In exploring the notion of culture, it is cultural anthropology—the study of the human person within culture—that provides the best available guidance.

Contemporary constructions of culture

Here there are two major contemporary schools of thought: the modern construction of culture and the post-modern construction. In this chapter we focus on the former which is essential to understanding the latter. Most of the educational literature on 'school culture' and 'cultural leadership' is based, often implicitly, on the modern understanding of culture. However, in the face of globalisation and advancing pluralism, the limits of this understanding have become clearer, giving rise to post-modern approaches. The major difference between the two constructions lies in the understanding of cultural values and the role these play in shaping the dynamics by which cultures adapt, or are manipulated, to deal with changing contexts. Both models contain important insights for school and system leaders, since shaping the culture of the school or school system is a major part of their role. Both models have important things to say about what 'evangelising culture' means.

At an intuitive level culture can be thought of as the patterns of interaction that characterise life within a particular group of people.[137] Whenever a group of people form a social entity, culture begins to take shape. This is true of nations, ethnic groups, communities, schools, churches, football teams, etc. What culture is and how it functions has been a subject of much discussion since the concept was first formulated in the nineteenth century. Prior to that time people spoke of 'civilisation' rather than of 'culture'.[138]

Modern view of culture

Cultural anthropology began in the late nineteenth and early twentieth centuries as an academic discipline. Its subject is 'the culture of peoples'. It grew in importance after World War II as the Allied powers sought to rebuild nations in the Pacific and began to realise that, without knowledge of local cultures, their task was doomed to failure. Anthropologists observed local cultures, often using ethnography as their methodology in order to identify patterns of behavior, and the values and meanings that gave these behaviors significance for local peoples. The basic assumption behind many early studies of culture was that *every people has a culture* and that this is unique to that people. Since the study of cultures was done empirically, this model of culture was called the 'empirical' or 'anthropological' concept. As it was formulated at the height or modernity, it is also known as the 'modern' concept of culture.

Culture of organisations and groups

As knowledge of local cultures grew, it was soon realised that findings at the macro level (culture of a people) could be applied to smaller social groupings within the culture (often referred to as 'sub-cultures'). Thus it became possible to talk about the culture of organisations, such as schools, or of groups within a society such as youth, football teams, etc. In the modern construction of culture, if any social grouping is to exist over time, then it is necessary for the members to work out a more or less

---

137 The classic Catholic work on mission anthropology is Louis Luzbetak *The Church and Cultures* (Maryknoll N.Y.: Orbis Books, 1988). For excellent contributions by a Protestant scholar see Paul Hiebert *The Gospel in Human Contexts: Anthropological Explorations for Contemporary Missions* (Grand Rapids: BakerAcademic, 2009), and Paul Hiebert *Transforming Worldviews: An Anthropological Understanding of How People Change* (Grand Rapids: BakerAcademic, 2008).
138 For a history of the concept of culture see Kathryn Tanner *Theories of Culture: A New Agenda for Theology* (Minneapolis: Fortress Press, 1997), 3ff.

comprehensive and reasonably successful design for living together that is appropriate to the times and to the environment in which they live.[139] This understanding is often abbreviated in common parlance so that culture is understood as 'how things are done around here' or, more simply, as 'our way of life'.

Two things need to be highlighted immediately. Firstly, since every people and every community has a culture, humans only ever exist as *persons-within-culture*. There is no escaping culture. This means that there is no 'objective' place in which we can stand to view another culture. Put another way, there is no such thing as a 'culture-free' space. We always look at other cultures through the lens of our own culture, and it is not possible to throw that lens away because our culture provides us with our primary frame of reference in making sense of life. Early anthropology was bedeviled by the fact that people 'observing' cultures did not recognise the cultural preconceptions they brought to interpreting their data. Rather than determining what things meant for locals, they tended to project their own meaning systems onto data. Their studies told the reader as much about the researcher's culture as they did about the culture being studied. Put simply, *it is not possible to take a 'God's eye' view of culture.*

The second point to note is that culture is a human construct. People create cultures and change cultures. All cultures are the consequence of human agency which may be intended or unintended. This point applies to Church culture, national culture, school culture, the culture of school systems and so on. 'The way things are done around here' is always the result of human aspirations lived out in the context of contested human decisions. Culture therefore is created, and so can be re-created, as contexts and times change. This will happen if a culture is to meet the 'more or less successful' criteria essential for its survival.

CLASSICIST VIEW OF CULTURE

In the modern period the term 'culture' also came to be used in another context, that of 'high culture'. The 'classicist' understanding identifies 'culture' with the longer-standing notions of 'civilisation' and 'human refinement'. Within any local culture dominant elites come to define 'what is best in the culture'.

High culture

In Western cultures 'what is best' in a culture is often defined by those holding power, or by tradition. In the classicist conception, the higher expressions of

---

139 Luzbetak, 74.

culture are found in the arts, in music, in science, in philosophy, in literature and so on. High culture also incorporates those patterns of behavior which define civility. High culture represents what is judged to be of worth. While in the short term this can be defined by those in power, power alone cannot define worth in the absence of general appreciation of 'what is best', which is conferred by tradition. In the classicist perspective culture is not the possession of a people but of individuals. People are, or are not, 'cultured'.

In the classicist understanding, judgements are made about the relative merits of civilisations and what represents their highest achievements. In the West the unstated assumption has been that European culture represents the pinnacle of human achievement, and so human refinement is best defined in terms of what is deemed best and appropriate in that culture. This conception was powerful in the nineteenth century when it became combined with that of evolution. European civilisation was seen as the endpoint of cultural evolution. This understanding led to European governments accepting responsibility for 'civilising' the less developed cultures encountered in their colonies. In its American interpretation, it led to the conception of a 'manifest destiny' to provide world leadership. Both of these conceptions are based in the cultural assumptions of elites and relate to the notion of power.

In the modern period the classicist notion was influential in shaping educational policy and practice. Education was seen as a universal means of inducting young people into their 'cultural heritage'—the highest expressions of their culture as determined by traditions and the elites who preserve, control and manipulate these traditions. Very often education has come to be the process by which the young are inducted into the value systems of these elites—academic, political and religious. The meaning of education is interpreted in terms of *cultural reproduction*. Its essential task is to hand on the values and myths that determine and underpin the cultural tradition.

Ethnocentric biases in high culture

All cultures have elites who determine what is best in the culture and seek to preserve this. Indeed this is widely recognised as one of the tasks of leaders. The problems arise in the way values are determined and employed to make judgements about what is best, and in the way elites seek to manipulate these. The classicist understanding tends to see certain values as 'universal' and is oriented to institutionalising them. In a liminal era the institutional values that elites rely on to define 'what is best' come under scrutiny, and notions of 'what is best' are open to re-negotiation. This is a defining feature of what has become known as the 'post-modern turn' which occurred in the 1970s. As an example, in the West for the last two hundred years, religion has been excluded by academic and political elites from the definition of 'what is best'. However, in the face of globalisation and advancing pluralism this stance is becoming untenable. Recent history demonstrates that international tensions cannot be resolved by the use of power alone; resolution has to be a matter of dialogue. However, as long as religion, which is thought of as integral to 'what is best' in Muslim societies for example, is excluded from 'what is best' in Western societies, the prospects for dialogue are limited.[140]

The empirical or modern understanding of culture makes no judgements about culture. Culture is something that simply is, and can be studied. In this perspective, education is based on the premise that, in order to thrive in a culture, young people must appreciate both its strengths and weaknesses, since they employ the resources of their culture to create life chances for themselves and to make sense of life. All human constructions, all cultures have both strengths and weaknesses. All contain biases to which insiders are often oblivious because these biases are part of a system that is taken for granted. In the modern perspective, education is thought of as helping young people engage critically with their culture. The aim is *critical transmission* of culture. Critical transmission assumes values come into play. The question in Catholic education is 'which values?' Discussions in Catholic education about 'integrating faith and culture' often confuse the two quite different understandings of culture discussed above, the modern and the classicist. This leads to a good deal of confusion about what this expression means in practice.[141]

In the balance of this chapter we want to explore in some detail the modern understanding of culture and its implications for school and system leadership, with a particular focus on leading for mission.

MODERN MODEL OF CULTURE

As a result of the work of cultural anthropologists we now know a good deal about culture and how it functions. We know that cultures operate at a variety of levels.

---

140 Tony Blair, former Prime Minister of the U.K., who played a key role in attempts to impose Western power on Muslim countries, after leaving government established the Tony Blair Faith Foundation which describes its goals as follows: [The foundation] 'Promotes respect and understanding about the world's religions through education and multi-faith action. We show how faith can be a powerful force for good in the modern world'. See http://www.tonyblairfaithfoundation.org.
141 In the various Roman documents relating to Catholic schooling the reader is referred back to the Vatican II document *The Church in the Modern World* for the meaning of culture. However, in that document (#53), the modern and classicist understandings are simply juxtaposed. Vatican documents on Catholic education have yet to address in depth issues raised by the post-modern understanding.

Dimensions of culture

Cultures have a surface level that corresponds to what can be observed. They also have depth dimensions which are by no means obvious to even the trained observer. While the question 'What is happening here?' can be quickly answered by reference to the surface dimension, questions such as 'Why is it happening?' are harder for the cultural outsider to answer because he or she often lacks the key needed to interpret behavior. The key is often found when one understands the place religion holds in the culture.

An outsider uses the models of the human and social sciences in an attempt to explain cultural behavior. Insiders do not explain cultural behavior; they interpret it. In early anthropological enquiry it was assumed that a social scientist could 'objectively' study a people and their culture. It was soon realised that such analyses tended to highlight the cultural assumptions the observer brought to the task rather than the cultural understandings of the people being observed. Secondly, it was realised that, when people are observed, they change to fit the expectations of the observer. People are not objects; they are, and remain, active subjects. Both these factors make it difficult to identify the meanings that sit behind culture and give cultural behavior its power and significance for insiders.

Depth dimensions

In order to understand a culture it is necessary to grasp its depth dimensions—what gives it meaning for insiders. To accomplish this the outsider has to enter into a dialogue with the insider. 'Dialogue' here involves more than just talking. It involves living together and doing things together, so that answers to questions such as 'why?' and 'what should?' emerge out of lived-experience.

Anthropologists, for example Paul Hiebert, hold that our culture provides us with the framework within which we think, value and feel.[142]

Culture is not just something of the mind, it is something of the heart as well. Culture then provides us with our primary frame of reference in making sense of the world we encounter, of our feelings towards that world, and of our judgements about it. All three are important.

We can only make sense of what we observe in a culture by exploring the values that give surface activity their coherence and meaning. For instance, we recently took a young relative visiting from Switzerland to her first game of Australian Rules football. The game was an important one, attended by a crowd of over 30,000 people. To our surprise our visitor

---

[142] Paul Hiebert *Transforming Worldviews: An Anthropological Understanding of How People Change* (Grand Rapids: Michigan Baker Academic 2008), 26.

got more amusement from watching the crowd than watching the game. Two of her questions, when it concluded, were: 'Why do people barrack so passionately for their teams?' and 'Why do they give the umpires such a hard time?' The answers to these questions tap into something deep in the Australian culture which is so taken-for-granted that many would be at a loss to explain what it is. The meaning of the crowd's behavior is not found in the game, but rather in the place the game holds in something bigger, affirming the values, myths and worldview that underpin Australian culture. These are the culture's depth dimensions.

Cultural values

Cultural values acquire significance over time as the result of lived experience. Dominant Australian cultural values such as 'every person is entitled to a fair go' operate at a conscious level; others operate sub-consciously, and we are often unaware of what they are until they are challenged by the way people act, and so are drawn to our attention. We recognise some forms of behavior as 'un-Australian'. 'Never dob in a mate' might fit into this category. Cultural values shape our behavior, but are rarely questioned because they operate 'behind our backs' or out-of-awareness.

Cultural myths

Cultural values take on the mantle of sacredness when they are incorporated into the mythology of the culture. Myth is often popularly understood as something that is not really true. This is not the way the term is used in social science, where it refers to a narrative that expresses what a people want to believe and feel about themselves as members of the social group. Myth conveys meaning based on beliefs that are unquestioned or unable to be questioned.

The mythic dimension of a culture encompasses the aspirations people hold for themselves, for their families, for the communities to which they belong, and for their social group as a whole. These hopes create expectations. Cultural myths are conveyed from generation to generation *in narrative form* and provide a basic means by which culture is transmitted. Mythic narratives do not have to be entirely factual, although most are based in historical fact. The ANZAC and Ned Kelly legends are examples of mythic narratives in Australian culture. They convey something essential about what it means to be Australian.

Cultural worldviews

The depth dimensions of a culture—values and mythology which includes narrative and symbol—provide the bedrock on which the culture's worldview rests. The worldview of a culture is a basic frame of reference that people living in a culture call upon in making sense of and responding to the events of life.

Culture provides 'a more or less comprehensive design for living' because its key components are ordered hierarchically. Myth and worldview reinforce cultural values giving them both interpretive value and salience. Values underpin cultural behaviors and render them meaningful. While it is relatively easy to change cultural expressions and what is readily observed at the surface area of culture, people are resistant to changes in cultural values, and making changes at the level of myth and worldview are more difficult still, since these impinge on identity—who we are as a people. Change at this level means re-interpreting historical experience and re-shaping the aspirations that flow from the present interpretation of this experience. People find this very difficult as it involves real loss.

We can represent the modern model of culture schematically as follows:

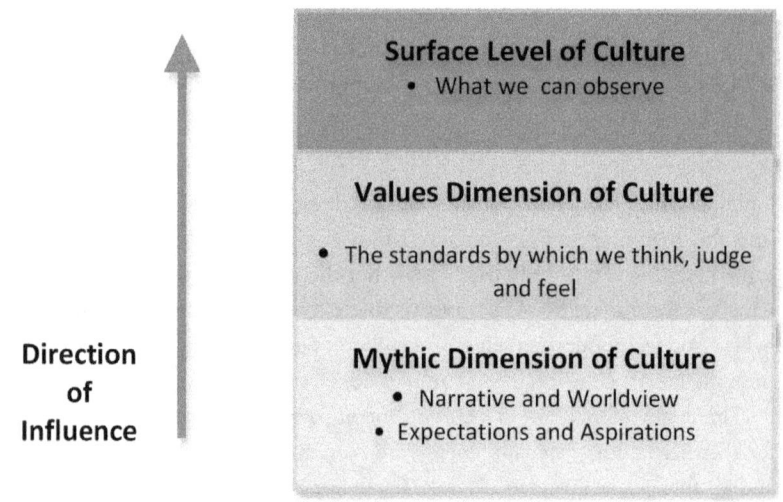

FIGURE 8.1 The Three Dimensions of Culture

Early anthropologists were surprised at the number of people living within the cultures they studied who seemed blissfully unaware of the mythic dimension and much of the value dimension of their cultures. This is not surprising, as the depth elements of a culture are so taken-for-granted that people simply do not think about them. You begin to realise this in terms of Australian culture when you think about why it is that people at AFL football matches give the umpires such a hard time!

CONCEPTUALISING CULTURE: ICEBERG MODEL

When it comes to conceptualising culture, icebergs provide a helpful image. The tip of the iceberg is readily observed above the surface of the sea. However, the bulk of the iceberg lies out of sight. Icebergs are hazardous precisely because one does not know what is out of sight. As a consequence the observer can easily be lured into underestimating what lies beneath.

Reflective cultural insiders have a good idea of what lies beneath because they understand the framework within which events are commonly interpreted, feelings expressed, and judgements made. They also understand the depth dimension of the culture because they are prepared to put questions to human experience and note the ways in which this experience is explained and interpreted. In this process, little by little, cultural values and norms come to consciousness. An unreflective person, on the other hand, is the prisoner of culture, and forced to make sense of life using a value system so taken-for-granted that its strengths and weaknesses are not recognised until some form of crisis forces deeper reflection. This is precisely what happens in a liminal era.

The fact that much of our culture operates outside of awareness means that the model outlined above needs to be adapted. This is done in Figure 8.2. The revised model indicates that most people are usually aware of only some of the cultural values by which they live because the mythic dimensions of their culture lie out of their awareness.

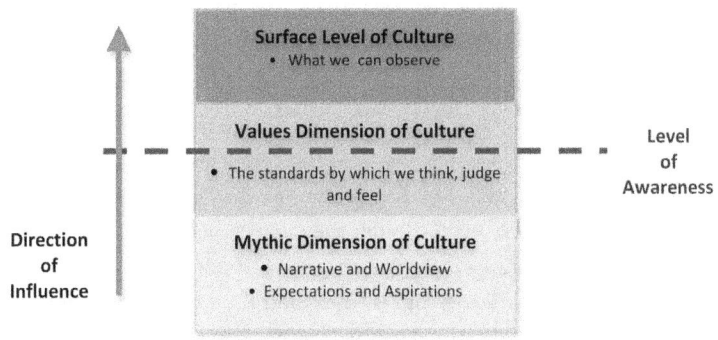

FIGURE 8.2   Culture: Conscious and Sub-Conscious Dimensions

Enculturation

People acquire their cultural worldview in a complex process called enculturation. Enculturation operates at two levels, the conscious and the sub-conscious. If, for instance, you are born on the northern beaches of

Sydney, you do not 'learn to surf' as you have to if you were born in outback New South Wales. Why? Because surfing is something that you have done since you can first remember. It is part of the 'beach culture' in which you grew up. Surfing is just something you do. People growing up in Switzerland have a similar experience with skiing. However, for young people growing up well away from the sea or the snow, surfing and skiing are something that they have to learn to do consciously. Enculturation happens sub-consciously as a result of trial and error, watching and learning from role models and in a social group, finding out what is rewarded and what is punished. Enculturation also happens consciously through the learning that goes on in the various communities in which people live. Children learn their culture—'how things are done around here'—by growing up in a family, being members of a football team, going to school, that is, in the rub of life. They do not always understand why the rules are the way they are, but learn to accept them all the same. When children question the 'way things are done around here', adults are often at a loss for an answer, since they themselves have acquired the norms and patterns of their culture sub-consciously. The only answer to the child's question often is: 'We do it this way, because we do it this way!'

One of the reasons culture is so influential is that it enables us to take things for granted and not to question them. It creates a world of meaning that enables us to interpret and make sense of life based on what previous generations have come to understand as 'what works for us'. This takes a lot of the stress out of life.

Culture and the imaginal horizon

While culture provides meaning, it also limits meaning. All cultures operate within an imaginal horizon that limits how people think, how they feel, and how they judge. They commonly seek the solutions to all life's challenges and problems within this horizon. Solutions that lie beyond these limits are simply out of reach, even though they may appear perfectly obvious to people operating within a different imaginal horizon.

One of the tasks of leadership is to expand the imaginal horizon within which colleagues customarily construe reality so that new hopes can surface and new possibilities arise. To do this the leader has to be aware of what the prevailing horizon is and the resources at his or her disposal in expanding that horizon. The vision of the leader becomes instrumental in this regard, especially if it brings meaning into a situation in which established meanings are losing their currency, as occurs in liminal eras.

In a situation of cultural liminality the taken-for-granted assumptions of the culture begin to break down and, as a consequence, people feel totally at a loss since they now have to consciously determine what things mean, why they feel the way they do, and why the standards by which they have always judged things no longer seem appropriate. When significant aspects of a trusted and taken-for-granted meaning system begin to collapse, people feel quite lost and disorientated. This is now recognised as a consequence of the 'post-modern turn' of the 1970s.[143] In this context people have little option but to put questions to their culture, that is, to adopt a critical stance towards it.

Critiquing culture: putting questions to culture

The modern model of culture as outlined above enables us to put questions to Australian culture such as:

- What cultural values anchor Australian culture at the present time?
- What cultural myths underpin what 'being Australian' now means?
- What are some of the narrative forms used to convey these myths within the Australian community?
- What unstated expectations and aspirations flow from these myths?
- How are the aspirations embedded in Australian culture being realized, or frustrated, at the present time?

Any attempt to answer such questions soon highlights how much of our culture is taken for granted, and how much of it lies out of sight. The same questions, in suitably adapted form, can profitably be put to sub-cultures—such as the local Catholic Church, the school system, or the culture of individual schools.

An important point to keep in mind in critically assessing culture is that *it is only in a dialogue between insiders and outsiders that such questions can be answered in any real depth.* The anthropological reality is that neither insiders nor outsiders ever see the whole picture by themselves.

The most enduring aspect of a culture in the modern model is its mythic level. This is the level leaders need to understand since it is the bedrock on which the culture stands, the most open to secularisation in a secular society, the most difficult to change, and so the most demanding to evangelise.

---

[143] A discussion of the nature and consequences of post-modernity can be found in Jim & Therese D'Orsa *Explorers, Guides and Meaning-makers: Mission Theology for Catholic Educators* (Mulgrave: Garratt Publishing, 2010), in particular Chapter Five 'Exploring the Post-modern Experience', Chapter Six 'The Narrative of Post-modernity' and Chapter Nine 'Contemporary Pluralism—the Rise and Rise of Difference'. Also in Jim & Therese D'Orsa *Catholic Curriculum: A Mission to the Heart of Young People* (Mulgrave: Garratt Publishing, 2012) especially Chapter 11 'The Post-modern Critique: Prophets of Deconstruction' and Chapter 12 'The Post-modern Critique: Prophets of Reconstruction'.

CULTURE IN SCHOOL AND SYSTEM LEADERSHIP

All cultures encompass a worldview which is passed from one generation to the next, not as propositions, but as cultural narratives owned by the communities to whom the culture belongs. We are introduced to these narratives from a very early age. Seeing them acted out on television, hearing them in stories read to us, and learning them at school are all part of enculturation. Cultural narratives form our attitudes, operating as they do at the sub-conscious level telling us who we are and who we are not, how we should act and how we should not act. By employing myth they become an important vehicle for the transmission of values and norms of behavior.

Cultural narratives and cultural bias

Cultural narratives always come to us in a moderated, rather than a 'pure', state. While these narratives can take many forms, they encompass common values and aspirations. It is the plural nature of the narratives that enables people from a variety of backgrounds to identify with each other and live together in a culture. Descendants of early Irish immigrants, for example, pass on the essentials of 'being Australian' in narratives somewhat different from those of post-World War II immigrants from southern Europe, Vietnamese boat people of the 1970s, or more recently refugees from the Middle East and Africa.

Cultural narratives are meaningful because they give people a way of interpreting lived experience. Different migrant groups living within the boundaries of the Australian narrative have come to interpret their story as somehow aligned with the depth dimensions of the culture, and this enables them to consider themselves as 'being Australian'. This identification enables large slices of life that previously had to be consciously negotiated, now to be taken for granted. When this stage is reached, migrants speak of feeling 'at home' in the culture. Sadly, this stage is not reached by all.

Since cultural narratives are conveyed in forms moderated by communities, they can contain various types of bias and therefore need to be open to critique. One of the roles of schooling is to challenge such biases by bringing them to the surface and opening them up to challenge. The greatest bias at present comes from secularisation, particularly its exclusion of religious language and narrative symbols from common discourse.

Leader as keeper of the story

Awareness of the moderated nature of cultural narratives should enable a Catholic school leader to be attentive to the way in which the cultural narrative of the school is held within the school community, underpinning the culture of the school. It seems the case that many Catholic schools have lost contact with their cultural narrative. When this happens, it becomes difficult to anchor values in a meaningful way within the community. Schools associated with religious congregations now use charism as a way of framing the cultural narrative of the school. This is a relatively recent and effective response to the cultural situation. However, it covers only a proportion of schools. At the system level it has generally been only in recent years that leaders have come to appreciate that school systems, as well as schools, have a cultural narrative that needs to be formally acknowledged, and in many dioceses work has been undertaken to research and make these available, often featuring a founding Director.[144] Such narratives are also an expression of how the Gospel has been lived out at this level of educational life, be it within a diocese or congregational jurisdiction.

Evangelising the culture of a school or school system is a matter of building on what is—that is, on the ways in which *the Gospel has been lived out in the story of the community*. This cannot happen if this story has been lost or never seriously interpreted. Leaders have a very real obligation to ensure that the story is kept alive, celebrated, and has a trajectory which leads to hope.

Cultural leadership

Because schools and school systems have cultures, life is played out against this background. The wise leader knows this, and seeks actively to use this as a resource in leadership. Thomas Sergiovanni was among the first to nominate cultural leadership as a criterion of excellence in school and system leadership.[145] Since this influential work was published, there has been a good deal of discussion about what cultural leadership involves. Because colleagues naturally seek to interpret the actions of a school or system leader, wise leaders use this dynamic to create meaning, rather than leave it to chance. Symbolic action and story-telling have become important tools in leading for mission. Story and symbolic action function together in the creation of both meaning and of hope.

---

144 Examples include: Maurice Ryan *From a Suitcase on the Verandah* (Ringwood: David Lovell, 2005) – Brisbane archdiocese; Terry Synan *A Journey in Faith: the History of Catholic Education in Gippsland 1850-1991* (Ringwood: David Lovell, 2003) – Diocese of Sale; James D'Orsa Monsignor John Slowey: *Servant of Education, Facilitator of Change* (Sydney: Catholic Education Office, 1999) – Sydney archdiocese, Jill Blee *From the Murray to the Sea: The History of Catholic Education in the Ballarat diocese* (Catholic Education and Indra Publishing, 2004) – Ballarat diocese.
145 Thomas Sergiovanni *The Principalship: A Reflective Practice Perspective* (Boston: Allyn & Bacon, 1987), 55ff.

Dialogue, cultural change and leading for mission

Cultures, as more or less comprehensive and more or less successful designs for living, are persistent. This being the case, culture is quite resistant to change, particularly if the change is perceived as impacting on its depth dimensions – values and myth. Culture is experienced more as a thing of the heart than of the head. It always encompasses how people feel and what they value, as well as what they think. Good ideas for educational change, the appeal of which lies mainly at the cognitive level, rarely succeed. This perplexes some leaders. Real cultural change demands re-orientation within a taken-for-granted frame of reference and a consequent loss of the familiar. A sense of loss accompanies cultural change and causes grief that has to be managed.[146] Failure to do this is one reason why it is often so difficult to evangelise cultures. The modern model of culture suggests why dialogue is an essential element in leading for mission, and particularly when the aim is to evangelise the culture of the school or school system.

The aim of this chapter has been to delineate the modern conception of culture as a *working model* that is useful in understanding important aspects of organisational life and leadership. We have distinguished this model from the classicist model which also has currency in Catholic teaching about culture. Both of these models are seen as limited, even defective, by post-modern thinkers, and their critique has given rise to a third model of culture— the post-modern model. This model also provides valuable insights for educational leaders, and it is to this that we now turn.

PRIORITIES IN LEADING FOR MISSION

PRIORITY 8.1 In leading for mission the leader has to be in touch with the depth dimensions of the school or system's culture

One of the more difficult transitions in Catholic education is that from school leader to system leader. An important reason for this is that, while the school and system share common values, they operate in quite different cultural contexts.

Continuing the Conversation

One way to explore the culture of a school (or system) is to listen to its 'great stories' and to find out who are its the 'heroines' and 'heroes'.

---

[146] Anthropologist Gerald Arbuckle explores this theme in *Grieving for Change: A Spirituality for Re-founding Gospel Communities* (Homebush: St Paul Publications, 1991).

- What do you know about the great stories and the heroes and heroines of your school (or system)?
- What does this knowledge tell you about people's aspirations and what they hold to be important? How can you validate this knowledge? How can it be mobilised in managing change and loss?

PRIORITIES IN LEADING FOR MISSION

PRIORITY 8.2 For leaders, symbolic action is an important tool in meaning-making and in communicating what is important.

For example, a principal engages in symbolic action in the way in which s/he uses time. The principal who always has time for the drama production but no time for the football match, or vice versa, is acting symbolically. Also, in a school it is important to observe which achievements are noted and rewarded, and which are not. The leader is engaged in symbolic action, a powerful vehicle for meaning-making.

Continuing the Conversation

- Recall up to three cases where leaders have consciously used symbolic action to 'get the message across' in a way that was highly effective.
- What aspect of the school's or system's cultural myths or values did these actions tap into in order to gain their salience?
- Symbolic action played a key role in Jesus' leadership as this is presented in the Gospels. Can you recall examples of this? How have these actions shaped the culture of Catholic faith communities?

9
WHAT LEADERS NEED TO KNOW ABOUT CULTURE: THE POST-MODERN CONSTRUCTION

When leaders try to engage with complex notions like culture, it is necessary to use what Gerald Egan terms 'working models'. Working models meet two important criteria—in the first place they are complex enough to embrace most features of the topic under discussion, and in the second they are simple enough to have predictive value. As the name suggests, working models direct action.[147] In this they differ from research models which are directed towards identifying and understanding the nature of relationships between carefully defined variables.

WORKING MODELS OF CULTURE

The modern understanding of culture discussed in the previous chapter is a good example of a working model. This model had currency in anthropology up until the 1980s when the need to explore the impact of advancing pluralism on cultures highlighted some of its inherent limitations as a working model. However, this did not devalue the model which still has currency in organisational literature and in official Church documents.

Modern model: two schools of thought

As long as cultures were thought of as more or less comprehensive and enduring wholes, they could be understood either as *organisms* or as *structures*. Schools of anthropology developed around each of these two notions. These became known respectively as the *functionalist* approach to culture and the *structuralist* approach to culture. These two schools of thought shared a common understanding viz. that anthropology is an explanatory science, and therefore cultures can be made the subject of objective study, that is that they

---
147 See Gerald Egan *Change Agent Skills in Helping and Human Service Settings* (Monterey: Brookes/Cole Publishing, 1985), 6.

can be 'put under the microscope', so that relationships can be established and predictions made. In both perspectives, functionalist and structuralist, cultures were seen as operating more or less independently of the people living in them. The functionalist approach sees culture as an organism or body, and so the aim is to establish how parts function in relation to the whole. The structuralist approach sees cultures as having inherent structures which are ordered hierarchically. The aim is to understand these structures and the way in which they are organised. The model set out in Figure 8.2 in the previous chapter can be analysed from either of these perspectives.

Post-modern critique

All working models are based on assumptions that may hold at a certain time and in a certain context, but which break down as times and contexts change, so that the model has to be revised or replaced. The modern understanding of culture fits this pattern. In the previous chapter we outlined how the model was progressively adapted as anthropology developed. Disquiet with the modern model accelerated in the 1980s giving rise to an alternative model, now called the post-modern model.

This model emerged in response to the post-modern critique of all things 'modern'. Since the late 1970s, the post-modern critique has taken three principal directions:

- critique of the way in which power was used in modernity to define what constituted knowledge
- critique of the meta-narratives of modernity (communism, scientism, liberalism, fascism and capitalism) as overarching narratives within which all local narratives were to be interpreted
- critique of the way in which modernity imposed uniformity and under-valued difference.

These forms of critique are associated, respectively, with the names of Michel Foucault, Jean-Francois Lyotard and Jacques Derrida, who grew up in mainland France, or in Derrida's case French Algeria, in the aftermath of World War II. Their thinking was strongly influenced by the cultural context in which they lived, and the tensions inherent in that context. The post-modern critique was to have a strong influence in shaping anthropology and gave rise to an alternative model of culture. The post-modern critique seeks to 'deconstruct' the meaning system of modernity by challenging the way power is used in its construction, its inflexibility, and the unstated assumptions on which it depends. It is not surprising then that the modern model of culture is caught up in this critique.

In the modern model, cultures are seen as *more or less clearly defined*. They serve the important social function of creating the boundary between 'us' and 'not us'. In the early twentieth century this may well have been a good description of the social reality. However, as communication technologies have advanced, and the possibility of rapid travel extended to more and more people, the social boundaries between 'us' and 'not us' in most Western cultures have become blurred. As a consequence, identity in both its psychological and political dimensions, has become a major issue. It was in this context that the need for an alternative understanding of culture and its dynamics developed.[148]

Not only was the modern model of culture put under the microscope by the post-modern critics, so too were the understandings of anthropology on which it rested, including the methodologies used to assemble and process cultural data. New schools of thought arose that understood anthropology as an *interpretive science* and rejected its role as an explanatory science. As an interpretive science, anthropology's major concern is with how a people negotiates meaning.

Post-modern anthropology: two schools of thought

Post-modern anthropologists hold that culture is a much more dynamic reality than the modern model suggests. Post-modern anthropology can be divided into two broad schools—the *anti-functionalists* and the *post-structuralists*. The first of these post-modern schools of anthropologists follows the lead of Clifford Geertz.

In Geertz's view, cultural anthropology seeks to interpret the symbolic data—symbol systems which include language, myths, narratives and rituals—present in all cultures, in the search to uncover their meaning and significance for the culture's participants.[149] In this task the anthropologist brings his or her meaning system to bear and, if not careful, will impose it when interpreting cultural data, irrespective of what that data means for the people being studied. There is therefore need for a high degree of reflexivity when approaching cultural data. Geertz's critique of the 'scientific' approach is that, in seeking to be 'objective', the anthropologist screens out the role that variables such as feeling and gender play in meaning-making and the search for significance. For Geertz, culture is not something people 'have'; rather it is something in which they are 'immersed'. He speaks of culture as a 'web of significance'.[150]

---

148 For a good introduction to this concept see Kathryn Tanner *Theories of Culture: A New Agenda for Theology* (Minneapolis: Augsberg Fortress, 1997) or Gerald Arbuckle *Culture, Inculturation and the Theologians: A Post Modern Critique* (Collegeville Minnesota: Liturgical Press, 2010).
149 Clifford Geertz *The Interpretation of Cultures* (New York: Basic Books, 1973), 4–6.
150 Arbuckle, Chapter 2 'Cultures as Webs of Symbols and Myths' in *Culture, Inculturation and Theologians*, 19–36.

In attempting to make sense of a culture, the anthropologist is caught up in a 'hermeneutical circle'. When interpreting cultural data it is important to realise that the parts have meaning only in relationship with the whole, and the whole takes on new meaning as we study the parts. For example, in Australian culture the value 'everyone is entitled to a fair go' stands in relationship to other values rather than alone, and its place in the 'web' throws light on the limits within which it applies. The relationship between the web and the particular value becomes a matter of interpretation, and is something that is contested by insiders. How such contests are resolved tells us important things about how the culture functions.

The second school of thought is strongly influenced by Michel Foucault's critique of power and its use in modern societies. In this perspective, the way in which contests over meaning are resolved reflects the often hidden manipulation of power within the culture. As a consequence, the post-modern model of culture is concerned with the ways in which power is used within a culture to legitimate knowledge, feelings and norms. This perspective acknowledges that power is used in ways that are dynamic and that evolve over time as contexts change. Liminal eras usually herald a major re-configuration of the culture.

Arbuckle sums up these two post-modern perspectives as follows:

> ...*cultures are not fixed entities, but processes in which people struggle for meaning in a threatening political environment. ... a culture tells members of a particular society how to view the world, how to experience it emotionally, and how to relate to one another and to the people of other societies.*

He goes on to offer the following 'post-modern' definition of culture. A culture is a pattern of meanings:

- encased in a network of symbols, myths, narratives and rituals,
- created by individuals and subdivisions, (groups within a culture) as they struggle to respond to the competitive pressures of power and limited resources in a rapidly globalizing and fragmenting world,
- and instructing adherents about what is considered to be the correct way to feel, think, and behave.[151]

POST-MODERN APPROACH TO CULTURE

The definition above incorporates many elements found in the modern understanding of culture discussed in the previous chapter. However it is

---

151 Arbuckle, 17. Words in brackets not in the original.

more expansive in specifically including two new issues: *meaning-making* and *the use of power*.

Mission anthropologist, Paul Hiebert, operates within this understanding in suggesting that, in order to understand cultures, it is necessary to look at the way in which worldviews play out in them.[152] He holds that all cultures, as meaning-making systems, contain a worldview. The *cultural worldview*, which corresponds to the third element in Arbuckle's definition, provides people with the basic frame of reference within which they make sense of life. It has a cognitive, affective and evaluative dimension. In other words this cultural worldview legitimates certain ways of thinking, feeling and acting as acceptable within a given society and at a particular point of time. However, the worldview of a culture also changes over time, which means that every culture contains inbuilt processes of re-negotiation by which change occurs. The post-modern model of cultures distinguishes between cultures, not on the basis of how they distinguish between 'us' and not us, *but on the basis of how the re-negotiation processes operate and, in particular, how power is used within them.*

Synchronic and diachronic dimensions

When leaders talk of 'organisational culture' their concern is usually directed to how the culture functions in the here and now. In anthropology this is called the *synchronic* dimension of culture. The modern model, discussed in the previous chapter, focuses almost exclusively on this dimension. Much of the literature on school culture also focuses on this dimension. However, culture has a second dimension called the *diachronic* dimension which is concerned with the dynamics by which the culture changes over time. This dimension is particularly concerned with the role played by narrative and myth in the re-negotiation of meaning and values as cultures adapt to meet the demands of changing contexts.

Operation of theme and counter-theme in cultures

In the post-modern approach, cultural values do not exist in a stand-alone form as the modern model suggests. Rather, they are present within cultures as *theme and counter-theme*. Theme and counter-theme represent competing goods that exist in tension, and between which a balance has to be struck. These competing goods—theme and counter-theme—are *both affirmed* within cultural myths and narratives. However, if taken to extremes, the pursuit of one restricts or denies the pursuit of the other. Power is used in a battle to determine where the balance point lies, and the battleground is meaning.

---

[152] Paul Hiebert *Transforming Worldviews: An Anthropological Understanding of How People Change* (Grand Rapids: BakerAcademic, 2008), 28.

THEME AND COUNTER THEME: TWO ILLUSTRATIONS

The pursuit of personal freedom and the pursuit of the common good stand as theme and counter–theme and as a distinguishing feature of most Western societies.

'Pursuit of the common good' and 'personal freedom'

However in Australian culture and in the cultures of the United States, for example, these values are understood in different ways, and people living in the respective cultures set the balance point differently.

For example in Australian culture universal health care is taken for granted in 'pursuit of the common good'. Australians at this point of history find it hard to comprehend the situation in the U.S. where universal health care is a hotly contested political issue because certain modes of its provision are seen to encroach on individual freedom. Citizens in Australia understand the 'social contract' between themselves and government in a somewhat different way from many of their contemporaries in the U.S.

A similar difference arises when it comes to gun control. We might represent the situation of the two cultures in regard to the issues named as follows.

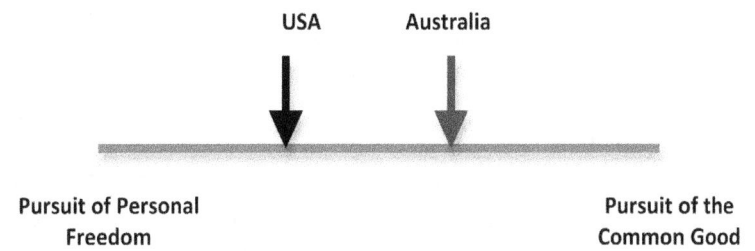

FIGURE 9.1 Theme and Counter–theme in the Post-Modern View of Culture

It is worth noting at this stage that a cultural value can be given such status in a culture that its counter-value is suppressed. This happened in the West in the late modern era, for instance, when the scientific method was adopted as the sole method of human enquiry legitimating knowledge, with the result that other forms of human enquiry which have helped people in making sense of the world, were substantially suppressed.

'Everyone deserves a fair go' and 'everyone needs to pull their weight'

In Australian 'everyone deserves a fair go' stands as a theme. What counter-theme balances this? To get at this we need to ask: What aspiration does this value set up? Here the national narrative and myth come into play. If everyone gets a fair go, what do we expect to be the consequence? When people are perceived to have been given a fair go in the context of the Australian narrative, they are expected 'to pull their weight'. People who are given a fair go and who are not seen to be pulling their weight fall into the cultural category of 'bludger'. No one wants to feel that they are 'bludgers' or be judged to be 'bludgers'. Being so tagged is a form of cultural sanction.

In Australian culture what people will tolerate to ensure that others get 'a fair go' is balanced by their perception of what 'pulling your weight' entails, and this understanding is then qualified by the access people have to resources. There is a strong concern in Australian culture for those who are marginalised economically, particularly the young. In this culture more is expected of those with more resources.

Building the web of significance

In Australian culture, 'pulling your weight' is linked to the cultural norm 'never let a mate down' which taps into the feelings and images Australians hold about 'mateship'. When elderly Australian war veterans were interviewed recently while visiting the site of the significant battles of El Alamein in Egypt to mark the seventieth anniversary of the turning of the tide of war in the North Africa,[153] they linked 'mateship' and 'pulling your weight' in a significant way. They spoke of how they had to learn to depend on each other, and of the mateship that developed among them as the battles raged. In their minds mateship was linked to survival. It became an inclusive ideal, one that extended beyond one's immediate friends, and transcended the divisions of class or creed that characterised the Australian culture of the time. The example illustrates how culture weaves its 'web of significance' by linking together themes in a culture and so shaping what people think, how they feel, and the norms by which they act.

Culture and identity in the post-modern model

In the empirical model of culture, values often define the boundary between 'us' and 'not us'. 'We' value this, 'you' value that, so you are different from us. The model encompasses an 'either-or' stance to values. You are with us or against us.

The post-modern approach, which analyses cultural values in terms of theme and counter-theme takes a 'both-and' approach to values. It suggests that the 'design for living' embedded in a culture needs to acknowledge

---

153 E.g. www.abc.net.au/news/2012-10-20/world-war-two-veterans-mark-el-alamein-anniversary/4322352

and address *the pluralism inherent in group life in a way that does not compromise identity*. The consequence of this change in stance is that cultures come to be seen as battlegrounds in which pressure groups vie to re-define theme and counter-theme and to shift the balance points between competing values in favour of their own interests. We see this starkly illustrated in Australian politics at the present time.

The use of power to bring about changes in a culture is not confined to the secular sphere. It also happens in Christian organisations when, as we saw in the case of the Johannine community, designated leaders attempt to co-opt the Holy Spirit in their own interests. As if alert to this possibility, the Spirit calls the prophet to speak on God's behalf, and also speaks somewhat less directly through the wisdom of cultures.

CHANGES IN CULTURAL CONFIGURATION

The configuration of themes and counter-themes within a culture at any point of time defines Geertz's 'web of significance'. As contexts change, this configuration can also change. In order to understand the culture, it is necessary to understand the way in which these changes are negotiated across time, that is, to understand the culture's diachronic dimensions.

Present and past in any group of people are linked by narrative and myth. The diagram below (Figure 9.2) illustrates the way in which the post-modern model attempts to make sense of cultural change. The model is applicable to a school.

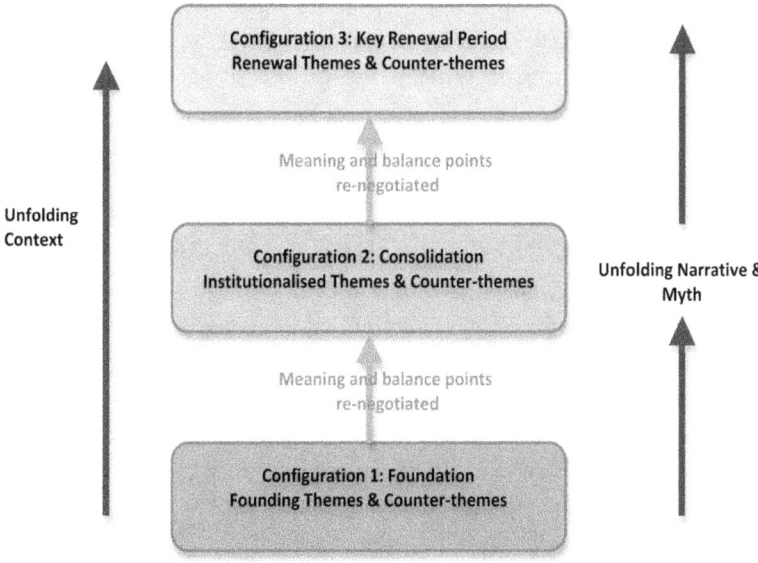

FIGURE 9.2 Post-Modern Model of Culture

Many church organisations are founded in response to local aspirations and needs. Their founders are often charismatic individuals charged to get things moving. The particular need the organisation addresses may be care for the marginalised, a new parish, or a new school in a developing suburb, etc. Founders attract to the cause people who are focused on 'meeting the need'. However, founders caught up in the moment often fail to put the group's work on a sustainable footing, because that is not their immediate concern.

In the founding phase the themes and counter-themes that give meaning to the work of the group usually *grow out of the work itself*. Once the founding period in which survival of the group is usually a major issue is over, it becomes possible and necessary to put the work of the group on a sustainable footing. Charismatic founders are more often than not succeeded by people who are organisers. Readers who have worked under a charismatic leader, such as a founding principal, will have experienced the dynamic described above at first-hand. As the work of a group is put on a sustainable footing, themes, counter-themes and balance points have to be re-negotiated. The result is a form of institutionalisation in which policies, plans, structures and roles are created. The often chaotic power structures of the founding period are tamed as the organisation takes on its institutional form. The charismatic power of the founder is replaced by positional power and the authority that goes with this. The organisation moves from its founding configuration to its consolidation configuration.

As history continues to unfold, some form of renewal will be called for, because the original needs which brought the organisation into being have changed with changes in context. Renewal may be brought about by a change in *scale* requiring the group to expand, or a change in *type* requiring a rethinking as the mission of the group as needs change.

As this movement from the founding configuration to the renewal configuration occurs, the group develops the *characteristic ways of re-negotiating meaning* which includes the ways in which power is used within the organisation. These patterns are embedded, often sub-consciously, in both the narrative of the group and its myth.

The post-modern model of culture focuses on *the way in which power is used* in the process of re-negotiating meanings, and the issue of *whose interests this serves*. That is, it pays more attention to the diachronic dimension of culture than does the modern model. As a predictive model, it suggests that unless a school leader is aware of the processes by which meaning is negotiated within the school's culture, then she or he will become deeply frustrated in trying to bring about cultural change.

Power in the post-modern model

In most cultures, including organisational cultures, power is used to negotiate the meaningful themes and counter-themes that characterise group life, and determine where the points of balance lie. Leaders can so emphasise one pole of the theme/counter-theme continuum that a value is given almost absolute status. The value then becomes part of the ideology of local leadership. This phenomenon can happen, often unwittingly, in well-intentioned projects to promote 'Australian values' or 'Gospel values' within the school curriculum. The promoters of such initiatives use the power at their disposal (which may be political or religious) to determine a value set to be introduced into the curriculum, and often fail to consider the way in which *values operate together within the 'web of significance' that defines the culture*. Such projects are premised on the modern view of culture and its understanding of how cultures function, and are compromised by the weaknesses inherent in that model. These projects, at least at school level, have proved difficult to sustain because as a working model the modern conception of culture has its limits.

THEME AND COUNTER-THEME IN NEW TESTAMENT LEADERSHIP HERITAGES

The post-modern understanding of culture can be used to explore leadership issues in the New Testament. Some examples highlight this way of interpreting the leadership heritages discussed in Chapters 5 and 6.

The Johannine heritage was developed in the context of polemic between two Jewish groups about who Jesus was. For one group, Jesus' humanity was the most important emphasis. For the other group, Jesus' divinity was central in their understanding. The Johannine community went somewhat 'overboard' in declaring the latter at the expense of the former. Rather than keeping these two important realities in balance, the community shifted so far to one pole that eventually it split into warring factions. And, although all factions believed that the Paraclete dwelt in every believer, they lacked a mechanism to resolve the fact that believers could hold fundamentally different positions.[154] Brown highlights another important issue viz. that, when a position is exaggerated for whatever reason in one generation, as happened in the Johannine community, it is the exaggerated position that is passed on to the next, and unless addressed, introduces distortions into a religious tradition.[155] We see other examples of this dynamic as the tensions in post-Vatican II Catholicism have become clearer.

---
154 Raymond Brown, 121–2.
155 ibid, 123.

The author of the *Gospel of John* uses Peter and the 'beloved disciple' symbolically to define an important balance point in Christian cultures. The writer juxtaposes authority (symbolised in Peter) with discipleship (symbolised in the beloved disciple), and sets the balance point clearly on the side of discipleship. The treatment is nuanced since, when it comes to discipleship, the writer evenly balances the role of men and women, the treatment of the beloved disciple being counter-poised by treatments of Mary the mother of Jesus, and Martha and Mary, giving the very clear message that gender is not an issue in discipleship.

The writer of the *Gospel of Matthew* is also nuanced in his treatment of leadership affirming the need for authority in the community, but balancing this by also affirming the need to exercise that authority according to the standards of Jesus. He thus steers his community clear of the pit into which the Johannine community eventually fell, as we know from the Letters.

POST-MODERN MODEL: RE-ENGAGING WITH PLURALISM

The post-modern understanding of culture places significant value on the role pluralism plays in a culture, holding that the theme/counter-theme dynamic has always been integral to the way in which cultures function. While certain social conditions do make it possible for those in power to shift a balance point so far in one direction that its counter-value is suppressed, if the suppressed value is held in the collective cultural sub-conscious, it will eventually resurface because it is carried in the aspirations that a people hold for themselves. It is at this level that the Spirit acts in human history.

An example of this phenomenon can be seen in the case of religion in some Eastern European countries since the fall of communism. We have seen a similar dynamic at work in religious congregations as they have become less institutionalised as a result of discerning in their narrative the founding charism of the group, and have sought to re-interpret this to address the needs of a changed context. In many cases this renewal process has led to deep cultural change.

While the advanced pluralism that we find in most Western societies draws our attention to the plural roots of Australian culture, it also invites us to reflect on the plural roots of Australian Catholicism, and in particular on some of the historical distortions to important themes and counter-themes at work there. It was these distortions that the Second Vatican Council sought to address. This reflection, in turn, puts the focus on the resources that are contained within a plural religious tradition, one that embraces many cultures. At the empirical level this may provide some insight into the reasons why people interpret 'being Catholic' in such a variety of ways.

Post-modern Catholic culture

The post-modern understanding of culture puts important questions to local Catholic cultures in looking at how important themes and counter-themes are identified. These are often recognised because they become tension points in Catholic life. These include community/institution, inclusiveness/ exclusiveness, global church/local church, unity/diversity and so on, all of which contribute to the 'web of significance' that is Catholic culture at the present time.

Perhaps the most culture-defining of these pairs, because it plays out at so many levels in Church life, is the tension between *Church as faith community* and *Church as global institution*.

FIGURE 9.3 Establishing a Vital Balance Point

In its founding configuration, the Church existed as isolated faith communities brought together under the authority of particular apostles. This structure was not sustainable once the apostles and those who knew them had died. In order to survive, the Church had to take on an institutional form independent of the communities that comprised it. While it is correct to say that Jesus founded the Church, the form the Church took once it was institutionalised is a human construct that has changed many times since its foundational configuration. While there is no question that the Church needs to have an institutional form, equally there is no question that the deepest aspiration of its members is to be a community of communities.

The post-modern critique asks whether important values have been suppressed by the way in which the present community-institution balance is determined, and if so, what are those values. This is a pressing question for school leaders who find themselves dealing with the new ways in which people define themselves as 'being Catholic' and of 'living the Gospel'. The balance point is also being determined by the low standing in which the institution is held among young people, partly as a result of the actions of delinquent priests and religious in abusing young people, but also because of the way the matter has been handled by their leaders.

The pressing challenge for every school leader in the present context is to ensure that, *as an institution, the school is always at the service of the community*.

When an inappropriate balance point is struck, the Catholic school quickly becomes secularised and its religious message muted.

In this and the preceding chapter we have looked at the two major approaches to the study of culture. The Church's understanding of culture, as expressed in ecclesial documents, including those on Catholic education, is framed mainly in terms of the modern and classicist understandings. There has been limited engagement with the post-modern model. In this chapter we have attempted to set out that model and identify important questions that it raises.

The models are offered as 'working models'. Their value lies in the questions they put to life and the insights they offer in directing action. Without a clear understanding of culture and how it functions, it is simply impossible to lead effectively in situations where the configuration of a culture changes.

The problem of liminality in the cultural sphere is compounded by liminality in the religious sphere. In such a situation the mission of the leader is to create meaning, *to become a meaning-maker*. It is to this challenging role that we now turn.

PRIORITIES IN LEADING FOR MISSION

PRIORITY 9.1 If a leadership group wishes to bring about cultural change, then they must be aware of the themes and counter-themes that shape the culture, and the ways in which power is used to change balance points with respect to these.

The exploration of themes and counter themes that have salience in a given organisational culture means getting in contact with the diachronic (across time) dimension of the culture. The following leadership development exercise is helpful in this respect.

Continuing the Conversation

Invite key people associated with the founding of the school, or eras in which it underwent major changes, to tell the story of that era, identifying the hopes and the values that were to the fore when crucial decisions were made. The speakers must be given both a brief and a time limit.

The brief should include some or all of the following questions:

- What were the dominant concerns in people's minds that seemed to shape key decisions in the period you are covering?
- Why was it that people thought in that way at the time?

- Who were the key decision-makers, and how did they go about making decisions?
- How did key decision-makers seek to involve important stakeholders in major decisions?
- How did stakeholders respond?
- How did leaders set about the task of building the energy needed to bring about change?
- How did the stakeholders respond to what was happening?
- What did you learn from your involvement in this stage of the school's or system's development?

Have the leadership group reflect on the various accounts they have heard, and explore the following questions about the school's or system's culture:

- What are the major factors that have driven change in this organisation?
- What are the recurring themes and counter-themes in this narrative?
- How have balance points been determined initially, and what has caused them to change?
- How are these changes reconciled with the deep myths that underpin the culture?
- How is power used most effectively in this school or system to bring about organisational development in response to a major change in context?

10
THE LEADER AS MEANING-MAKER

Two essential elements in leading for mission are meaning-making and the communication of meaning. Both faith and culture are important resources in meaning-making, and therefore play a crucial role in missional leadership. Leaders know that at times they must make sense of complex situations even when they have only a part of the information needed to carry out the task well, so they come to trust their intuition as a resource in meaning-making. In this chapter we explore the role that faith, culture and human experience each play in the meaning-making process. We are endeavouring to help leaders develop an approach to meaning-making which, with practice, becomes not only a well-honed skill, but also shapes intuition. In doing so we call on the resources available to us from both anthropology and hermeneutics.[156] Essentially, the argument of the chapter is that, in the present experience of liminality within our cultural and ecclesial contexts, meaning-making is a critical skill in effective leadership.

The three questions we consider in this chapter are:

- How do we make meaning?
- What is the role of culture and faith in this process?
- What implications does an understanding of the meaning-making process have for school and system leaders in a post-modern context?

MEANING-MAKING IN A LIMINAL ERA

In the last chapter we saw that in transition eras the configuration of a culture is re-negotiated by the cultural community. Under the post-modern model this can happen in a number of ways: new themes emerge, older theme/counter-theme relationships are re-interpreted, a new balance is struck between the themes and counter-themes that help define the culture, and so on. These developments, occurring in response to changes in human aspiration that arise as contexts change, open up new chapters

---

[156] Moderate hermeneutics is usually associated with the work of Hans Georg Gadamer and later Paul Ricoeur. See Shaun Gallagher *Hermeneutics and Education* (New York: State University of New York Press, 1992) for an account of moderate hermeneutics.

in the cultural narrative. The factors driving change in the two transition eras featured in Chapters 3 and 4 make this clear. Today the post-modern era is increasingly recognised as a transition stage in which deep change is occurring, not only in the cultural community, but in the faith community as well. For many Catholics the experience of living in an in-between-time in *both* their cultural and faith worlds is perplexing.

To be effective in such a context senior leaders in Catholic educational settings must be able to *speak meaningfully* to the situation confronted by their colleagues and students. This is made more difficult if the Church authorities with whom they relate seem distant or disengaged from the major themes of post-modern thought and its critiques of the ways in which institutional power is often abused. In any liminal era *the essential function of the leader is that of meaning-maker*. Put another way, the educational leaders, at both the school and system levels, have a duty to ensure that the education the schools offer is meaningful for teachers, parents and students.

Schooling seeks to prepare young people to enter a life-world in which the major relationships that shape it—to family and friends, to the wider society, to the natural environment, to the faith community, and to the transcendent—*are all being substantially re-defined*. The uncertainties this generates make systematic preparation difficult. The changing ecclesial context of Catholic schools adds a further degree of complexity to an already complex situation.

When school leaders help people make sense of the context in which they work, then ultimately it is the teachers, children and the faith community who benefit. Otherwise, excellence quickly comes to be defined in narrow terms and, in consequence, children become less than they can be, and the school has less influence on their development than it should. *Excellence in Catholic schooling can only be pursued if it represents a meaningful ideal.*

How then are the dynamics of meaning-making to be understood and tapped? This is perhaps *the* essential question in mission thinking. In outlining an answer we call on the insights provided by moderate hermeneutics.

However, first we need to establish some basic hermeneutical constructs, particularly those of 'worldview' and 'public worldview'.

PERSONAL WORLDVIEW AND ITS ROLE IN MEANING-MAKING

When we attempt to interpret or make sense of our experiences, we do so with reference to our *personal worldview*. This is a frame of reference that each of us develops in the process of growing up, and which enables us to make sense of life and so situate ourselves meaningfully in our cultural and faith communities.

Personal worldview as a source of meaning

Our personal worldview enables us to orient ourselves in our life-world more or less automatically. Our worldview has three dimensions: a *cognitive dimension* – what we know, aspire to, believe and take for granted about our life-world; an *evaluative dimension* - what we judge to be of worth in the people, events and things we encounter in our life-world; and an *affective dimension* which determines, in large part, the way we react to the people, events and things that make up our life-world – how we feel about ourselves, about others and about life in general. Our personal worldview is an important part of who we are and a filter through which we interpret all our experiences.[157]

Cultural anthropologist, Paul Hiebert describes a person's worldview as the lens through which she or he views the world, makes sense of it and responds to the demands of living in it. Put another way, we all see the world through the lens of our worldview. No one is able to view life from some 'worldview-free' position. Expressed in more poetic terms, we can never take our worldview glasses off! We never get to interpret the world from some 'objective', worldview-free place. The consequence is that we *interpret all the data that comes to us through the lens of our worldview.*

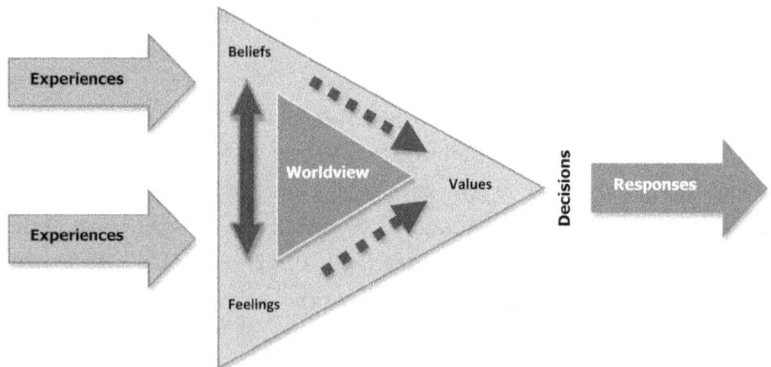

FIGURE 10.1 Worldview as Interpretive Lens[158]

Hiebert uses the diagram above to bring home how our personal worldview functions in the way we make sense of life.

Of course, our personal worldview is not inherited. It does not just appear out of the air, nor is it something that we construct in an intentional way. We acquire the fundamentals of our worldview as part of

---

157 This understanding of worldview is based on the work of Paul Hiebert and David Naugle. See Paul Hiebert *Transforming Worldviews: An Anthropological Understanding of How People Change* (Grand Rapids: BakerAcademic, 2008), 13ff and David Naugle *Worldview: History of a Concept* (Grand Rapids: W. B. Eerdmans, 2002).
158 Hiebert, 26.

our enculturation and refine it though formal education. Our worldview provides us with a set of dispositions which we employ in making sense of all life situations. We are more often than not unaware of the way these affect us. Since our worldview is integral to who we are, we take it and the role it plays in meaning-making for granted.

PUBLIC WORLDVIEWS

The process by which we develop our personal worldview is, at best, only partially understood. Moderate hermeneutics provides us with a useful *working model*[159] in exploring how it functions in making sense of experience.

In hermeneutical theory people develop their personal worldview by reference to *public worldviews*. These worldviews are public in the sense that they are traditions that are *the possession of a community*, are sustained over time, and so can be formally studied. The public worldviews involved in meaning-making are *the worldview of our culture* which is primary, *the worldview of the age* or era in which we live, and the *worldview of our faith tradition*. Each of these worldviews constitutes a frame of reference with a cognitive, an evaluative and an affective dimension. Each embodies a specific understanding of what it means to be human, how we should behave, and how we should feel and react in a predictable range of situations. All three are in constant interaction and are reshaped as a consequence.

Worldview of culture

The 'plan for living' at the heart of any culture depends on the worldview of the culture. This is transmitted from generation to generation as narratives that children encounter from their early years. A child's personal worldview is shaped by the cultural worldview long before he or she is aware of what is happening. The worldview of our culture provides us with *a primary frame of reference in making sense of the world*. It becomes our default frame of reference because we are constantly immersed in culture as are all other players in the events we seek to understand. If we grow up in a secular culture, this means that the frame of reference in which we make sense of things will generally be secular, *unless we consciously choose to bring another frame of reference into play*.

Worldview of the age

This worldview of the age provides people with a way of looking at life that has currency *across a number of local cultures* in a particular historical

---

[159] As we have pointed out previously a working model is one that attempts to portray a complex phenomenon by simplifying it. To be effective it must be complex enough to encompass the essential features of the phenomena while being simple enough to make predictions.

period and reflects the best aspirations of people living in that period. Classic examples are *the modern worldview* which is premised on unlimited human progress driven by science, and the particular version of *the Christian worldview* dominant in Europe in the late Middle Ages which held that the social/political structures of the day were divinely ordered. The modern worldview developed out of disillusionment with this worldview and, in turn, disillusionment with the modern worldview in the late 1970s gave rise to the 'post-modern' worldview.[160] Major changes in human aspiration accompany, or bring about, major changes in the cultural outlook of an age.

Worldview of faith

All religions encourage hope by promoting understandings about what it means to be human, and about how humans should relate to each other, to the environment and to God. Religious worldviews encompass an understanding of the transcendent and its significance in making sense of life and the matrix of relationships that define life. The three Abrahamic faiths—Christian, Jewish and Muslim—share a common belief in a God who exists *outside the created universe* and is the source of meaning for those living within it. This belief is axiomatic in the worldview of these faiths. In the perspective of these religions, there can be such a thing as a 'God's eye view of the world' because God chooses to communicate with humankind, as mysterious and remarkable as this seems to many people. Difficulty arises when God's communication is translated into human categories and must pass through the filters of human culture. Our human understanding of what God communicates can be as problematic as the communication itself is mysterious.

In cultural anthropology, collective worldviews such as the three public ones discussed above *underpin public commitments and sustain common efforts.* Cultures would not survive very long without the commitment to the 'plan for living' which they encompass. Religious communities would command little attention without the commitment members show to the beliefs and norms of faith. The aspirations that drive an age, for example for freedom or peace, also depend on commitment—what people are prepared to do. In summary, then, a worldview is not just a *thing of the mind; it is a thing of the heart.*[161] 'Worldview', as understood in cultural anthropology, is close in meaning to the biblical notion of 'heart'.[162]

---

160 There is considerable debate about whether or not post-modernity can be described as having a worldview because some of its supporters question the validity of worldview as a construct.
161 The term 'worldview' was first coined by the philosopher, Immanuel Kant, and as used by him the emphasis was on the cognitive element. This meaning lingers on in common usage of the term. See David Naugle *Worldview: History of a Concept* Cambridge UK: William B Eerdmans Publishing Company 2002.
162 Jim & Therese D'Orsa Catholic Curriculum: A Mission to the Heart of Young People (Mulgrave: Garratt Publishing, 2012), 237–251.

Public worldviews mediated by the communities that hold them

Public worldviews *never exist in a pure form*; their form is mediated by the way they are held in communities. We encounter the worldview of culture, for instance, through our families, through television and through education. It is transmitted to us as children in the form of narratives that tell us who we are and who we are not; what we should do and what we should not; how we should feel and how we should not.

The worldviews of faith and of the age are also mediated by family, school and the other communities of which we are part. Our understanding of them *is as much caught as taught*. Recognising that this is so has always been important for Catholic educators, introducing young people to the worldview of Christian faith as a source of meaning in making sense of life in a secular culture.

Public worldviews are interrelated sources of meaning

The three public worldviews are not separate sources of meaning, but are *inter-related*. Each affects the other two. Faith has to be expressed and transmitted through the language and symbols of culture. Changes in the worldview of an age lead to changes in cultural worldviews. As cultures change, so too do our insights into the meaning of faith. These are normal patterns of interaction.

Of particular importance is the relationship between the worldview of culture and that of the age. We live in a bifurcated age which can be represented diagrammatically as follows

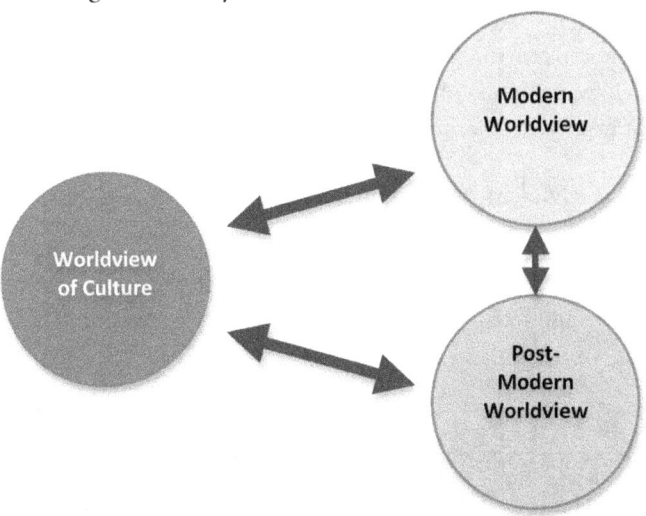

FIGURE 10.2 Post-Modern and Modern Influences on the Worldview of Culture

The worldview of our Western cultures has for the last four centuries been shaped by the modern worldview which reigned more or less supreme in the academic world until the mid-1970s. The modern worldview still stands behind most of the academic disciplines. It is a secular worldview which defines knowledge as that which can be determined by the methods of science, and is based on the belief that the meaning of the world can be found only in the world. In this perspective 'God' is an unnecessary construct. The post-modern worldview critiques the assumptions on which modernity is built. In particular, and with good reason, it rejects as delusory, the exaggerated optimism expressed in the grand narratives of modernity such as communism and liberal capitalism.[163] While discounting these grand narratives, post-modern thinkers are in fact creating a new grand narrative. Post-modern thought often applies critiques to other worldviews which it does not apply to itself.

It seems part of the human condition that we have to put our trust in something. Ambivalence about what this something should be lies at the heart of the post-modern condition. History and anthropology suggest that people cannot live in a transition state for any length of time. They either go backwards, or move forwards. What seems true is that young people are currently being educated in the cultural space between modernity and post-modernity, and this is unsettling for many because it destabilises the worldview of culture which is their primary frame of reference in making sense of life.

HOW PEOPLE MAKE SENSE OF THEIR EXPERIENCES[164]

We do not often think much about the processes by which we make meaning; we just do it. Model A below provides a simple working model of what happens in meaning-making.

Making sense of experience: Model A

'Events' are the stock in trade when it comes to meaning-making. An event may be the way in which students react to a new teacher; how parents respond to the teaching of Religious Education at VCE level; or

---

163 The problematic element in post-modern thought is that, while it is important to critique the often covert ways in which power is used in modern cultures, it is impossible to build a coherent system of thought around a hermeneutic of suspicion. If you suspect everything, you also need to suspect the position that you suspect everything!

164 The work of Shaun Gallagher *Hermeneutics and Education* (Albany: State University of New York Press, 1992), 149–158 is acknowledged as important source material in the discussion which follows in this chapter.

how the Parish Priest relates to students when celebrating a class Mass, and so on.

Leaders are expected to 'read' such situations. In doing this they access their personal worldview, and this shapes what they 'see' to be 'the facts of the matter'. In reading situations leaders bring a range of 'pre-understandings' into play which determine in large part what they include or exclude as 'facts'. These pre-understandings operate largely outside of their awareness.

We can use the case of a student misbehaving in class to show how this process operates. When Johnny X misbehaves, the matter is referred to the Year Coordinator, Ms Y. More or less without thinking she puts a series of questions to the event: What is going on? Why is it going on? What should be going on? In doing this Ms Y interprets the event with respect to *what she already knows about the context in which it occurred*—this might include knowledge about Johnny X, about the teacher, or what the school expects. This knowledge exists in the form of pre-understandings that Ms Y brings to the task of interpreting what is happening without her even being aware of it. These pre-understandings shape the way Ms Y makes sense of the event and the actors in it.

In making sense of the event, Ms Y fits it into a 'whole' in which the student's behavior becomes an element. The 'whole' provides a framework for making more sense of the part (specific behaviors), revealing that the case is not as simple as perhaps the teacher thinks it is. This puts further questions to the 'whole' and so on. Interpreting the event creates a hermeneutical circle in which interaction of whole and part generates deeper insight into the significance of the event.

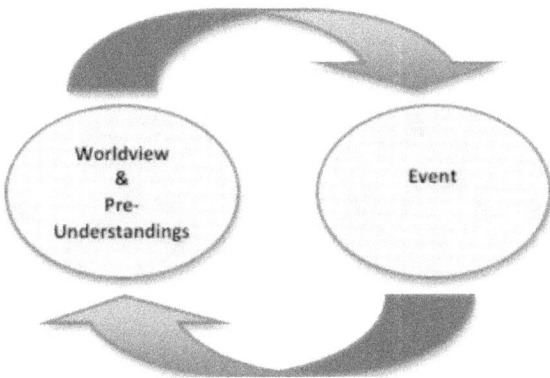

FIGURE 10.3 Model A and the Hermeneutical Circle

The hermeneutic circle is not always benign, as in the case above. What we see as 'the facts of the matter' often depends on the biases encoded in our pre-understandings. It requires self-awareness on the part of leaders to become aware of what their biases are and how these shape the way they read situations. For instance some leaders are always harder on people's poor behavior when they discover it themselves than when this is reported by others! Without critical reflection a leader can easily become trapped in the hermeneutical circle. To avoid this trap the leader has two important options. The first is to be aware of the way in which her or his worldview shapes reaction to situations. The second option is always to approach situations inter-subjectively. That is, to realise that 'my' reading of the situation is as strongly influenced by subjective biases as is every other reading of the situation. It therefore requires dialogue – listening to people, working closely with them, being present to them – to make real sense of a situation. A leader can, and in some cases must, impose meaning on a situation, but this always carries with it risk, and sometimes real human cost.

Making sense of experience: model B

Model B, is a development on Model A, and provides a more accurate portrayal of the meaning-making process. As the diagram indicates, standing behind the personal worldview of the interpreter are *traditions of meaning* which are the source of the pre-understandings that leaders bring to bear in making sense of events. With this element included, we can re-examine the process which occurs in three movements.

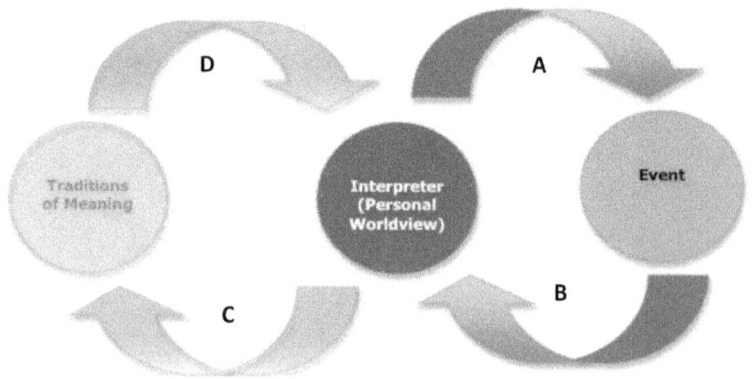

FIGURE 10.4 Making Sense of Experience: Model B (after Gallagher)[165]

In the first place we look at the facts of the situation (Arrow A). We then bring our pre-understandings and worldview to bear in making sense of it (Arrow B), and enter the hermeneutical circle as in Model A. Having read the situation we then choose to respond. If our reading of the event is

---

165 Gallagher, 156.

sound, and the response is deemed appropriate, we think no more about the matter. Model A has done the job!

However, the situation changes if the response does not produce the desired result. Then we ask: How did I get it so wrong? In seeking an answer we are forced to examine the process and the understandings we brought to it. That is, we begin to question the taken-for granted assumptions that stand in the background. This may even lead us to question the *traditions of meaning* themselves (Arrow C). This examination may lead to a rejection of some aspects of the tradition, or it may lead us to recognise limitations in our grasp of it. A third option is to contribute to the development of the tradition. All three of these options can lead us to re-shape our worldview (Arrow D).

Model B highlights a major issue in meaning-making. When people lose confidence in a public worldview, this impacts on how they understand situations. For instance, when religious people lose confidence in the worldview of faith, then the concept of sin often fades from view. Bad behavior comes to be seen as pathological, unethical or illegal, rather than as sinful. People who operate within the worldview of faith find this stance hard to comprehend.

As people have lost confidence in the modern worldview, the concept of 'objective knowledge' becomes meaningless. What we know becomes a 'matter of opinion', and relativism results. Once people lose confidence in the possibility of objective knowledge, then they have great difficulty in making sense of the worldview of faith. It is hard for people of faith, in turn, to understand the strange psychic space in which post-moderns live.

Adrift on the post-modern sea

One of the major problems presently confronting young Catholics sailing on the post-modern sea is that its form of critique often undermines the trust people invest in traditions of meaning, and offers little in its place, except meaninglessness. As a result, many *lack a coherent frame of reference* with which to make sense of their lives, which become aimless. Some retrieve the situation by appealing to fragments of public worldviews that are leftovers from their enculturation. However, most do not realise that their understanding of these is too naïve.

Dean Hoge, in an important study of young Catholic adults growing up in the post-modern era, suggests that they now live in a 'culture of choice' that enables them to put their worldview together by making a selection in the 'values supermarket'.[166] Such a stance is hermeneutically

---

166 Dean Hoge, William Dinges, Mary Johnson and Juan Gonzales *Young Adult Catholics: Religion in a Culture of Choice* (Notre Dame Indiana, Notre Dame University Press, 2001).

impossible as it assumes that a person's worldview is consciously constructed. This notion is also anthropologically unsound because it fails to appreciate the influence enculturation plays in the development of our worldview. It is against this background that missiologists are rapidly coming to the view that meaning-making and the construction of knowledge are new mission fields – vitally important areas in which the Kingdom of God needs to be made present in the interests of improving human lives.

'Befriending' as a stance to worldviews

Since public worldviews are owned by communities, and are internally contested, they evolve over time. Not all developments are positive, and so they need to be critiqued, but some need to be trusted as well. In this context practical theologians such as James and Evelyn Whitehead suggest the need to 'befriend' traditions of meaning. In befriending someone we *accept them for what they are, aware of their strengths and limitations.* Critique and trust are held together in friendship. In befriending a tradition, whether faith or culture, the aim is to hold trust and critique in tension. The opposite of befriending is alienation. Many Catholics today seem to live in a space between these options. They have lost confidence in the worldview of faith as a total interpretive system, but still hang on to fragments of it. Rather than engage in critique which can lead to a development of the tradition, they prefer to disengage and remain distant. What is remarkable is that, despite this, many obviously retain a loyalty to Catholic schools and support them. The questions that educational leaders have to ask are: Why? For how long?

The analysis of meaning-making suggests that leaders need to befriend both their cultural and faith traditions and appreciate the role each plays in how they make sense of life situations. Befriending a tradition, whether, faith or culture, is a life-long process because the traditions are dynamic and continuously evolving.

PRIORITIES IN LEADING FOR MISSION

PRIORITY 10.1 To become meaning-makers it is necessary for leaders to 'befriend' both their faith tradition and their cultural tradition.

'Befriending' means having sufficient perspective on a tradition to move beyond a critical stance to accepting the value of the tradition despite its limitations. This enables the leader to work within the opportunities that are available to address limitations within the tradition.

Continuing the Conversation

The following questions explore issues which impinge on how schools and systems promote 'befriending' as a stance in the development of staff.

- What opportunities, if any, does your school or system provide for enabling teachers to befriend their faith tradition?
- What options exist, or could be created, that might achieve this goal?
- Readiness is a major factor in determining whether or not a person can or will move from a critical stance to that of befriending in matters concerning the Church. In your own experience what factors shape this readiness and how can these be best facilitated?
- How does post-modern thinking surface in the contemporary classroom? Among parents? Among staff?
- What would you name as its characteristics? How do its assumptions compare/contrast with traditional religious thinking?
- What implications does such an analysis have for Catholic educators?

PRIORITIES IN LEADING FOR MISSION

PRIORITY 10.2 **In leading for mission it is always important firstly to understand the worldviews that people bring to the table when addressing problems, and secondly to work inter-subjectively in seeking to resolve those problems.**

Continuing the Conversation

Consider the following case study:

John is the REC at your Catholic primary school. Most of the students' parents have little to do with the Church. Few ever attend Mass outside of Christmas and Easter. John organises liturgies to celebrate major feasts and events such as ANZAC day. There is a high level of student participation in these events and parents are invited. Because they are held at the start of the school day, there is usually a good level of parental presence. John has encouraged some to play a role in the events. However, there is not the same support if a class or school Mass is provided in this time slot.

The local parish priest has come to you about this. His view is that there should be more Masses for the students so that they can get a better understanding of the Mass. His attitude is that, if this is not what Catholic schools are on about, then what are they about?

You call John in to discuss the matter and find out that he does not want to organise more class or school Masses as he is encountering resistance from the staff. They feel that their main role at these events is as children-tamers – ensuring order. In their view this is counterproductive of their other work with the students in Religious Education.

John's view is that children like the liturgies that he puts on, but are put off by the Mass. In this they reflect the attitude of their parents who also like the liturgies, but not Mass.

Three important questions in exploring this event meaningfully are:
What is going on? Why is it going on? What should be going on?

Examine each of these questions from the perspective of three of the major players: John, the Parish Priest and the staff.

- What does such an analysis tell you about the worldview they are employing in making sense of the event?
- What clues does this give you as leader in knowing how to address it?
- How would you address it?

Part D
LEADING FOR MISSION:
Contemporary practices and perspectives

As we have noted in earlier chapters, in the past Catholic educational leaders have had to negotiate liminal crises, and their experience provides both hope and insight. Contemporary leaders are not without resources in meeting the present challenge. Part D outlines some of the approaches currently being taken and what can be learned from these experiences.

If meaning-making is essential to mission thinking, then understanding the processes by which meaning is created is important. As we saw in the last chapter, traditions of meaning play an important role in how we create our personal worldview. We also saw that these traditions come to us moderated by the communities in which we live: family, peers, school, parish all play a part. The relative influence which these groups exercise shapes both our understanding of what a tradition is, and the value we place on it as a resource in meaning-making. This hermeneutical understanding has important implications for Catholic schooling. To what extent are schools aware of the ways in which, for instance, students understand the worldview of faith, given that differing understandings are likely to exist at the family, school and parish levels?

The *Enhancing Catholic School Identity Project* sponsored by the Catholic Education Commission of Victoria and the Catholic University of Leuven seeks to profile the way in which key groups in a school community—students, staff and parents—understand the worldview of faith. In Chapter 11, Paul Sharkey outlines the framework underlying this project, its theoretical foundation in hermeneutical theory, and the instruments developed to explore the perspective that key stakeholders bring to bear in supporting Catholic schools. The project provides schools and systems with accurate and reliable data, and suggests a way of establishing the mission demands of working with particular school communities. While still in its early days, in that the project has yet to fully develop processes for utilising the data it provides, it offers an important step forward in negotiating liminality.

In Chapter 12 Br Michael Green suggests an alternative approach in helping young people to incorporate the worldview of faith into their own personal worldviews, and that is by aligning themselves with one of the great spiritual traditions alive in Catholic schools. In his case it is the Marist spiritual tradition. A spirituality tends to gain traction in people's consciousness because it provides a way of integrating an understanding of the worldview of faith with that of the prevailing culture. For this reason there are a number of Catholic spiritualities. Those that survive over time do so because they are the possession of a community which sponsors them and around which a culture develops. Marist spirituality is unique not only in the way it understands the worldview of faith and the commitments this leads to, but also in the culture that has developed around Marist educational institutions which are an expression of that culture. Many Catholic schools in recent years have tried to address the crisis of liminality by re-aligning themselves with the spiritual traditions of the congregations that have played a part in their story. Some leaders have great difficulty in understanding why this works. Michael Green brings anthropology and theology together in explaining why it does so.

Over the past thirty years Australian Catholic University has provided a principal source of training for people aspiring to leadership in Catholic schools and school systems. This has lead to the implementation in 2012 of a Masters program designed specifically for leaders from within systems such as Catholic Education Offices. Although not designed specifically to address the issue of leading in liminal times the program, devised in consultation with the CEOs, covers many of the bases outlined previously. System and school leadership is exercised in an increasingly complex environment and requires the adoption of models that are appropriate to that environment. In Chapter 13, professors Michael Bezzina and Anne Benjamin suggest that Catholic school systems today form complex adaptive systems, and that there are useful models available to school leaders in understanding the 'rules' by which these function. Complex adaptive systems, of which flocking birds is a good example, function on both rules and instinct in negotiating hurdles that stand between the flock and its destination. The discussion highlights the roles 'intelligent inter-dependence' and instinct play in the operation of complex organisations. It reminds leaders of the need to trust the religious instinct at work in driving mission forward – a theme we return to in the final chapter.

Chris Barrett brings the section to a conclusion by examining how one complex adaptive system functions (Chapter 14). He details efforts made by the CEO Sydney to implement a specific leadership model which sought to address the mission thinking issues that are thrown up in a liminal era. He draws attention to the issues this experience raises for the leadership of CEOs in sustaining mission directions across time, and as personnel change. The implementation of a leadership model implies the development of a framework and processes which need to be consciously aligned. This becomes an exercise in 'intelligent inter-dependence'. The chapter outlines the particular form intelligent inter-dependence took in the development of the Sydney CEO models of school and system leadership, and the place of reviews in these models.

The common theme across all models discussed in this section is the need for leadership and mission to be contextualised in the sense that they are made meaningful for those who lead, those entrusted with mission responsibilities, and those whom mission embraces.

11
HERMENEUTICS AND THE MISSION OF THE CATHOLIC SCHOOL: ECSIP AS A CASE STUDY

Paul Sharkey[167]

Those of us who have given our professional lives over as a vocation in Catholic education know that our schools are confronted by a range of complex and stimulating challenges in regard to their Catholic identity. We know that we need to develop new strategies and approaches if we are to continue creating spaces which engage students with the mystery, substance and richness of Catholic faith. Hermeneutic theory can provide Catholic educators with important compass bearings as they navigate their way through the issues associated with developing a strong Catholic school identity at that this time. The chapter begins with a reflection on the place of hermeneutics and religion in an individual's quest for truth and meaning. The hermeneutic theory of Hans-Georg Gadamer and Paul Ricoeur provides a foundation for these reflections as do a number of key concepts developed in a research project called the *Enhancing Catholic School Identity Project* (ECSI project).

The ECSI project arose in the context of a fruitful partnership between Professor Didier Pollefeyt from the Catholic University in Leuven (Belgium) and the Catholic Education Commission of Victoria. While still in the early stages of development, the ECSI project provides a valuable framework for understanding and addressing the challenges that go hand in hand with educating young people in a liminal age. In the second section of this chapter I examine the concept of post-critical belief which is a key construct in one of the ECSI project research instruments. The third section focuses

---

167 Paul Sharkey is Director of Catholic Education in the Archdiocese of Adelaide. He has previously been a diocesan director of religious education and has completed a PhD which considered school identity from a hermeneutic place.

on what hermeneutics has to say about developing a Catholic identity in the midst of difference and diversity and how this is addressed in the ECSI Project. The chapter concludes by considering hermeneutics as a process which unfolds in the space between strangeness and familiarity. Once again the ECSI project is considered in the light of this insight.

HERMENEUTICS AND RELIGION: MAKING SENSE OF HUMAN EXPERIENCE

The term 'hermeneutics' can be defined as the science of interpretation and its origins have sometimes been associated with Hermes, the tricky god who runs messages between the gods and humanity. There is something evocative about this image when it comes to considering what Catholic educators are doing today as they seek to open up the tradition for their students. In antiquity, hermeneutics was an academic discipline concerned with the interpretation of texts that were difficult or problematic in some way. Over the past two centuries the field of hermeneutics has broadened so that instead of asking how a difficult written text might be understood, contemporary hermeneutics now considers how understanding or meaning-making is possible at all.

German Philosopher Martin Heidegger gave central significance to the importance of hermeneutics in his analysis where he presented the human inclination to interpret and make meaning as being a fundamental mode of human existence. Human beings are fundamentally oriented towards interpretation which means that *we only understand our world as we make sense of our experience of it*. It is this human orientation towards meaning-making that forms the basis of the hermeneutic approach to Catholic identity being advocated in this chapter.[168]

Hans-Georg Gadamer (1900–2002) is the philosopher whose hermeneutic theory is particularly useful for anyone considering how a religious or a cultural tradition is formative for those who experience it. Traditions are comprised of elements such as symbols, language, stories, beliefs, values and rituals which provide a world of meaning for those who live inside them. The human condition is to live inside cultural and religious

---

168 Space does not permit a discussion of the stances that hermeneutic theories take to the relationship between truth and meaning-making. Some of these stances were acknowledged earlier in this book in Chapter 4. The orientation of this chapter could be classified as 'moderate' in the survey of hermeneutics given in Shaun Gallagher's *Hermeneutics and Education* (Albany: State University of New York Press, 1992). A moderate hermeneutics holds that, whilst understanding is always situated in the interpreter's horizon (and therefore always contextualised by life experience and culture), interpretation is not reduced to the nihilism of radical hermeneutics where a tradition's capacity to lay a truth claim on the individual is minimised. Moderate hermeneutics accepts the claim of the tradition and the need to appropriate it in culture and life.

traditions which shape us long before we shape them. Rather than being static and closed, traditions carry riches as a living reality into the present and are recreated anew for future generations.

Catholic schools are explicitly grounded in the Catholic tradition. A good Catholic school is one where the school's founding tradition is brought to life daily so that it permeates the school's culture and curriculum, richly shaping the way students see the world and their place in it. Catholic traditions always develop within a particular cultural setting and are always shaped therefore by the values and beliefs associated with that setting.

Cultural anthropologist Clifford Geertz described human persons as *being suspended in webs of significance that they themselves have spun.*[169] Educators in Catholic schools need some of the skills of the cultural anthropologist as they develop the school's culture so that its 'webs of significance' reverberate with Catholic symbols, values, beliefs and action for those who are suspended in it. The formative impact of the Catholic school is amplified when students encounter Catholic faith as a living reality in their family and in their parish. Catholic faith powerfully shapes the lives and outlook of all involved when it is experienced in this holistic way.

Catholic educators know however that such a grand vision for Catholic education is rarely realised in practice. Very few students now come from families that are actively involved in the life of the Church beyond the school. Now, more than ever, those who lead Catholic schools need to understand the pluralistic context and the diverse cultural currents that shape the worldviews of members of their school community. School leaders need to understand the opportunities and constraints for realising the mission within the prevailing socio-cultural context.

Religion and the context of meaning-making in Australia

The writings of Charles Taylor, a Canadian philosopher, and Philip Hughes, an Australian social scientist, can help us understand what is happening in the relationship between religion and culture in Australia at this time. Taylor has characterised the modern age as being shaped by an 'ethic of authenticity'[170] where the fundamental task for each individual is to realise their humanity by fashioning *their own unique way of being human*. 'My way' is not an imitation of someone else's way, and neither is it a conformity to a model imposed externally from society, the previous generation, nor is it given to us as a package from a religious or political authority. Each individual must discover the point of their life themselves: *what being human means for them.*

---

169 Geertz, C. *The Interpretation of Cultures* (New York: Basic Books, 1993).
170 Charles Taylor *The Ethics of Authenticity* (Canadian Broadcasting Corporation, 1991).

Whilst the ethic of authenticity is commendable, it can also degenerate into subjectivism and narcissism where an individual understands his or her identity simply as a self-creation: 'entirely an act of self-determining freedom'. This slide is self-defeating as it 'detaches the individual from the very connections that we require for our lives to have meaning'.[171] Catholic schools can support the individual's meaning-making quest within *webs of significance that resound in a Catholic key*.

Our sense of identity is neither free-floating nor simply an instinctive response to realities we find attractive. Detached from horizons of significance and identity-defining relationships, human identity would be meaningless.[172]

The point here is that it is the community not just individuals who hold the traditions of meaning that give significance and meaning to human experience. Taylor's analysis is illuminating for leaders in a Catholic school. Ours is an age where students and staff 'put life together' in their own way as distinct from having a 'way' imposed on them from the outside. Appeals to tradition have little impact unless the individual is able *to engage with those traditions* in the context of a *personal and unique search for meaning and authenticity*. The individual's quest loses its anchor when it is detached from the wider community that gives the individual search its context and significance. Authenticity easily degenerates into narcissism and bricolage[173] when detached from the communities and relationships which deepen and broaden an individual's worldview and challenge incoherence or inconsistency. It is interesting to examine the online social networks accessed with such intensity by many students to evaluate whether they provide a community which enlarges or ossifies the worldviews of those who engage with them. Online communities are not unlike their face-to-face counterparts in having the potential to either broaden or diminish the outlook of the individuals who belong to them.

The Catholic school can provide an enriching and broadening community and it can engage individuals with the richness of Catholic faith, not as an imposed tradition that substitutes for the individual's quest for truth, but as a rich context in which that quest might unfold. As has been indicated, the Catholic school is best placed to support the individual's quest when its contribution is offered in concert with what is experienced in the home and the broader Church.

Philip Hughes is the author of a book called *Putting Life Together* which reports on a large scale Australian youth spirituality research project.[174]

---

171 James McEvoy 'Proclamation as dialogue: Transition in the church–world relationship' *Theological Studies*, 70, 2009, 892.
172 ibid., 891.
173 A term originally used in the visual arts to indicate a work constructed from whatever is at hand.
174 Hughes, P. *Putting Life Together: Findings from Australian Youth Spirituality Research* (Fairfield: Fairfield Press, 2007).

Hughes found that young Australians typically do not employ categories such as 'religion', 'spirituality' or even 'what gives meaning to life'. The young people he interviewed looked at him blankly when such terms were used as they were not part of their language. Hughes therefore shifted the focus from religion and spirituality to discussing 'what life is about'. He did this by discussing *what was important for the young people*: the values and priorities that guided their behavior. He found that young Australians talk about their beliefs as *something that they put together themselves in a creative fashion* (hence the title of his book). Whilst about 20% of young people in his sample identified themselves as belonging to a religious community, the majority had not explored a particular religious tradition in any depth. They tended instead to 'dabble', often being fascinated by elements drawn from a variety of disconnected fragments of traditions—both cultural and religious.

Faced with the reality of this eschewal of commitment by young people to a particular religious tradition and recognising the students' quest for authenticity, it is easy to understand why some Catholic educators are tempted to opt for a generalised spirituality for their students, rather than creating spaces which engage more explicitly with Catholic religious commitment. Writers such as Sandra Schneiders, Anthony Kelly and David Tacey have argued that spirituality and religion need to be seen as partners which complement each other, rather than mutually exclusive options between which one must choose.[175] *Religious commitment without spirituality is sterile. Spirituality without religious commitment lacks a tradition of meaning* which draws upon the rich resources of language, symbol, history, theology and ritual. Catholic educators need to be sophisticated in their approach if they are to create spaces which genuinely engage their students with the Catholic tradition in an era where so much value is placed on the individual quest and putting life together oneself from one's own resources. Hermeneutics can provide important compass bearings for educators as they navigate their way through this challenging and stimulating territory.

POST-CRITICAL BELIEF

In his first encyclical, Pope Benedict XVI surprised many with his strong emphasis on *the experience* of the love of God as being at the heart of Christian faith. The experience of this love shapes the image one has of God and of the nature and destiny of the human person. Benedict indicated that, as this

---

175 Sandra Schneiders 'Religion and Spirituality: Strangers, rivals or partners?' in *The Santa Clara Lectures* 6(2), 2000, 1–26; Anthony Kelly 'Reflections on spirituality and the Church. *The Australasian Catholic Record*. v 78, n 3, 2001, 309–320; David Tacey 'Mind the gap: Youth spirituality and formal religion'. Keynote address given at Catholic Education Conference, Adelaide, 16 August, 2001.

was his first encyclical, he wished to focus on the love which God lavishes upon us and which we in turn must share with others.[176] For this Pope, being Christian is 'not the result of an ethical choice or a lofty idea, but an encounter with an event, a person, which gives life a new horizon and a decisive direction'. At the heart of Christian faith is an encounter with the risen Christ, and this *encounter is ongoing and life-changing for those who experience it*. Those who lead Catholic schools are challenged to ensure that spaces are created for their students that invite them into the experience of God's love which lies at the heart of Christian faith.

The Hermeneutics of Paul Ricoeur

The hermeneutic theory of French philosopher Paul Ricoeur throws considerable light onto how this challenge might be addressed in our time. Ricoeur argues that in today's world the myths, rituals and stories through which traditions are conveyed are no longer accessible to us in the way they were before the rise of science and critical consciousness. In order to be 'scientific' or 'critical' a person has to step back from the world in order to explain it. In this 'distanciation' (or stepping back) the naïve meaning of the symbols (myth, ritual or story) is lost and the symbol loses its initial meaning. Ricoeur's reflections on the critical dimension of human understanding addresses a deficiency that some have found in Gadamer's work that there is too little acknowledgement of the need to engage critically with traditions. A new connection with a symbol (in Ricoeur's language 'a second naivete') is only possible when the hermeneutic process moves into critical engagement and *then beyond it* into a post-critical appropriation.

Many school leaders have experienced this process in their study of Scripture as they have moved from naïve literalism into a critical engagement with the text, then a post-critical appropriation of the text's meaning for their own life. The development of a post-critical understanding not only applies to faith as a tradition of meaning, but also to culture. The post-critical understanding is 'no longer, to be sure, the first faith of the simple soul, but rather the second faith of one who has engaged in hermeneutics, a faith that has undergone criticism, a post-critical faith'.[177] *This process of moving from naïve belief, through criticism and into post-critical belief is ongoing throughout life.*

---

176 Benedict XVI *Deus Caritas Est*, #1
177 Paul Ricoeur *Freud and Philosophy: an essay on interpretation* (trans. Denis Savage) (New Haven: Yale University Press) 1970.

Critiquing traditions

Traditions of meaning are far from naïve. They are the products of history and culture and are therefore enriched and diminished as a consequence. The Church is described in the Vatican II document on the Church as being 'at the same time holy and always in need of being purified'.[178] The meaning-making process for individuals and communities unfolds within a continuous rhythm of belief, critique and post-critical belief.

In Ricoeur's analysis, whilst critical engagement is normal and necessary, the critical stage *is not the last stage or even the most important stage in the meaning making process*. It is only when the interpreter is able to move on from critique into a post-critical appropriation of the cultural or religious tradition that a new sense of meaning (and potentially of faith) emerges.

Ricoeur's insights have particular relevance in Catholic schools where staff and students are at various places in their faith journey. Those who have recognised the love of God reaching into their lives are forever changed by the experience. Christians appreciate this love in the context of their experience of the incarnation and the paschal mystery. Catholics appreciate this love in the midst of their Church, its people, teachings and sacraments and through their participation in its mission.

Some Catholics interpret the tradition literally and experience Catholic faith as a 'deposit' of truths that *are fixed and forever unchanging*. Other people who work in Catholic schools do not frame their lives in specifically religious terms and may not believe in a God at all. Some of these people are quite hostile towards religion believing it to be based on an illusion that has no place in the modern world. Others are quite open to the religious views of others, even though they do not see the world in these terms themselves.

A fourth approach to Catholic faith is to appreciate that it is only ever grasped in particular historical circumstances and therefore has to be expressed anew in every age as expressions and understandings of the faith continually develop in an ongoing interaction between faith and culture. In the words of John Paul II: 'a faith that has not been fully inculturated is a faith that has not been fully received'.[179]

The ECSI Project Post-Critical Belief Scale

With the above options in mind, those who lead Catholic schools need to develop and enact a sophisticated array of pastoral responses with

---

178 *Lumen Gentium* # 8.
179 John Paul II. (1982a). 'Letter to Cardinal Agostino Casaroli.' *L'Osservatore Romano*, 28 June 1982.

members of their school community, according to where they are in their experience of the transcendent God who moves in the midst of human experience. Those students or staff who take a literal approach to religious faith need different strategies of engagement from those who believe that the tradition must be interpreted before its symbols will speak meaningfully in our time. Those who are hostile towards religious faith require different strategies from those who tolerate religion but have no belief themselves in a God who reaches out in love to them. These latter people may understand that each person needs to construct their own world of meaning but see each construction as being equally adequate because there is no sense of there actually being a God beyond the construction. Where there is no sense of God as the referent, there can be no evaluation of the adequacy of signs which point towards this referent. Those who lead Catholic schools face the challenge of *creating spaces which lead each of these types of people to contribute more effectively to the mission of the school.*

In the *Enhancing Catholic School Identity Project* the categories that have just been discussed are profiled in the Post-Critical Belief (PCB) scale developed by Dirk Hutsebaut.[180] The PCB scale can be used by school leaders to profile the religious attitudes of members of the school community, thus enabling pastoral strategies to be designed and enacted which enhance the school's Catholic identity in the light of its particular profile. The four categories from the PCB scale were discussed above in the following order: Literal Belief, External Critique, Relativity and Post-Critical Belief. Further information about the scale and its use in Catholic schools is available in the work of Pollefeyt and Bouwens and in the reports from the ECSI project which are currently being published.[181] The ECSI project is still in its initial stages of development, and it will clearly take some time and experimentation to develop a range of pastoral strategies which respond to the profiles generated by the research instruments.

PLAY AND DIALOGUE IN MEANING-MAKING

In his analysis of what it means to make sense of life, Gadamer used metaphors such as 'conversation' and 'play' to convey the indeterminacy that is necessary for genuine understanding to occur. New meaning only emerges when, like a good conversation, we allow ourselves to be led by

---

180 Hutsebaut, D. 'Post-critical belief. A new approach to the religious attitude problem' in *Journal of Empirical Theology* 9(2): 48–66, 1996.
181 Pollefeyt, D. and Bouwens, J. 'Framing the identity of Catholic schools: empirical methodology for quantitative research on the Catholic identity of an education institute' in *International Studies in Catholic Education*. 2(2), 2010, 193–211

the subject matter we are seeking to understand. If we know ahead of time what will be said in a conversation, the interaction is better characterised as a series of monologues in which each party says only what they had always intended to say and is not affected by the insights of the other. No new understandings emerge in such a process and the dialogue partners remain the same. *New meaning only arises when the person seeking to understand something is genuinely open to what it is that the life expression has to say*, rather than being sure before the process begins what will eventuate.

Another metaphor that Gadamer used to amplify this point was the experience of playing a game. He suggests that in play the *game draws the players into its power and fills them with its spirit*. The whole point of a game is that, unless the result has been rigged, *the outcome is undecided*. 'The attraction of a game, the fascination it exerts, consists precisely in the fact that the game masters its players'.[182] In Gadamer's schema, the interpreter not only makes sense of a life expression *but is also interpreted by it*. By entering into the world that an expression of culture or religious faith opens up, the interpreter's world of meaning has the potential to be enriched and changed.

It is only through entering into genuine conversation with life expressions (human experience) that truth is disclosed and authentic understanding occurs. Gadamer calls this the experience of 'being transformed into a communion in which we do not remain what we were'.[183] This applies whether we are seeking to make sense of secular or religious experiences.

THE ECSIP VICTORIA SCALE: DEALING WITH RELIGIOUS DIVERSITY IN CATHOLIC SCHOOLS

Employing Gadamer's metaphors, Catholic educators are challenged to foster Catholic 'conversations' and 'games' in their schools. A well-intentioned, but misguided response to the growing diversity in Catholic schools is to seek to ensure that the only voice heard is 'the Catholic voice'. Staff with this orientation seek (implicitly, if not sometimes explicitly) to suppress non-Catholic voices as the means of safeguarding the school's Catholic identity. The problem with this option is that the dialogue needed to create meaning is reduced to a monologue and so students disengage from the conversation. Secular culture then, by default, provides the tradition in which students make sense of their world. The irony in this situation is that, while the intent is to evangelise, the opposite effect occurs because of a lack of

---

182 ibid., 106.
183 ibid., 379.

understanding of how people make sense of life and commit themselves to particular beliefs, values or practices. In the absence of genuine dialogue the secularisation/evangelisation balance is tipped in favour of secularisation.

We have seen above that ours is an age where people expect to 'put life together' themselves and will not engage with an imposed worldview. With this in mind, a second response to faith pluralism in the school is to create a space where anyone who has anything to say can do so with little moderation or challenge. The specifically Catholic voice becomes lost in a confused cacophony in this type of school. In this situation the secularisation/evangelisation balance also tips decisively in favour of secularisation.

Another response to pluralism is to suppress the religious conversation, so that religion is banished to the private sphere. Rather than run the risk of disrespecting any view, staff simply avoid religious conversation altogether. The Catholic school's mission is obviously thwarted when the faith dialogue is privatised in this way. The school may preserve the forms of Catholic identity for a time but its Catholic core eventually erodes and disappears. This has been the experience of Catholic schools in parts of the world where the secularisation process is more advanced than it is in Australia.[184]

The preferred approach in the ECSIP is to engage with the Catholic tradition even as the diversity of students is respected and acknowledged. Hermeneutics can provide a framework for this approach to be enacted so that students are 'transformed into a communion' in which they do not remain what they were. The engaged approach advocated here is predicated on the belief that cultural and religious traditions are *rich and disclosive of truth for those who engage with them*. Rather than trying to discourage students from bringing their diverse views into the 'Catholic' conversation, educators seek to create a space that engages those diverse views strongly with the tradition so that new understandings and meanings emerge. This is the sense in which 'befriending' is used in earlier chapters.

Of course, if the student has already closed his or her mind to the Catholic tradition as a potential source of meaning prior to engaging with it, then genuine 'conversation' is not an option. This situation can easily arise when the student's understanding of the faith tradition is at the first naïveté stage and his or her understanding of the cultural tradition is at the level of critical engagement. Equally, when a teacher has already decided what the Catholic tradition should mean for the students, the students quickly sense that the game is rigged and they walk away from the field of play. What we are talking about here is the distinction between indoctrination and education. *Authentic education always leads the students and teachers out into a*

---

[184] See Pollefeyt and Bouwens 'Framing the identity of Catholic schools' for further details of the Victoria Scale and the analysis of the dialogue options in the Catholic school.

new place. Obviously teachers need to know how to create spaces where strong engagement with the students' traditions of culture and faith can occur. The present writer is currently working with colleagues to identify exemplary practice in this regard with a view towards publishing examples of it in due course. The study of hermeneutics suggests the need to encourage and educate each other as colleagues in our ongoing endeavours to create Catholic spaces for our students that are formative for them at this time.

HERMENEUTICS: BETWEEN STRANGENESS AND FAMILIARITY

For Gadamer, hermeneutics unfolds in the space between familiarity and strangeness. Each of us lives within a horizon of meaning where some things make sense to us and are meaningful and familiar whereas others are strange and devoid of meaning.

The horizon is the range of vision that includes everything that can be seen from a particular vantage point. Applying this to the thinking mind, we speak of narrowness of horizon, of the possible expansion of horizon, of the opening up of new horizons and so forth.[185]

Hermeneutics is only necessary in the middle space between familiarity and unfamiliarity. It is unnecessary when encountering a life-expression that is totally familiar because the expression is already meaningful and does not provoke interpretation. If the life-expression is totally strange (for example a text written in hieroglyphics), then interpretation is an impossibility because the interpreter has no place to begin the meaning-making process.

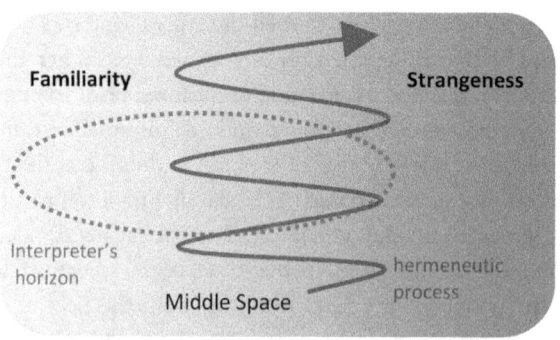

FIGURE 11.1: Hermeneutics Unfolds in Between Strangeness and Familiarity

---

185 Gadamer, *Truth and Method*, 302.

The ECSI project Melbourne scale: new expressions of an ancient tradition

Those who lead Catholic schools can find increasingly that the students they are enrolling and the staff they are employing are less familiar with Catholic faith than they once were. Some of the responses to this pastoral context are profiled in the ECSIP *Melbourne Scale* under the headings Reconfessionalisation, Values Education and Recontextualisation.[186] The first two of these options are rejected from a hermeneutical standpoint because they take students (and staff) away from the 'middle' hermeneutic space between strangeness and familiarity where understanding deepens and meaning is made.

Leaders who take the purest form of the Reconfessionalisation option would only enrol students and employ staff who are thoroughly familiar with the Catholic tradition. The gap between strangeness and familiarity is resolved here by only enrolling or employing 'insiders' who create a Catholic world apart from the broader social context. The 'reconfessionalising' option faces a number of difficulties, not least of which is a practical one because the number of Catholic insiders is reducing all the time. Another problem with this option is that it lacks an orientation towards evangelisation and will therefore be rejected by those with an outreach commitment.[187]

A second response to the gap between culture and faith is to *reduce Catholic faith down to only the concepts and expressions that sit comfortably within the students' cultural horizons.* Once again this option takes students away from the space between strangeness and familiarity where meaning is made and understanding deepens. Over time, the tradition becomes hollowed out and drained of meaning when this reductionist option is exercised and the opportunity for the tradition to lead members of the school community into new understandings and meanings is taken away. This 'hollowing out' occurs in *some*, but not all, forms of values education when an attempt is made to reduce the call of the Gospel to a series of culturally acceptable values.

The preferred option in the ECSI project is *recontextualisation* where challenging 'middle' spaces are created which lead students and staff to grapple with the tradition so that there are rich opportunities for truth to be disclosed and formation to occur. Instead of 'dumbing down' the

---

186 See Pollefeyt and Bouwens for further detail on these three options in the Melbourne scale. Two further options in the Melbourne scale (Institutional, Secularisation, and the Confessionally based institution) are not considered here because they do not reflect an authentic engagement on the part of the school leader with the identity challenges of our day.
187 This option is specifically rejected by the bishops of NSW in *Catholic Schools at the Crossroads* (Sydney: 2007, 6) and in policy documents of the Congregation for Christian Education for example *Catholic Schools on the Threshold of the Third Millennium* #15.

challenges which the faith tradition offers in such a school, its sharper edges are highlighted as opportunities for learning, formation and growth. Instead of suppressing diversity within the staff and students, their differences are highlighted as an opportunity for developing a deeper understanding of what the tradition might disclose to each person in their own hermeneutic place. As has been indicated above, it would now be timely to document some of the effective practice that is currently underway in this area.

Considerable skill is needed on the part of school leadership to ensure that the right processes and people are involved so that an authentic encounter with the tradition is provided. Pope Benedict in a 2005 address to the Curia repeated the remarks of John XXIII as he opened the Second Vatican Council: 'transmit the doctrine, pure and integral, without any attenuation or distortion'. Whilst the tradition must be presented faithfully, it should also be expounded 'through the literary forms of modern thought' for the 'substance of the ancient doctrine of the deposit of faith is one thing, and the way in which it is presented is another'.[188]

Catholic educators are challenged to present the tradition authentically but they must do so in *terms that are meaningful for members of their school community*. New forms and expressions are required if this is to occur and this creative process needs to be characterised by respect. If each person's worldview is respected during the formative process, then the school is entitled to be just as strong in its respect *for the particularity of the Catholic tradition and the challenge it offers to those who engage with it*.

Those who engage with this type of formative process not only interpret the tradition, they are interpreted by it. The process is predicated on the belief that *Catholic faith speaks to people when there is an openness to hear, when it is proclaimed well, and when the spaces for encountering the tradition are appropriately structured*. New and authentic Catholic expressions are created in this engagement and these expressions draw people more deeply into the truth of what the tradition has to disclose.

Conclusion

The hermeneutic theory considered in this chapter has the potential to help students and staff to engage more deeply with the faith tradition that gives the Catholic school its reason for being. Students and staff are challenged to become aware of the ways in which religious and cultural traditions intersect and interact in the meaning-making process for each individual. Traditions have strengths and weaknesses and are always in a process of

---

188 Pope Benedict XVI. 2005 address to the Roman Curia in M. Lacey and F. Oakley eds *The Crisis of Authority in Catholic Modernity* (Oxford: Oxford University Press, 2011).

development as human experience expands, new concepts, images and symbols are invented, and as new meanings develop.

As has been indicated throughout the text, a number of jurisdictions are currently profiling their school communities to establish how Catholic identity options are being taken up in the life of the school. This empirical data will help school and system leaders to understand the nature of the challenges presented by their school's particular profile. Profiling school communities will not however, of itself, change or improve them. *A deeper understanding of the mission context does, nonetheless, provide a firm foundation for system or school leaders to identify strategies of engagement which can be effective for the various types of families and staff who are in our Catholic schools at this time.* The next step will be for us to share insights and effective practice with each other so that we are better equipped to realise the great mission that animates the schools in which we work. *The way ahead could provide a marvellous example of mission-thinking-in-action as system and school leaders work together to respond to the identity challenges which confront us so richly at this time.*

PRIORITIES IN LEADING FOR MISSION

PRIORITY 11.1 In leading for mission in Catholic education it is necessary to identify, acknowledge and address the range of faith stances alive in the broader Catholic community, and in the Catholic school in particular.

Continuing the Conversation

In a liminal era assumptions that could once be taken for granted begin to erode. Some of these assumptions concern the way in which people understand what 'being religious' means. This theme translates in a number of ways when it is played out in a Catholic school.

- What are some of the variations that play out in your school among
  » the staff?
  » the students?
  » the parents?
- What implicit assumptions does the school/school system seem to be working from in its educational planning as it seeks to acknowledge (or fails to acknowledge) these differences?
- Do school/system leaders have any working model in mind such as the one offered by Paul Sharkey, as they seek to meet the challenge that difference in faith-stance now constitutes in a Catholic school? If so, what model is used and how effective is it in directing action?

PRIORITIES IN LEADING FOR MISSION

PRIORITY 11.2 Leading for mission in Catholic education involves assisting key personnel reach a post-critical stance with respect to both faith and culture.

Ricoeur's notion that meaning-making requires leaders to take a post-critical stance to faith and culture corresponds to the Whiteheads' idea that to make sense of faith or culture it is necessary to 'befriend' them.

Continuing the Conversation

Most teachers have been introduced to the modern worldview as a result of their secondary and tertiary education. It is a worldview that holds that science defines what constitutes real knowledge, and gives other forms of human enquiry a secondary status. The post-modern critique challenges this understanding in important ways. It points out that all public worldviews are built on axioms which are usually unstated, and so are open to critique. Unless such critique is acknowledged, the modern way of construing knowledge is quite problematic.

- When you look at your own teaching areas, is there a consistent theory of the knowledge embedded in them? If so, what are its major assumptions?
- If not, what are the competing theories and how do students understand the differences?
- The post-modern mentality holds that all knowledge contains a degree of uncertainty. In your experience how does this mentality play out
  » in the media?
  » in the classroom?
  » in the staffroom?
- What would be involved in taking a post-critical stance to the post-modern mentality?
- In your experience, what sense do people with a post-modern mentality make of the worldview of faith? What challenges does this present to the religious educator?

12
CHARISMIC CONTRIBUTIONS IN LIMINAL TIMES[189]

About forty kilometres from the famous pilgrimage city of Le Puy in southern France is the shell of the once grand abbey of *La Chaise-Dieu*. For eight centuries before the French Revolution it had flowered as a vibrant centre of spirituality, not only for the hundreds of monks in its community at any one time but also for the up to three hundred minor monasteries dependent on it. The scale of its structures and the reach of its influence stagger a modern visitor. It was the medieval Church alive. Today most of its former buildings are private apartments or shops, its majestic abbatial church cold and vacant, the local parish trying to generate a few euros from visitors inspecting the tapestries and works of art that have survived. Do we blame the faithless and militant revolutionaries of 1790 for its destruction? Had it not been for their irreverent and insensitive sack of it, would it not be still a hub of Christian faith and culture? No, that is a misrepresentation of history. The sad fact is that by the time of the Revolution the Abbey had already shrunk to a community of fewer than twenty old monks, their relevance and their purpose quite out of step from the world in which they found themselves. They were an anachronism.

The demise of *La Chaise-Dieu* is instructive for the Church in any age, not least our own. It was founded and thrived on Benedictine spirituality: one of the great spiritual traditions of the Church, one that has provided and continues to provide countless Christians with a richly effective way to embrace the Gospel of Jesus. There was and is nothing anachronistic about the essentials of Benedictine spirituality. Where the *Chaise-Dieu* monks went wrong was their failure to engage it with the spirit of their age. They continued in a medieval time warp, coddled away from the liberating movements of thought and profound societal realignment that marked the Enlightenment. It was a liminal time, and they did not read its signs. Their ruin was not so much at the hands

---
[189] Br Michael Green is National Director of Marist Schools Australia.

of external adversaries, but the result of their own lack of readiness to renew and re-imagine their spiritual heritage for their own times.

There have been many examples over the centuries when the Church has become disconnected, resulting in its members becoming dispirited, discredited, and disenfranchised. What has happened? One of two things, typically: either it has wallowed in its old ways and remained removed from the lives of most ordinary people, or it has been open to the fresh ways that the Spirit has offered people to satisfy the God-thirst in them, personally and communally, ways that suited their time and place. Witness, for example, the paradigm-changing emergence of the Franciscans and the Dominicans in the medieval Church, the Jesuits in the Counter-Reformation, or the explosion of apostolic movements in France in the decades that followed the revolutionary-Napoleonic period. In our own country, look at the contribution of religious institutes in saving and building our Catholic education and health sectors. The Spirit will always be seeking to irrupt when the needs are greatest. The inspirational people and the inspired movements that emerge in such situations—for example the apostolic religious institutes of the nineteenth century—sometimes have a short lifespan that allows the Church to meet the needs of a particular time and place. This has been the fate of most. They are established, they serve the Church's mission for a time, and then they fade. Others—a smaller number, and what *Lumen Gentium* may have understood as the 'more remarkable' ones[190]—enter the life of the Church, and become a continuing part of its spiritual and missionary fabric. They do this by their facility for adaptation to different times, ideas, places and cultures, and their accessibility to many different people. For example, the Middle Ages saw the birth of both the Franciscans and the Knights Templar. While they both grew exponentially and influentially, one proved to be a creature of its time and today seems weirdly anachronistic, the stuff of a Dan Brown novel, while the other continues to be one of the most attractive spiritualities of the Church, still capturing the hearts and imagination of the young, still giving a graced way of Christian discipleship, inclusive in its membership and adaptable in its expression. This seems to be the way of the Spirit. For a spirituality to be one that will serve the Church of the third millennium, and particularly one that is going to be embraced by a contemporary Catholic school, it will need to be one that allows for the universal call to holiness that was proposed by Vatican II: it must be inclusive of lay people as its main constituent group.

It is this line of thinking that is shaping the Marists' approach for continuing to offer their distinctive spirituality and educational practice to serve the needs of Catholic education. Like most religious institutes in

---

190 *Lumen Gentium* #12

the West, the numbers of Marist Brothers have markedly decreased. At the same time, interest in Marist spirituality and the Marist way of educating is growing enormously. The challenge is to look for ways to encourage this growth within a broader Marist ecclesial movement, while at the same time to redefine and to reposition the smaller number of consecrated Marists within it. It is to find new structures and fresh expressions for the graced intuitions of its charismic[191] essence as a Gospel path and missionary orientation.

LIMINALITY AND THE CHURCH'S SPIRITUAL FAMILIES

'Spiritual families'

The history of the Church reveals that it has been the founders of religious orders who have had some of the 'great Gospel ideas',[192] the inspired ways of discipleship that have stood the test of time and have proven fruitful, that have inspired generations of Christians to recognise and to love their God, and to share in God's mission in the Church. They have given them a story to join, a community of mission to which to belong, a work to do, a way to pray, a face of God to see. The Spirit-gifted intuitions of these founders first inspired like-hearted people to gather around them, and then gradually to have grown into rich and wise schools of spirituality and of missiology. Over time, they have developed a way of articulating the Gospel that people find both compelling and impelling. The Church has always been revitalised by such movements of grace. The great 'spiritual families'[193] of the universal Church have been the result. The last century gave birth to newer ones, often called the 'new ecclesial movements'. At the present time, the Church looks to these spiritual families, through their inclusion of lay people within them, as 'one of the great hopes for the future of the Catholic educational mission'.[194]

---

191 My preference is normally to use 'charismic' as the adjective relating to 'charism', and 'charismatic' with 'charisma'.
192 The phrase is Claude Maréchal's, the then Assumptionist Superior General, who delivered an insightful paper on this topic at the 56th Conference of Superiors General, in Rome, in 1999: 'Toward an effective partnership between religious and laity in fulfilment of charism and responsibility for mission'.
193 The term is the one used by the Congregation for Catholic Education (2007). See *Educating Together in Catholic Schools, A Shared Mission between Consecrated Persons and the Lay Faithful,*# #28–30.
194 Ibid.

Embracing a post-conciliar ecclesiology

An imperative shared by both the older and newer spiritual families of the Church is for them to be shaped by the inclusive ecclesiology of Vatican II, one based on *communio*. The universal call to holiness espoused by the Council challenges them to be open to all Christian women and men who are attracted to the distinctive ways of being a Christian disciple of a particular spiritual tradition. While the newer ecclesial movements have often been shaped by this kind of thinking from their inception, it can be more of a challenge for some older ones, especially those which have had their identities rather tightly framed around the religious or clerical state, or narrow patterns of life or ministry, or an identity that is more sourced in a type of work rather than a spirituality.

The Marists are among those spiritual families of the Church which are quite deliberately and strategically attempting to re-imagine how their particular spiritual heritage can be appropriated more broadly, for the mission of the contemporary Church. They, like many others, are responding to the spontaneous phenomenon of so many people being no longer satisfied merely to serve professionally within the works of religious institute or attach to themselves to it in a kind of lay-associate way, but calling for a radical re-imagining of what it might mean to be, for example, Augustinian or Ignatian or Lasallian. They are calling, in fact, for *communio* as Vatican II proposed it.[195]

The spiritual families that will most effectively serve the Church in this century are those which can re-imagine themselves in this way. The administration and staffing of the *ad extra* works of the Church—especially in the service ministries of education, health, and social welfare—are today almost entirely in the hands of lay people. If the spiritual traditions of the Church are to continue to help to enliven these ministries with their inspired paths of discipleship and their efficacious means of mission, as they have done so effectively in past centuries, then they need to be wide in their embrace of the Christian people who serve in them.

The greatest challenges facing today's Catholic schools

There are, at the present time, arguably no two greater challenges to the integrity and the effectiveness of Australian Catholic schools as agents of evangelisation than the depth of spirituality and the degree of ecclesial commitment of those who teach and work in these schools. In world terms,

---

195 For a succinct discussion of this see the article by Pope Benedict XVI when as Cardinal Ratzinger he penned an editorial piece for the twentieth anniversary of the theological journal *Communio* of which he was one of the co-founders. See Ratzinger, J 'Communio: A Program', in *Communio*, Fall 1992 (American edition).

our Australian Catholic schools are built and resourced outstandingly. They are led and staffed by well-educated professionals, indeed people who, in the history of Catholic education in this country, have never been more highly qualified. Their public funding levels and resources are the envy of most countries. The schools are serviced by Catholic Education Offices and Catholic Education Commissions that provide high level curricular, financial, legal, and personnel support for policies, programmes and governance. They allow our dioceses and religious institutes to conduct a world-class network of schools, and to be able offer these to virtually anyone who is seeking a Catholic education. But to what extent is it still a *Catholic* education that is being offered? Or, to put it more pointedly, to what extent are these schools communities places where the Gospel of Christ is proclaimed unambiguously and received openly, where Jesus is known and loved personally, where the reign of God pervades all that is done there and how it is done? Do what extent are they places that satisfy the God-thirst in people and promote Christian discipleship? Let us hope that the answer to each of those questions is strongly affirmative. The degree to which it is the case in a school will be largely a function of the depth to which the staff who lead it can personally answer yes to each of those questions posed.[196]

The Congregation for Catholic Education goes to the heart of the matter:

> *The project of the Catholic school will be convincing only if it is carried out by people who are deeply motivated because they witness to a living encounter with Christ, in whom alone 'the mystery of man becomes clear'.*[197]

Competent, even excellent, management of the professional aspects of Catholic schooling should not be confused with *management for mission*. The latter is only likely to occur when system leaders, local administration, and the staff of Catholic schools can respond to questions such as these with compellingly authentic answers: What is their personal sense of being disciples of Jesus, their being Christian educators? What is their understanding of the Church's mission in education and their own role as evangelisers? What is their working knowledge of Scripture and of the teachings and traditions of the Church? What is their parish involvement? What are their social justice involvements?

---

[196] See the Pastoral Letter of the bishops of NSW and the ACT, *Catholic Schools at a Crossroads*, for a discussion of important issues around the identity and mission of the Australian Catholic school of the future.
[197] Congregation for Catholic Education *Educating Together in Catholic Schools: A shared mission between consecrated persons and the lay faithful.* (Rome: Libreria Edrice Vaticana, 2007).

If we are going to avoid significant 'mission drift'[198] as the next generation of teachers moves into middle-management and senior leadership—a larger number of whom have grown up in families that have not been active in their practice of the faith in the traditional sense—then we need to look for effective and engaging means for developing their personal spirituality of these teachers and connecting them to the life of the Church. If not, then Catholic schools will move subtly but inevitably towards becoming just low-fee private schools—albeit ones that may be quite professionally run and with a solid value base and not in conflict with the values of the Gospel—but with little capacity for explicit evangelisation or catechesis, or much understanding of it or vision for it. As far as connection with the life of the Church goes, the main point of connection may be through their Catholic Education Office rather than any parish, pastor, or religious institute.

The world of young Australian people, including younger teachers, is for the most part a post-Christian and post-modern one. Their world is pluralist, secularist and relativist. There are quite notable exceptions, and there are certainly differences among ethnic communities across the country, but most people under fifty are not the 'ecclesial natives' that their grandparents were, and perhaps some of their parents. Church is another country. They don't always feel at home there, or understand its language. They do not intuitively connect with it.

Renewal and mission are in the DNA of the Church's spiritual families

The revitalisation of the Church to align it with new and emerging times is well-trodden ground for most of the great spiritual families of the Church. Indeed it is where, at their best, they are most at home. It was from a need for renewal and re-interpretation that most of them grew. It is in their evangelical and ecclesial DNA; this is what gives them life. The Marists are typical of the many apostolic movements that grew out of such origins. It was to young people who had yet to hear the Good News that they felt called. Their own intuitions in post-Napoleonic France were that the Church needed a Marian approach if it was going to speak to people of its age: one that had a maternal heart, that was grounded and simple, merciful and hopeful, apostolic without being judgemental or punitive. Like other movements they have, over time, built up a rich store of means for giving effect to their purpose. The Church would be advantaged to

---

198 See Peter Nicholson 'PJPs: Issues in Formation', paper delivered at the Sydney Conference on Public Juridic Persons in the Church, 2009, for a discussion of this phenomenon. Conference paper available from Government and Management bookstore.

look to its spiritual families, both old and new, to give impetus to the 'new evangelisation' of the present time.

In the context of a Catholic school community, the potential evangelising benefits of belonging corporately to such a spiritual tradition or movement are immense. If it is one that suits that school community and its present realities, one that is attractive to its members, then it can provide a graced way to give compelling life to the Gospel. First, it will give people a means of deepening their personal and their communal spirituality, a way of quenching their thirst for God, a path to meeting Jesus. Second, it will give a treasure chest of resources, solid formation programmes, literature, symbols and rituals, strategies for ministry, extra-parochial and extra-diocesan links, and collected wisdom, from which the principal and staff can draw. It becomes the glue that binds the community and concretises its mission.

The 'charismic gap' in the leadership of Catholic education

One of the characteristics of the contemporary Catholic education scene in this country is the enhancement of the Catholic education bureaucracy, a growth that has not usually been paralleled in the more charismic dimensions of the life of the Church. As religious institutes have become less directly involved and less influential in the education sector, they have left a vacuum into which lay people have not adequately stepped. Whereas lay people occupy places in the diocesan curia, both comfortably and competently, they are yet to assume their rightful positions of recognised leadership and practical influence in the spiritual families of the Church in ways that impact sufficiently on the life and mission of the Church in education. The result? Diocesan education offices can be left, often on their own, to look for ways to meet that most pressing of all challenges that faces us: the development of staff spirituality. Despite the best of intentions and the deployment of resources, they can be less well oriented to be as successful or as inspirational. At its worst, it reduces to a tick-the-boxes or count-the-hours approach, or externally imposed minimum requirements. Spirituality, however, is not something that can be mandated. It is something of the heart. Certainly, the practice of particular spirituality and an understanding of it can be taught and learnt; the term 'school of spirituality' rightly implies this. But, first it has to attract and to inspire, and it has to suit each person at the intuitive level. Each has to feel at home with the spirituality itself, and with his or her spiritual companions.

The best spiritual families and the ecclesial movements work first on this inspirational level; people are attracted to join them intuitively. They provide ways of incarnating Christ-life into time, place, mission and the hearts of people. As a founder's charism moves over time to become a spiritual tradition, it develops a wealth of accumulated wisdom and resources into which others can tap, to learn from those who have walked and are walking the same spiritual path. In offering people a literature to read, songs to sing, accessible language and symbols to use, and saints from whom to draw inspiration, it provides them with a narrative of holiness and mission. It offers powerful means to receive and to promote the Gospel of Jesus—a 'do-able discipleship'.

RE-IMAGINING MARIST LIFE AND MISSION

With other spiritual families of the Church, the Marists have had an ever deepening engagement with the liminality that is the legacy of Vatican II. For the first two post-conciliar decades this was predominantly concerned with the renewal of consecrated life. It has been the time since the late-1980s that has witnessed an increasing shift of focus to lay people. It seemed to take some time for the implications of a more inclusive ecclesiology to mature in the collective mindset of the Marists. While this remains a work in progress, there appears to be an inevitable evolution from a narrower sense that Marist life and mission belonged to Marist Brothers alone to one that is open to a variety of expressions, indeed one that calls for it. Over the last twenty years this has moved from being simply intuitive and ad hoc to something that is much more considered and strategic.

Marist education today is essentially no different from what it has been since its foundation two centuries ago, one may hope, as it will be always: *Marist education is what Marists do in education, and why they do it.* To put it that way is not to describe Marist education tritely or simplistically, nor to imply that it does not have a depth that cannot be expansively articulated or subtlety nuanced. On the contrary, the educational approach that is known today as 'Marist' is an enormously rich, efficacious and compelling way through which to undertake the Christian education of young people. It is important, however, to recognise that the basis of Marist education is not sourced essentially in an educational philosophy or in a pedagogical theory, but in a spirituality, and in a spirituality that was shared and lived by an ecclesial community. It is to the intuitive Gospel-response of Saint Marcellin Champagnat and that of the founding generation of Marists that one must go to understand the essence of Marist education. The many thousands of Marists who followed these founders in responding to the Gospel of Jesus in a distinctively Marist way—Marist Brothers initially, and more lately so many Lay Marists—have created 'Marist education' and they continue to create it. While the external characteristics of Marist education can be readily enough described, these are not its essence. At its core it is something much deeper, much richer. That essence can only be appreciated by touching into the hearts of the people who have been inspired by the Marist movement, who feel at home in it, who have been fulfilled by it, who have been graced to find their passion for God and their passion for young people in and through it. The future of the Marist education movement will depend on its attracting, sustaining, and associating people who can do the same, in ways that suit their time, their culture and their general circumstances. The vitality and capacity of Marist education will depend entirely on the vitality and capacity of Marist educators, individually and collectively.

In all parts of the world where there is a desire to develop Marist education, the essential questions are common: Who are those who seek to do this? Why do they want to do it? Do they see themselves and understand themselves as *Marist educators*? If so, are they well-formed and well sustained in their sense of Marist identity and mission? Do they feel called to the conversion of heart that is at the core of Marist apostolic spirituality? How can the viability and authenticity of this be guaranteed? How do they associate themselves with one another in Marist life and mission? The answers to these questions need to provide ways for these people to bring into harmony and interplay the three elemental dimensions of any Christian life: the faith/discipleship element, the shared life/community element, and the apostolic/mission element. If Marist education is what Marist educators do, it is important that attention be focussed on forming, associating and sustaining contemporary people as authentically Marist. The rest is likely, in large measure, to take care of itself. The strategy of the Marist response to these liminal times emanates from this and can be seen broadly within four lines of action: developing 'spiritual capital', reimagining new canonical structures that foster communion and co-responsibility, building and sustaining 'charismic culture', and developing Marist leadership capacity.

Developing 'spiritual capital'

This phrase of Gerald Grace[199] offers a conceptual way into an understanding what is most important in securing the future of Marist education. The primary objective of Marist education is evangelisation, 'to make Jesus Christ known and loved', or to 'bring Christ-life to birth' in young people.[200] While the chief medium for this is education, and while Marists operate out of a

---

199 Grace, Gerald (2010) 'Renewing spiritual capital: an urgent priority for the future of Catholic education internationally' *International Studies in Catholic Education*, 2, 2, 117–128.
200 *Water from the Rock. Marist Spirituality flowing in the tradition of Marcellin Champagnat*, #26 Institute of the Marist Brothers (2007) See also #11. The phrase sharing in 'making Jesus Christ known and loved' comes from the Constitutions of the Marist Brothers (#2).

strongly incarnational theology that does not dichotomise the sacred from the secular, it is an essentially religious endeavour to which Marist educators are called. Marists understand that it is 'as Mary', sharing in her eternal role as Theotokos, that they can give birth to Christ-life. To be as Mary is not simply to have a motherly instinct for nurture or a sisterly disposition to solidarity. It is not merely to have a Marian style of relating, of hopefulness, of humility, of resilience, of inclusion, of simplicity, or of generosity. To be as Mary is first of all to be open to the movement of God's spirit in the depths of one's being; it is to be submissive to that Spirit so that God's very life can take root and flower. To be as Mary is to be, like her, a disciple. It is to set out into the 'hill country'[201] of the world of the young, bringing them good news of a faithful, merciful and just God; bringing them Jesus. It is to gather with and to sustain the dispirited and hopeless in what Marists call l'Église naissante: the Church as it comes to birth. Similarly, to be like Marcellin is not simply to be warm and compassionate, confident and big-thinking, hard-working and unpretentious, or courageous and daring. To be like Marcellin is, in the first place, to be a person of deep and profound faith who has come to know the love of God deeply and in a way that has seized one's heart. It is not to be perfect, as Marcellin himself was not perfect, but it is to have a basically religious orientation and an abiding yearning for spiritual growth.

The future of Marist education will depend first on the forming and sustaining of Marist educators to have these Marian and Marcellian dispositions. This is not to imply that they are somehow to be conformed to a pre-determined Marist personality, but rather that they become disciples of Marcellin in the sense that they learn from his spiritual intuitions and his responses of practical love; that they find in Marcellin and the founding Marist generation a way to come to know and to love God, and to want to make God's love known and loved by the young. It is their own encounter with Jesus, their own faith journey, that is pivotal. To become a Marist is to learn to have a personal faith lived out in a ecclesial community; it is not merely to support a set of religious values or to be able to name the characteristics of Marist ministerial style. The formation of Marist educators will be founded on experiences and learnings that allow them to go more deeply on their personal journeys of faith, and in doing this to take advantage of the graced Marist way to which they find some attraction and through which their own personal spirituality can be expressed. The major contribution of the great spiritual traditions of the Church is that they have developed language, strategies, resources, practices, literature and accumulated wisdom for guiding people in their spiritual journeys.

---

201 Cf. Luke 1:39.

For such spiritual capital to be accumulated, formation—both initial and ongoing—cannot be haphazard or left to chance. By definition, a school of spirituality such as the Marist one, is something that teaches. Inversely, it is something than can be learned. Marist formation is constructed with these elements in mind:

- Comprehensive study of theology and doctrine
- Instruction in Christian spirituality and in prayer
- Opportunity for prayer, retreat, and personal accompaniment
- Study of the Marist story, including the canon of Marist documents
- Study of Marist spirituality and pedagogy
- Exposure to the local Marist story and to the present international Marist reality
- Ongoing membership of an active group of Marist companions who gather regularly for Eucharist and prayer, for faith sharing, and for social activity.

In all of this, it is important for the formation to be Christocentric and avoid all sense of cultism around Marcellin or tribalism around a Marist identity. It needs always to lead from and to Jesus.

Re-imagining how Marists are associated and structured

A challenge closely related to the enhancing of the spiritual capital of Marist educators is to develop ways for them to associate with each other. It is about fostering communion and co-responsibility. History has shown that for a spiritual tradition to remain alive, its adherents need to act, to live, and to pray communally, and to share ownership for the movement's integrity, relevance, and future. Christian spiritualities have vitality as *movements* of people; they are essentially ecclesial. The universal Church is enriched, and often renewed, when such movements build momentum through cumulative energies. The first aspect of this is a quite human one: people need to know each other. To belong to a 'spiritual family' implies at least this. The metaphor of family also suggests that they know each other well, that they share a collective memory, that they gather in places that are special to them, that they know and can re-tell their shared story and honour the people who have written it, that they share ownership of it and responsibility for its continued vitality. Marists therefore need to come together physically not only for experiences that are more explicitly spiritual, but also for simple socialising, sharing, celebrating, story-telling and, of course, working together in common endeavour. They see themselves as the spiritual and apostolic companions of one another in a shared Marist mission.

It will be helpful if this community of people also has a juridically recognised identity in Canon Law. This is a line of action which the Marists are carefully pursuing. It will allow the Marist expression of Christian life—in all its forms, not only consecrated—to have a recognised place within the Church, and so be able to relate to other entities in Church such as bishops and pastors.

Building and sustaining a charismic culture

When the concept of organisational culture is brought together with the theological concept of charism it is possible to propose a way of understanding how the Gospel can be made incarnate, as it must. Story, legends, heroes, rituals, sacred places, song, language, customs, dress, symbols, characteristic patterns of behavior, special days and celebrations, intuitive ways of acting and reacting, ways of judging and perceiving, preferred manner and style, sensitivities in relating: all these are the stuff of culture. When they are expressions of Gospel living, particularly built around the graced and compelling response of an especially inspired disciple of Jesus, then the concept of 'charismic culture'[202] can be proposed as a way for an educational community such as a school or university to strategically develop its capacity as an evangelising organisation.

A charismic culture, such as the Marist one, when it is well established in the life of an educational community, will play itself out as a powerful dynamic. First, it will offer a constancy of orientation as teachers and students come and go. Although the temporal expressions of its culture do and should change as new needs and circumstances emerge, its core cultural components remain secure. What is more, this core is a graced way of the Gospel, and a rich source of spirituality and culture for those in leadership across the generations. Second, in an educational setting or within a network of them such as the Marist schools of a country, a charismic culture can lead both teachers and students to identify with the Gospel in ways that make sense to them and to which they can commit themselves. It provides a story to learn, to tell and of which to feel part, sacred places to visit, a folklore that carries the values and beliefs in normal human ways, even books to read and songs to sing. It is well for people to feel part of a story, one that is big enough to expand their horizons, but small enough that

---

202 For a full discussion of this topic see Michael Green (1997) *The Charismic Culture of Marist Schools in the Province of Sydney*. Unpublished doctoral dissertation submitted in the University of Sydney, and available from the Fisher Library. See also the monograph *Charisms: What possibilities and challenges do they offer school leaders for developing cultures and spirituality in Catholic schools*. Edited text of an address to the Australian Catholic Schools Principals' Conference, Melbourne, Australia (2000); and *Lay Spirituality and Charism*. Keynote address at Catholic Education Conference, Townsville. July 17, 2009.

they can feel it is their own story. It allows them to feel both 'at home' but also challenged to act. For a school seeking to make the Gospel of real and inspirational, these are solid pegs on which to hang the evangelisation hats. So student leadership programmes, apostolic youth groups, founders and saints days, house patrons, social justice programmes, school symbols and rituals, school songs, material for newsletter editorials, teaching of prayer, methods and names of awards and rewards, school retreat programmes, can all have a power and grace that make them engaging for students, and give teachers a language to speak that students will understand. For the teachers, the charismic tradition can facilitate spiritual formation programmes to be constructed, conferences to occur, pilgrimages to be undertaken, journals to be published, and local communities of spiritual and apostolic companions to gather. Third, one of the useful opportunities afforded by affiliation with a broader movement such as the Marists are the links it gives the school, locally and internationally, with other areas of ministry within the Church. Examples include social welfare, young adult ministry, health care, ministry to marginalised groups, social action, and overseas missions. A natural sense of association and a crossover of personnel and information can give educational institutions a sense of solidarity with and an entrée into these other fields of the Church's mission. Such an international network can also facilitate and encourage an individual school to connect with the broader Church, beyond the limits of its own diocese.

At the same time, an educational institution needs to be alert for lurking dangers when they are working out of a cultural discourse, pitfalls that can actually compromise their work of evangelisation or at least diminish it. For example, when an institution or administrative unit becomes more concerned with telling the story of its past rather than engaging in the needs of today's young people, then the charismic punch may have gone out of its life; it may no longer be relevant. This is likely to have happened if there has not been sufficient induction of new Marist educators in the ways discussed above, or sufficient adaptation of old structures and mindsets. It can also happen when the temporal expressions of a charism lose touch with its spiritual core, and become ends in themselves. Charismic traditions, to remain authentic, are about the Gospel of Jesus Christ and about incarnating it in ways that are relevant and engaging. It is a way of integrating faith, culture and life. It is sometimes the case, however, that these incarnations can take on a life of their own that lose connection with the centre. The school culture loses its Christocentrism. Distinctive sporting, music or curricular foci, loyalty to the school and a strong sense of bonding, particular expectations on student conduct, are all examples of how a school may seek, legitimately and vibrantly, to *express* its core charism. But these are not the charism. Its authenticity as a Catholic school can begin to diminish when the leadership of a school or too many members of its staff start to confuse these leaves with the tree from which they have grown. A second trap to avoid is that of cultism around a founder, or of creating any kind of parallel church, as has been already discussed.

The challenges for today's Marists in their building and maintaining of a strong charismic culture in and among their educational institutions and other ministries rest in their attending to the induction and development of Marist educators as *culturally Marist*. This is something that can go hand-in-glove with their spiritual formation.

Enhancing leadership capacity

There has been much researched and written on educational leadership, and rightly so; the health of an educational institution rises or falls on the quality of those in leadership of it. Whatever is true for the need for solid formation of Marist educators generally is even more the case for those in leadership roles within Marist educational communities and within the Marist movement more broadly. In any assessment of the 'critical mass' that is required for an institution to call itself Marist, an indispensable element will be the principal and leadership team. If those people are not Marist in heart, mind and spirit, it is unlikely that the institution will be able to be coherently or effectively Marist in its identity and mission. The leader will be someone who is not only Marist in his or her educational approach, but someone who is spiritually Marist and culturally Marist. In this way that person will be able to build a Marist community, inspire and accompany others who see themselves as Marist spiritual and apostolic companions of one another, articulate a Marist vision and perspective, and induct new members into the Marist way.

CONCLUSION

Let us return to *La Chaise-Dieu*. In the faded glory of the abbey church, to the side of the choir, there is a famous series of large mural sketches depicting *la danse macabre* (the 'Dance of Death') a frequent motif in churches and monasteries in post-plague Europe. It depicts a set of people—a prince, a bishop, a merchant, a man about town, and others from all rungs of society—each of whom is 'dancing' with a skeleton. It is reminder of mortality. The confronting irony for today's visitor is that all of these medieval personalities have indeed passed to death, as has the society they inhabited, and indeed the grandeur of the huge church building which hosts their images. What remains is a museum, a historical curiosity, a visualisation of the spiritual wrestling of another age and, in the end, a memorial to a once-vibrant ecclesial community that ceased to speak with credibility and relevance to a new age.

The Spirit will always be seeking to empower members of the Church for mission in ways that are new, relevant and engaging, ways that suit who and where they are and the needs they face. As the present-day Church moves to an ecclesiology centred on *communio*, albeit more slowly that many would want, the broadening of the embrace of the different spiritualities is really not surprising. What remain unclear are the future forms and structures that these charismic movements might take. Some see this as both the adventure and the frustration of a founding time, or, as some others would see it, a re-founding time.[203] The challenge for spiritual families themselves is to re-imagine and re-cast themselves in an emerging Church; the opportunity for the Church is to draw on the rich Gospel intuitions and resources of these families to give life to God's mission.

PRIORITIES IN LEADING FOR MISSION

PRIORITY 12.1 In leading for Mission it is necessary to be aware of how the Spirit is at work in the life of a Christian community, and the empowerment that the Spirit's presence brings as gift to the world.

Religious congregations have had to live with the painful experience of loss as the present liminal era has unfolded. This has led to much creative thinking. While the present chapter deals with the approach of Marist Brothers, there have been comparable developments in other congregations.

As noted in the previous chapter, public worldviews come to us moderated by the communities in which we live. This dynamic can unfold either haphazardly or in a considered way. Michael Green outlines how the Marist Brothers seek to employ the dynamic in such a way that Marist educators become 'spiritually and culturally Marist'. To be spiritually and culturally Marist is to develop a spiritualty (a way of living the Gospel), and to become part of a community committed to a mission. Spirituality, community and mission, become integral to identity and to the Spirit's activity within the world.

---

203 Father Bruno Secondin, Carmelite Superior General, claims that the Church is going through a developmental phase with regard to lay involvement. Like any founding time it is 'exploratory, adventurous and contradictory'. See, 'Sharing Charisms and Spirituality, New Directions for Communion and Propagating the Mission', in *Charism and Spirituality*. Proceedings of the 56th Conference of the Unione Superiore Generali. Rome: USG.

Continuing the Conversation

- When you consider your own school community (or CEO) is there a corporate spirituality into which members are consciously inducted, or is this left to chance?
- What resources can leaders draw on in shaping the culture of the organisation by developing its corporate spirituality?
- What values provide the glue that holds the community together? How are these sustained over time?
- Do members understand the corporate identity of the school principally in terms of what it does, or is there some other basis for identity? If so, can you articulate what it is?
- Do colleagues have any real sense that mission and spirituality are linked, or are these seen as more or less discrete categories, one corporate, the other personal?

13
A MINISTRY TO MEANING-MAKING AND TO THE IMAGINATION: TEACHING CATHOLIC SYSTEM LEADERSHIP AT ACU

Anne Benjamin and Michael Bezzina[204]

Australian Catholic University (ACU) plays a privileged role in Catholic education in Australia, one with which there are no real parallels internationally. As a government–funded, national university with the sanction of the Australian church, it educates a significant proportion of teachers in Catholic schools, at least in the Eastern states, and is the major provider of postgraduate study in the key mission-related areas of Educational Leadership and Religious Education for Catholic schools. Indeed its educational leadership program is one of the largest in the country.

This book highlights the importance of leadership for Catholic education in a time of liminality, and poses two major questions: *How should we construe the mission of the Catholic school and Catholic school systems in this situation?* and *How should the school or system be managed and led?* It explicitly draws attention to the role of leadership at both school and system levels. These same questions have, in some ways, given rise to ACU's offering a new Masters program explicitly tailored to the needs of leaders of systems of Catholic schools, both diocesan and congregational.

The emergence of such a course at this particular time may well be understood as a response to the challenges of liminality, in the face of a growing awareness that to a great degree, the capacity of schools to live out their espoused purposes is a *whole-of-system enterprise*, and that system leadership calls for *capabilities which are different in some ways from those which work well in schools*. Moreover, while the label 'liminality' which has been so well elaborated in the earlier chapters of this text was not explicitly a

---

[204] Anne Benjamin is an Adjunct Professor of Australian Catholic University and Michael Bezzina is an Associate Professor of Australian Catholic University.

consideration in the new Masters degree, it has strong echoes with the way in which it treats the related concepts of 'emergence', and 'creative adaptive systems'. The first section of this chapter will explore the rationale for, and development of, the Master of Educational System Leadership course at Australian Catholic University, and illustrates the ways in which it can be understood as a response to the times in which we find ourselves in Catholic education. The second part draws out the ways in which the 'secular' literature on living systems might offer possibilities for system leaders in liminal times.

EVOLUTION OF THE MASTER OF EDUCATIONAL SYSTEM LEADERSHIP

Educational leadership courses have been a feature of postgraduate offerings at Australian Catholic University and the predecessor constituent colleges since 1980. Beginning with the Graduate Diploma in Education Studies, Leadership Development in 1980, then developing through to the Master of Educational Administration and finally to the current Master of Educational Leadership which began in 1996, educational leadership has been a signature of the postgraduate courses at the University.

This course has proved popular with students and employing authorities, both in Catholic and other faith-based education systems in Australia and overseas, including Lutheran Education Australia and the Association of Independent Schools. In 2011, 801 students from Australia, New Zealand, Mauritius and Pakistan were enrolled in the Master of Educational Leadership or the Postgraduate Certificate in Educational Leadership. Feedback through both formal reviews and informal communication indicates that Catholic education authorities have appreciated the availability and ways in which the offering of course units to cohorts of teachers and administrators from those systems has strengthened the level and quality of leadership skills in those areas and dioceses. In addition these bodies have also appreciated the opportunity for direct input into these courses, by developing specialist units tailored to their specific contexts and leadership needs or by taking advantage of those units in other programs to provide for a broader postgraduate academic experience.

Between 1997 and 2011, 1,794 students graduated with the Master of Educational Leadership degree from ACU and between 2003 and 2011, 120 with the Postgraduate Certificate. A significant number of these have gone on to doctoral studies at ACU. Amongst the graduates are a large number of senior executive members of Catholic education systems, including a number of directors and former directors.

The need for a postgraduate course that went beyond the Master of

Educational Leadership began to emerge from around 2000. Educational *system* leadership was identified as a priority in research conducted by the ACU Flagship for Creative and Authentic Leadership. One example of this was the *Service Organisation Leadership Research (SOLR)* Project;[205] this investigated the challenges and ethical dilemmas faced by leaders in a selection of frontline human services organisations, including, as well as Catholic Health and NSW Police, the Parramatta Catholic Education Office. This research highlighted the complexity of the education system leadership role in the context of radical change and the importance of preparing future leaders in respect to vision and realisation, accountability, staff relations and people management and balancing demands, expectations and responsibilities. In particular, this research proposed that: '...leaders in contemporary service organisations need formation in terms of the development of ethical and moral frameworks for action, as well as in competencies.'[206]

Research efforts in respect to leadership frameworks for Catholic and Lutheran school systems clarified the need to move beyond competency training and develop programs for holistic leadership formation and capacity building. Discussions with the National Catholic Education Commission in 2006 added support to the impetus to explore the unique needs of system leaders.

Recognising that there was little available by way of formal preparation and formation for those entering into system-level positions, ACU's School of Educational Leadership opened up consultations with a range of stakeholders. This led to two significant developments.

The first came in response to interest expressed by Catholic education systems for ACU's School of Educational Leadership and the Flagship for Creative and Authentic Leadership to initiate a workshop to develop a *Framework for Leadership at the System level in Catholic Education*. The collaborative development of the *Framework* occurred in 2007, and involved eleven Diocesan education systems from across five states, the networked schools of the Marist Brothers' and Christian Brothers and other NSW congregational schools. The presence of some of the largest and some of the smallest Catholic systems (or networks of congregational schools) enabled the group to remain mindful of the varied size, scope and resources of these varied systems.

---

205 Patrick Duignan et al (2003) *SOLR Project: Leadership challenges and ethical dilemmas for leaders of frontline service organisations. A three-year ARC funded research project.* (Sydney: ACU National, 2003).
206 Australian Catholic University Flagship for Creative and Authentic Leadership, (Sydney: ACU, 2003), 19.

The second development was the establishment of the new Master's degree, the Master of Educational System Leadership. Like the *Framework*, this new course was planned as a response to the unique challenge of system leadership which is both 'more than' and 'different from' those faced in individual schools. It was designed to examine the distinctive purposes, structures and processes of Catholic education systems, and the value that these organisational entities can add in supporting schools in their evangelising mission and in providing quality teaching and learning opportunities for students.

Consequently, the Master of Educational System Leadership and the Postgraduate Certificate in Education System Leadership courses were designed to improve professional practice by the application of advanced knowledge, skills and research findings to the problems, issues and challenges that face professionals responsible for leadership at system level in educational settings. The primary aim of the course was described as being *to prepare professionals who are reflective, independent and flexible thinkers open to new ideas, and who will be capable of applying their knowledge and skills to lead change in their school communities and develop leadership at all levels in their school or other educational setting.*[207]

Teaching and learning within the course emphasises the praxis of leadership in a faith based context. It is governed by the key principles of providing sufficient flexibility so that each participant's program is built on that person's individual profile; a significant integrative experience; and action-research on real issues from participants' education systems.

Within the new course, 'leadership' is presented as a service, promoting the good of the community. The course is structured around the following core and specialisation units.

COMPULSORY CORE UNITS	AT LEAST 1 OF THESE SPECIALISATION UNITS
• Leadership in Education Systems Education System Futures (Group Integrative Project)	• System Leadership in an Ecclesial Context Consultancy skills for System Leaders Educational Policy and Governance Education System Development Project
Electives as appropriate for each student from relevant Masters units, eg, in Educational Leadership, Education, Religious Education, Theology, Business.	

---

207 Australian Catholic University Master of Educational System Leadership and Postgraduate Certificate in Educational System Leadership, New Course Proposal, 5 November 2009, 8.

When the course was approved by the University's Academic Board in 2009, it was believed that there was no comparable course making provision for system leadership in any sector on offer elsewhere in Australia, and none with a consistent and explicit focus on the realities of a faith-based, and specifically, of the Catholic sector.

The course enrolled its inaugural intake in January 2012.

LIMINALITY IN THE MASTER OF EDUCATIONAL SYSTEM LEADERSHIP

While the Master of Educational System Leadership was developed without explicit reference to the concept of *liminality*, it is salutary to reflect on the emergence of the Master of Educational System Leadership in the context of this theme of 'being on a threshold', or of being in an 'in-between' state. A key indicator of this state of liminality is in the use of the concept of system—the distinguishing descriptor for the new ACU course.

In early discussions during the development of the new course, there was some sensitivity around what was the most accurate term to express the networks of schools for whom the course was being designed. Ultimately, the Course Development Committee that was convened by the university as part of its normal processes in course development, and which included key external stakeholders from Catholic education as well as ACU academics, settled for using system as part of a *working* title. The course proposal defined the term system as including any way in which any group of Catholic schools forms a 'community of schools' in order to enhance the mission of those schools. Following approval of the course by the university's Academic Board the term was retained in the title.

It is pertinent to the theme of *liminality* running through this book to reflect on how the notion, nature and priorities of Australian Catholic education systems, as *systems*, have shifted in the last decades. In retrospect, there would appear to be at least four major aspects that have bearing, both on the practice of Catholic education system leadership and, hence, on ACU's course in Educational System Leadership.

Changes in the nature/function of 'system' for Catholic education

The formation of systems has become a key element of the way in which Catholic education is led and governed, especially in Australia. Catholic education systems in Australia are distinctive. While government funding to Catholic schools began to flow again from the 1960s, a watershed in system developments was in 1983 when the Australian bishops needed an administrative facility to disburse government funding to schools and to address the accountability requirements.

Since that time, Catholic education systems have become increasingly sophisticated and have developed structures for supporting and leading Catholic diocesan schools that go far beyond disbursing and accounting for funding. Contemporary Catholic education systems are focused on supporting and leading quality Catholic schooling in all its dimensions, and not in simply being administrative facilities. With this shift has come the need to articulate the nature of the service offered by an education office towards its network of schools and the nature of the relationship between itself and schools in that network.

Diverse nature of contemporary Australian Catholic education systems

Catholic schools are a major educational enterprise within the nation, and form the largest proportion of the non-government education sector. In 2011, there were more than 723,000 students enrolled across 28 dioceses in 1704 Australian Catholic schools. The majority of these students were enrolled in Diocesan system schools. Consequently, a very significant proportion of the teachers and school leaders in Catholic education work within these diocesan school systems. Within these diocesan systems, however, there is great diversity. They differ in size, from the diocesan system of schools in Broome enrolling fewer than 2000 students to those in Melbourne which enrol nearly 144,000. Geography and different demographics shape the different operations of these diocesan systems. Similarly, Catholic education offices are structured, on behalf of their bishops, in different ways with varying degrees of centralisation of function, including Religious Education and ethos, finances, educational oversight and direction, human resource practices, and models of governing boards and councils.

More recently religious congregations have also begun working in a variety of ways with the schools within their congregational network. The communities of schools emerging around Religious Congregations (or Religious Institutes) are likewise diverse in their management, leadership, organisation, governance and function. Some religious institutes have a very traditional legal and canonical structure, while a number such as the Sisters of Charity and the Christian Brothers have moved, or are moving, towards Public Juridic Persons and separate civil incorporations for the operation of their schools. Other institutes have more informal networks of schools.

Recognition of the need for formation for those in system leadership

For both Diocesan school systems and those associated with Religious Institutes, the role of the system has become increasingly complex. It is anticipated that this complexity will continue to increase, both from internal shifts within systems and from external requirements imposed by government, legislative and administrative changes. For systems of Congregational schools, there are additional issues, such as, the linkages between mission and founding charisms to the new structures; and the tension between internal management of schools (which in Canon law resides with the Religious Institute) and the role of the bishop in coordinating the ministries and religious teaching of the diocese.

For all systems there has been generally a lack of specific formation for those who are entrusted with leadership at system level. Michael Fullan[208] argues that the *challenge is to create 'system thinkers in action' at all levels of the system, who proactively work with large parts of the system.* He calls these leaders the new theoreticians, doers with big minds, who relentlessly translate sound theory into practice during their daily interactions.

Changing profile of those in system leadership

It could also be argued that, compared to 1980, those working at 'system' level in Catholic education—the target group for the course—that is, women and men who are working, or who aspire to work, in the system offices of Catholic dioceses, or the congregations and religious institutes come from a wider range of professional disciplines. As well as curriculum specialists and administrators, the group includes people with backgrounds as diverse as Finance, IT, Property, Counselling and Planning, as well as curriculum specialists and administrators, and now represents *a changed demographic in terms of age and religious background*. In the context of this ongoing shift in the internal characteristics of systems, there are indicators that ACU's new Master of Educational System Leadership was responding to a context of *liminality*.

Changing context: concern with Catholic identity issues

In examining the concept of *liminality* in the context of the Master of Educational System Leadership, there are clear signs that ACU was responding to the issues raised in earlier chapters in this book. For example, the course proposal explicitly cites the following:

---

208 Michael Fullan quoted in ACU Course Proposal, 2009, 7.

The extreme pluralism pervading contemporary society leads to behavior patterns which are at times so opposed to one another as to undermine any idea of community identity, and new requirements have given force to the demand for new contents, new capabilities and new educational models besides those followed traditionally. Thus education and schooling have become particularly difficult today.[209]

In response to this situation, the Master of Educational System Leadership requires students to analyse their context and to address critically many leadership issues that stimulate positive interaction and dialogue between the University faculty and the School-based professionals.

Despite this certainty of shared mission, one doesn't need to look far to see that concern with *Catholic identity* or *ethos* has been a dominant concern amongst Catholic education systems in recent times. ACU's course, designed to meet the professional needs of leaders in Catholic school systems, situates itself within an understanding of leadership that acknowledges the societal, cultural and ecclesial dimensions of education, and the changes that are occurring within them.

Since all religious expression is in some form of *liminality*, it is conceivable that at future stages, ACU could offer some units that are modified for other faith-based education systems, not just Catholic education systems.

In the service of meaning-making and imagination

Certain elements of the Master of Educational System Leadership are consistent with providing a service in meaning-making and imagination for students. Taking up the challenge to educate students to lead Catholic education 'to be effectual in the Church and in society',[210] the course content and processes set out to include:

- a capacity for deep and authentic listening to the community;
- a critical analysis of relevant educational, political and social issues within a climate in which issues of justice and ethics can be researched and
- a Gospel-based approach to leadership.

Consequently, the new course makes a commitment to quality teaching and learning that offers holistic leadership formation. In particular, this course recognises the importance of providing for the creative integration of new knowledge bases and paradigms of system leadership and organisation; and a grounding of educational leadership in pedagogical, teaching and learning

---
209 Congregation for Catholic Education *The Catholic School on the Threshold of the Third Millennium*, 1997, ##1, 2
210 *The Catholic School on the Threshold of the Third Millennium*, #4.

concepts; Catholic theological, scriptural, ethical, moral, spiritual and social justice perspectives on leadership as well as legal and industrial imperatives.

Especially in the Core units, the course incorporates a focus on interdisciplinary approaches, a futures orientation, personal reflection, cross-sectoral interaction, prayer and spirituality, and community interaction. The instance of ACU's Master of Educational System Leadership is perhaps itself an example of the way that the Church responds in liminal times. As systems have grown and become more complex, and the contexts in which they operate have evolved in similar ways, leadership makes new demands, not least of which is leading in a time of uncertainty. One means by which the course seeks to better equip its students for this type of leadership is by engaging them with some of the recent thinking about complex adaptive systems.

COMPLEX ADAPTIVE SYSTEMS THINKING

It seems to us that the experience of liminality, of being in an 'in-between' state, is one that is not only experienced by individuals, but shared in community. Throughout this volume, reference has been made to the fact that any consideration of leadership in Catholic education needs to consider both school and system domains as *the loci within which the negotiation of liminality takes place*. While the challenges of meaning-making are the same whether one is seeking to exercise leadership in a school or a system, the dynamics are different, not only in scale, but in substance and style. In other words, leadership in Catholic educational systems calls for unique approaches to the challenges identified by D'Orsa and D'Orsa in the first chapter—the discovery of a new process for identifying vision, a new perspective, and new skills in leading the community towards the vision.

The introductory unit of ACU's new Master of Educational Systems Leadership degree course is called *Perspectives on System Leadership*. It seeks to expose students to a wide range of perspectives on this form of leadership. It provides access to case studies of leadership in extended systems such as businesses, not-for-profit organisations and Catholic school systems. It taps into research such as that conducted by the McKinsey Company[211] and the Grattan Institute[212] on the world's best performing school systems. Of particular interest in this chapter, however, is the material on recent 'living systems' thinking about organizations, which seeks to understand them more as living organisms than machines. We believe that these concepts have a great deal to offer Catholic system leaders in a time of liminality.

---

211 See M. Mourshed, C. Chijioke & M. Barber, (2010). *Executive Summary: How the world's most improved school systems keep getting better*, at http://mckinseyonsociety.com/how-the-worlds-most-improved-school-systems-keep-getting-better/
212 B. Jensen, A. Hunter, J. Sonnemann & T. Burns (2012). *Catching up: Learning from the best school systems in East Asia*. (Melbourne: Grattan Institute, 2012).

At such a time, one temptation, described in Chapter 1 as a 'traditionalist approach', is to respond to *new challenges with old thinking and old paradigms*. While such approaches have a natural attraction for many, and may have merit for technical problems, it has been argued that they are of limited use when adaptive challenges raise their head.[213] Liminality presents such adaptive challenges, in seeking to transition from one set of realities while shaping another.

If not a technical way of responding, then what? Uhl-Bien and Marion[214] argue that what is needed is for leaders to find a way of operating within what they call *complex adaptive systems*. A complex adaptive system is a natural phenomenon in which a group of interdependent individuals organize themselves in ways that allow them to respond to a complex, changing environment. A liminal era provides such an environment.

One example of a complex adaptive system in nature is the flocking behavior of birds. In a flock, there are often hundreds, even thousands, of individuals, all seeking to arrive together at the same destination. And despite the fact that the birds have neither rulebooks nor strategic plan nor maps, and have no obvious hierarchy, nor leadership structure, they somehow manage to navigate large distances and deal with capricious and sometimes violent weather to arrive at their destination.

To get a sense of how this is different from more mechanistic ways of organising, consider how animals are herded. The internal drive of the flock is replaced by the whip of the herder. The fundamental relationship is not interdependence among members, but dependence on that same herder. Responsiveness to challenge or new environmental circumstance is in the hands of the herder. Both the locus of control and the sense of direction reside not within the herd itself but with its drivers. This is the obverse of a creative adaptive system.

What, then, can we learn from nature as system leaders? Jansen et al.[215] point to the work of biologists which shows that while it may not be possible to predict flocking behavior, neither is it chaotic. Such behavior is responsive to external influences, and fundamentally purposeful. These are qualities to which all systems would aspire. It has been posited that the underlying rules for flocking are very simple: (1) separation – steer to avoid getting too close to nearby members of the flock; (2) alignment – steer in the general direction of nearby members of the flock; and (3) cohesion – steer to stay close to the general position of nearby members of the flock.

---

213 C. Jansen, P. Cammock & L. Conner, (2011). 'Leadership for emergence: Exploring organisations through a living systems lens'. *Leading and Managing*, 17(1), 59–74.
214 M. Uhl-Bien & R. Marion. (2009) 'Complexity leadership in bureaucratic forms of organizing: A meso model', *The Leadership Quarterly*, 20(4), 631–650.
215 Jansen et al, 59–74.

The capacity of these simple rules to generate flocking is a consequence of *a high degree of sensitivity to all the others in the flock*. When combined with a powerful migratory instinct, it ensures that the chances of the whole flock arriving at their destination are maximised. Some of the parallels between this example from nature, and human organisations may already be apparent.

When we factor human intelligence into the framework of complex adaptive systems we move from a process of instinctive, unthinking interdependence to one of *intelligent interdependence*, and from the comparatively simple matter of moving a group of individuals, to that of working collectively towards complex human outcomes - like Catholic education. In our systems, not only are the behaviors more complex, but the individuals who engage with these are also complex and unique.

In a time of liminality, in which we are seeking to create new meanings, these meanings need *to be owned and shared* if they are to become the wellspring of action, or to use the flocking analogy, the homing instinct. Traditional, authoritarian/bureaucratic approaches have more in common with herding than with flocking, placing too much emphasis with the central 'drivers', and too little confidence in the members of the community. Meaning-making within Catholic school systems calls for *a coherence of view*, and such coherence, according to Jansen, et al., relies more on immediate interdependencies than central control if they are to engage in the 'co-construction and co-production of new knowledge.[216] This calls on system leaders to move from the role of doer to enabler. They need to focus on the building of collective capacity in multiple communities of learning so that the movement through liminality is truly owned by all, and is, in the words of Sharratt and Fullan 'systematic, self-sustaining and unstoppable'.[217] This kind of leadership does not mean 'getting the followers to follow the leader's wishes; rather leadership occurs when interacting agents generate adaptive outcomes'.[218]

What does all this mean for leaders in Catholic educational systems? First of all, it points to the limitations of traditional 'command and control' regimes. *The McKinsey Report* emerging from the field of best-practice research, demonstrated that *the better the performance of a school system, the less central control was necessary*. The challenge here is that central control comes with its own built-in measures of comfort, because in this mode, at least

---

216 A. Harris & M. Jones (2010). 'Professional learning communities and system improvement'. *Improving Schools*, 13(2), 172–181.
217 L. Sharratt & M. Fullan *Realization: The Change Imperative for Deepening District-Wide Reform* (Thousand Oaks Ca: SAGE Publications, 2009), 92.
218 B. Lichtenstein, M. Uhl-Bien, R. Marion, A. Seers, J. Orton & C. Schreiber (2006). 'Complexity leadership theory: An interactive perspective on leading in complex adaptive systems' in *Emergence: Complexity and Organization*, 8:4 (2006), 2–12.

system leaders know what schools are *supposed* to be doing. The problem here is that in a time of liminality, holding control at the centre implies that those in central roles have all the answers, when in actual fact they may not have many at all. Moreover, such a stance deprives the system of the insights of literally hundreds of insightful and experienced educators in the schools, and the kinds of synergies that might emerge from greater interaction. Moving away from bureaucratic approaches requires a degree of *tolerance for ambiguity* that does not come naturally, and a capacity to *manage the balance between coherence and randomness*.

The role of leadership in a creative, adaptive system is to create the spaces within which shared meaning can emerge from the process of engaging with challenges in a time of apparent uncertainty. This requires developing ways in which networks of genuine sharing can be created and developed, crossing boundaries between school and centre, between school and school. If new meanings are to emerge for Catholic education systems, they will rely on processes of influence that are more subtle than a new organizational chart, and more sophisticated than reliance on a new mission statement. At the same time, this does not happen in a vacuum. Like the homing instinct discussed previously, *the deep moral purpose of Catholic education*—what D'Orsa and D'Orsa call the mythological roots in the first chapter—*provides the force that ensures coherence and shared direction*. As systems and their leaders engage with the challenges of transition, it is this purpose that provides the coherence, and maintains direction.

Engaging with moral purpose within any community or system is a leadership challenge in its own right. It requires leaders to help colleagues to become sensitive to the fundamental aspects of their identity and mission and to have the skill to think and plan in a way that is respectful of core values. It calls on leadership that builds capacity and a sense of agency and efficacy, both for individuals and the community/system as a whole. If this is done well, systems will be better equipped to 'live with liminality' and to make well based decisions in a time of uncertainty.

CONCLUSION

The authors welcome the discussion of 'liminality' posed by this book. The concept opens up new ways of understanding and practicing educational leadership, especially within the faith-based context of Catholic educational institutions. Likewise, as academics closely associated with the development and implementation of Australian Catholic University's new postgraduate course in Educational System Leadership, it has been enlightening for us to consider this course within the perspective of 'liminality'. As mentioned within the chapter, the concept was not an explicit reference point in the course's development, but it is clear that the course is itself a response to the circumstances of being in a 'threshold' state.

Some of the clear take-home messages for system leaders in such circumstances are *to re-imagine their roles*: from doer to enabler; from central control to building collective capacity in multiple communities of learning; *to develop a capacity for managing the discomfort of ambiguity, and the balance between coherence and randomness*. And in re-imaging their roles, and analytically assessing the value of current practices, system leaders will need to maintain that demanding challenge of *creating spaces within which shared meaning can emerge*, precisely from engagement with the dissonance and uncertainty of the times in which we find ourselves.

The moral purpose of system leadership within Catholic education at this time will only be found in the times and places within which we live and work. That, to us, is the essential message of our creedal commitment to the Incarnation of Jesus Christ.

PRIORITIES IN LEADING FOR MISSION

PRIORITY 13.1 In a liminal era leading for mission involves accepting the gift of uncertainty, and using it both in the search for meaning and in determining the system's moral purpose.

The writers invoke the metaphors of flocking and herding as possible leadership stances in complex organisations. In the case of humans, the flocking model requires internal control and 'intelligent interdependence', whereas herding requires some form of external control based on the assumption that the leader (or leadership group) 'gets things right'. In situations characterised by uncertainty, this assumption can prove highly problematic.

Continuing the Conversation

- What expectations do your colleagues hold about the leadership group 'getting things right'? How realistic are these expectations?
- How would you describe the faces of 'intelligent inter-dependence' in your school system?
- In a flock the direction that the birds take is guided by instinct. Your Catholic school system is considered as a 'complex adaptive system'. What guides its choice in regard to directions? Is there a religious instinct or intuition at work in such choices? If so, how would you name it?
- If flocking and herding can be regarded as theme and counter-theme in describing the leadership culture of your school system, where does

the balance point lie, and what are the principal factors determining its position?

PRIORITIES IN LEADING FOR MISSION

Priority 13.2 In a liminal era leaders have to be able to carry the community with them in negotiating ambiguity. They do this by pushing out the imaginal boundaries within which colleagues customarily think, thus making it possible for new meanings to emerge.

Continuing the Conversation

- What are the principal sources of ambiguity in contemporary school leadership? In school system leadership? What are the commonalities? Where are the principal areas of difference?
- In what ways do your school leaders (or school system leaders) seek to push out the imaginal boundaries within which colleagues think? How effective do you think these efforts are? How could they be improved?
- How does your school system set about the task of creating the critical mass of leaders needed to sustain school communities in achieving their mission? How many strands can you identify in this endeavour, and how effective do you judge each of these strands to be?

14

MODELS, FRAMEWORKS AND PROCESSES IN SCHOOL IMPROVEMENT: A CASE STUDY

Christopher Barrett[219]

The focus of this chapter is the relationship between mission and strategic thinking as these inter-relate in school improvement and the pursuit of excellence in Catholic schooling. The approach is to use the experience of the Catholic Education Office (CEO) Sydney as a case study which is then referenced against the approaches adopted by other major Catholic school systems. Treated as a case study, the Sydney experience is significant as the CEO there was first into the field in linking the management of schools to an integrated set of 'system processes' which sought to drive school improvement and the pursuit of excellence. That the system achieved what it set out to do has been publicly acknowledged by the internationally recognised Australian Business Excellence Awards in 2006 and 2008.[220]

NSW: A UNIQUE EDUCATIONAL CULTURE

The way the Sydney experience unfolded was determined in significant ways by the unique educational environment that exists in NSW. Aspects of this have been touched on in Part B which covered the impact of the NSW *Education Act 1961*.

Educational culture of NSW

The *Education Act 1990* provided the charter for the NSW Board of Studies to put in place the centralised regulatory system under which schools

---

219 Christopher Barrett has been integrally involved in the development of strategic planning and whole-of-system planning in NSW for over two decades, and currently serves as executive officer of the Conference of Diocesan Directors of Education NSW & ACT.
220 These awards are made against the criteria set out in the Australian Business Excellence Framework which are a licensed adaption of the more generic Baldridge Framework. Baldridge also have a specific framework for education. See www.nist.gov/baldrige/publications/education_criteria.cfm

function in NSW. Under this system school review and annual reporting—both deemed essential to school improvement—became obligatory. However, rather than supervise this regime directly, the Board of Studies opted to delegate the responsibility (along with the costs) to 'systems' of independent schools. The CEO in each of the eleven dioceses became 'the system authority' charged with the responsibility of developing a review process accredited by the Board of Studies. The review process had to provide evidence that each school in the system was 'continuously compliant' in meeting all statutory requirements with respect to its educational and legal obligations. This ushered in the new era of school improvement in NSW. The first round of school reviews had rolled out across a six year cycle which meant in practice that the length of the strategic planning cycle for schools was set by government, not by the situation of the schools. Subsequently, the review cycle was reduced to five years giving schools greater flexibility with respect to the length of the strategic planning cycle.[221]

Catholic schools in NSW operate under tighter constraints than is the case in other states, reflecting the highly centralised nature of educational provision in this state.[222] Systems in other states operate with more 'degrees of freedom'. The issues which the NSW experience highlights are important in defending those freedoms as pressure continues to mount for educational practices across states to 'converge'.

Mission and strategic thinking in the design of a Catholic system

Of particular interest to this study is the interplay between what we have called 'mission thinking' and 'strategic thinking' as these terms came to be understood, and the relationship between them worked out in practice, as the Sydney model of school and system management was developed and institutionalised under the leadership of long-serving Director, Br Kelvin Canavan.[223] As I proceed, I cross-reference the Sydney experience with that of other Catholic systems.

The management framework of a school system is a real life setting in which *faith intersects with culture* and so is a place where the relationship between the two is forged. Clearly, how this relationship is understood

---

221 These developments recognise implicitly, if not explicitly, that a 'one size fits all' approach to strategic planning can be counter-productive in bringing about school improvement.
222 This has to do with the size of the system which is one of the biggest systems supervised by a single authority in the world.
223 Br Kelvin Canavan joined the Catholic Education Office in Sydney in 1968 as the Wyndham scheme was being implemented. He completed post-graduate degrees in the U.S. at Cornell and later at San Francisco Universities. In 1987 he was appointed Director, a position he held until his retirement in 2009.

is implicit in a school system's management model. Secondly, the experience highlights the complex interactions between mission thinking and strategic thinking as this works out in practice in an educational system as contexts change.

At the outset we need to make a distinction between what we mean by a 'model', a 'framework' and a 'process'. As used here a *model* has two components: a *framework of meaning* and *a process (or set of processes)* that seek to translate meanings into effective management practices. Since meaning can be translated into practice in a number of ways, a framework can be implemented in a number of ways, thus giving rise to a variety of processes.

CEO SYDNEY MODEL OF SCHOOL AND SYSTEM IMPROVEMENT

The management framework adopted by the CEO Sydney has its theoretical basis in the *Management by Objectives* (MBO) model developed by Peter Drucker.[224] The focus in Drucker's framework is 'obtaining results'. However, what constitutes 'results' varies from organisation to organisation. In the case of the CEO Sydney, 'results' have been consistently interpreted in terms of 'educational excellence' as measured by *internationally recognised educational criteria*.

CEO Sydney model in outline

The MBO model has the following components.

FIGURE 14.1 MBO Approach to School and System Objectives (after Drucker 1993)

---

224 Peter Drucker *The Practice of Management* (New York: Harper Business, 1993).

Across the past two decades elements in the MBO model have been translated into a number of officially designated processes which, when taken together, constitute the CEO Sydney management model. The generic processes associated with this model are:

- School Review
- Strategic Planning leading to the development of Annual Improvement Plans
- Annual Implementation Processes
- Annual Reporting of Achievements to the community: outcomes, benefits, results and improvements[225]
- Annual Performance Review for school leaders and teachers.

Sitting behind the model is a second set of processes, which are not officially recognised, but are integral to the model. These are the *consultations* that shape both the frameworks within which processes have been developed and the processes themselves. The development of frameworks and processes becomes *an exercise in collective meaning-making* which involves input from school leaders and other professionals in the field. The model set out in Figure 14.2 *illustrates the way in which the subsidiarity and co-responsibility principles can function in a centralised system* such as the Sydney Catholic school system. In some Catholic school systems individual results-oriented processes are linked together to form a cohesive set of 'system processes' operating within a development cycle; in others they function in a more or less 'stand-alone' mode.

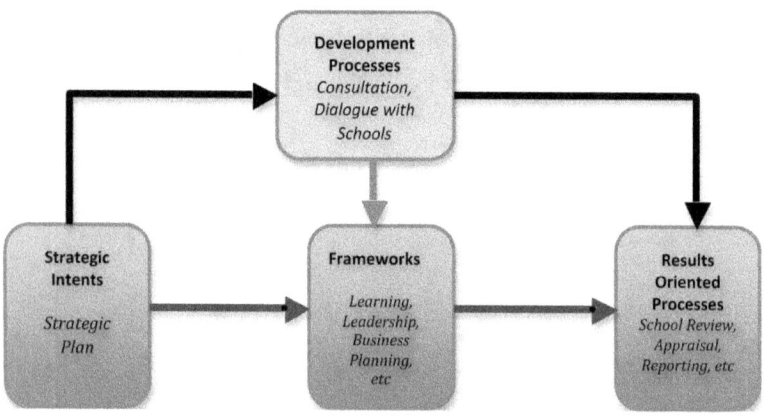

FIGURE 14.2 System Development Model in Sydney

---

225 In systems theory a system is analysed in terms of inputs, processes, and outputs. Reporting in the CEO Sydney model focuses on outputs, not on inputs or processes.

School management and school improvement

As the third generation[226] of school improvement projects has been developed, CEOs in NSW first attempted to integrate Catholic school improvement and compliance requirements *into a single school review process*. Compliance covers state-based requirements for the registration of non-government schools and a variety of legislation/public policy matters such as child protection, occupational health and safety, privacy, state-based teacher accreditation, etc. This approach however is now seen as compromising Catholic school improvement, and the recent trend is to view these two elements as separate element in a model. This has freed schools up to match the length of their strategic planning cycle to the situation of the school. As a consequence, there is now a range of school review processes operating in Catholic school systems in NSW. The level of central office support to assist schools with the implementation of results-oriented processes has depended on system-level policies and the availability of planning and process consultancy support provided either by CEO personnel or sourced independently by the schools.

The capacity of the smaller school systems to develop their own system processes is often quite limited, and they are increasingly dependent on developments in the larger systems (Sydney, Parramatta and Broken Bay) often adopting or adapting processes developed there to suit local contexts and resource levels. Resource levels place a major constraint on the types of processes that small school systems *can actually implement*.

Development models such as that outlined in Figure 14.2 make assumptions about the capacity of school leaders to understand and effectively use 'system processes' and from time to time these assumptions need to be questioned. For instance, it took school leaders in NSW nearly a decade to effectively integrate strategic planning into the practice of school management. This suggests that strategic thinking does not come easily because it requires a complex range of skills which require some time to identify, practise and master. A major learning from the Sydney experience, in this regard, is that all school leaders need to recognise that *strategic thinking is a permanent feature of leadership* and not a process that occurs once each school improvement cycle.

---

[226] First generation projects such as *Vision and Values* were imported from the United States. These sought to stabilise Catholic identity of the school. The second generation were developed locally and sought the same objective but by a different method. They focused of articulating the mission of a Catholic school and developing a plan to pursue this mission.

INCORPORATION OF EVIDENCE-BASED APPROACHES TO EFFECTIVENESS

Since the turn of the century there have been progressively increasing demands on schools to provide valid evidence to support claims of improvement. NAPLAN and MY SCHOOL stand at the end, rather than the start, of this development in NSW.

Development of effectiveness indicators

School improvement models in NSW, particularly those used by the larger, better-resourced systems, assess achievement using processes of *evidence-based review* leading to *self-evaluation*. These processes often use a set of *effectiveness indicators sourced in frameworks* to make informed, evaluative judgements about the adequacy and impact of present performance and the possibilities for future improvement. These processes assume that school and CEO unit leaders understand what constitutes 'evidence of achievement'. Experience to date indicates that this is not always the case.[227]

In Australia, the development of review processes that place a premium on evidence-based self-evaluation can be traced to the influence of Dr Ian Gamble who chaired the 2004 External Review of the Sydney CEO. This approach to school review created the need to *develop the expertise and processes required to assess and evaluate the school and system outcomes*, with respect to stated or agreed targets. In the light or more recent developments in Commonwealth educational policy, this intervention was timely, to say the least. How schools interpret, assess, communicate and best utilise the data that is available demands levels of strategic thinking that have to be developed, and cannot be presumed.

The incorporation of effectiveness indicators into school improvement models can be directly linked to the use of these indicators more generally in evaluating performance in education systems and not-for-profit organisations. For instance, the CEO Sydney has used the Baldridge Education Framework[228] to good effect. The McKinsey Report 2010[229] provided something of a wake-up call to look more closely at what *highly effective systems* were doing to improve educational excellence as distinct from what works at the school level.

---

[227] It has not been uncommon, for instance, for external review panels to be 'snowed' with documentation as evidence of achievement which confuses inputs and processes with results.
[228] See, for instance, the Baldrige Education Criteria for Performance Excellence at www.nist.gov/baldrige/publications/upload/2011_2012_Education_Criteria.pdf
[229] See The McKinsey Report: 'Shaping the Future: How Good Education Systems can become Great in the Decade Ahead' (2009) at www.mckinsey.com/locations/southeastasia/knowledge/Education_ Roundtable.pdf

In developing a set of effectiveness indicators for a Catholic school system two important questions have to be asked:

- what constitutes excellence in schooling given the context—cultural and ecclesial—in which the schools now function (the question of meaning)?
- how can this understanding best be translated into practice (the question of process)?

How good is our school?

The work of Ian Gamble, Chief Inspector for Education in Scotland, has provided useful guidance to the CEO Sydney and other Catholic school systems[230] in answering these questions. The work of his team in Scotland resulted in the development of a model of school improvement named *How Good is Our School? The Journey to Excellence* (2006).[231] This model has been influential in shaping the framework for excellence used by Catholic schools in a number of Australian Catholic school systems.

The Scottish model has two major components: a *conception of excellence*, 'Ten Dimensions of Excellence', and a *process of review and self-evaluation*. The *five-step* process invites school communities to develop an agreed conception of excellence using the conception of excellence framework (create meaning), then evaluate their performance against this conception. Judgements made about the level of performance against an agreed understanding of what constitute excellence then provide the basis for planning improvement. The five-step process combines both mission-thinking (addressing issues of meaning) and strategic thinking (creating a sustainable pathway to the preferred future).

Mission Thinking: Focus is on Meaning-making in Context

STEP 1 AIMING FOR EXCELLENCE: invites a school community to work out what excellence can mean in their particular context.

STEP 2 EXPLORING EXCELLENCE: here the community explores how the ten dimensions of excellence can be incorporated in our conception of excellence.

---

230 Dr Gamble was invited to Australia to chair the external review of the CEO and Sydney Catholic School System in 2004. He has worked as a consultant with Catholic school systems in Sydney, Perth, Brisbane and Bathurst.
231 HM Inspectorate of Education *How Good is Our School?: The Journey to Excellence* (Livingstone Scotland: HM Inspectorate of Education, 2006).

Strategic Thinking: Focus is on Translating Meaning into Action

STEP 3 HOW GOOD ARE WE NOW? the community completes a self-evaluation and so identify strengths and areas for improvement.

STEP 4 PLANNING FOR EXCELLENCE: having identified areas for improvement the school develops a plan for improvement.

STEP 5 JOURNEYS TO EXCELLENCE: the school learns from 'the heroes' in making the journey to improvement.

The Scottish learning and teaching framework as pioneered by Gamble sets out to produce students who are: successful learners, confident individuals, effective contributors and responsible citizens. It aims to engage young people in the highest quality teaching and learning activities. The effective school:

- Promotes student wellbeing and respect
- Develops a culture of ambition and achievement
- Develops a common vision among children and young people, parents and staff
- Fosters high quality leadership at all levels
- Works in partnership with other agencies and its community
- Works together with parents to improve learning
- Reflects on its own work and thrives on challenges
- Values and empowers its staff and young people.

In working towards these objectives, the school develops processes that focus on outcomes and which maximise success for learners. The framework and processes together constitute a school improvement model. The mission of the school is articulated in terms of this model and evaluated in terms of achievements (outcomes) made against the criteria set out above.

Largely inspired by the model outlined above, the CEO Sydney set out in 2006 to create its own model of excellence 'How Effective is our Catholic School?' as a means to implement the major priorities in its system level strategic plan *Towards 2010*.[232] The model was devised as a template that could be *adapted by local schools*. The indicators of excellence it employs are built around the *seven recurring themes* that have emerged in over three hundred school reviews across the first eleven years of school development. These are:

---

[232] Chris Barrett was the principal developer of this instrument, and subsequently developed a system-level instrument *How Effective is Our Catholic School System?* (CEO Sydney, 2010). The schema for this document was subsequently made available to all Catholic school systems.

Core Business Indicators

Key Area 1: Catholic Life and Religious Education
Key Area 2: Students and their Learning
Key Area 3: Pedagogy

Supporting Indicators

Key Area 4: Human Resources, Leadership and Management
Key Area 5: Resources, Finance and Facilities
Key Area 6: Parents, Partnership, Consultation and Communication
Key Area 7: Strategic Leadership and Management[233]

The consultation process used to fill out this framework saw the principals in the school system leaders confer for two days at a Sydney conference centre. The close involvement of school leaders in the development process led to the final schema winning a high degree of acceptance in the schools.

The Melbourne CEO has developed its own model for school development using the framework and process approach to address system level *strategic intents*. The model is called *Learning-Centred Schools: A Sacred Landscape*.[234] The Melbourne model is set out in a *framework* document and an accompanying *strategy* document. The framework is sourced in the CEO's 'ecclesial and educational vision' for the school system, *One Body, Many Parts*. The reference in the title to 'Sacred Landscape' draws attention to the fact that in a Catholic school, teaching and learning is the meeting place in which faith intersects with culture.

Major Catholic school systems including Melbourne, Sydney, Hobart, Parramatta and Brisbane have, as part of the third generation of school improvement initiatives, developed *Learning Frameworks* that seek to place teaching and learning in a meaningful Catholic setting.[235] These frameworks are usually aligned with the CEO's strategic plans.[236] The development and alignment of these frameworks provide sound examples of mission thinking at the system level because they seek to make teaching and learning meaningful in the context of mission and, in doing so, articulate a conception of what constitutes excellence in Catholic schooling.

The emerging pattern in these developments is summed up in the

---

233 CEO 'Sydney How Good is Our Catholic School?' (Sydney: Catholic Education Office, 2006), 4.
234 See at www.ceomelb.catholic.edu.au/learning-teaching/learning-centred-schools
235 These learning frameworks are available from the respective CEO websites. See *REACH* (Parramatta), *Learning Framework: a Discussion Paper* (Sydney), *Learning-Centred Schools: A Sacred Landscape* (Melbourne) and *Learning Framework* (Brisbane). Brisbane was the first into the field in 2002.
236 Melbourne and Parramatta use the language of 'strategic intents'.

diagram below which draws on the Sydney data, by way of example. The general approach raises a number of questions: Is the process of developing indicators of excellence best done at the CEO level, the school level, or, as happens in the Scottish model, at the school level with assistance from the CEO? In other words, should documents such as *How Effective is Our Catholic School?* have a normative standing, or are they better used as templates to be adapted at the local level?

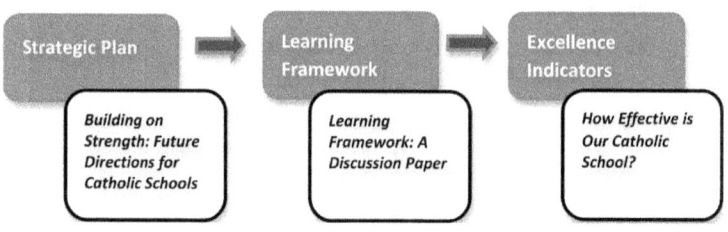

FIGURE 14.3 Mission Thinking and the Alignment of Strategy with Excellence

Secondly, what would be involved in developing indicators of excellence for the school *system as a whole?* What framework should underpin this development and how should it be developed? These were questions that came into play in the Sydney CEO in 2009 and resulted in the development of a system level model called *How Effective is our Catholic Education Office?* which was published in 2010. The intention in developing this document is that the CEO Sydney would model at the system level what it expects of schools, thus aligning the system with the school in the development of its next strategic plan.

DETERMINING THE DIMENSIONS OF EXCELLENCE IN CATHOLIC SCHOOLING

Initiatives such as the ones described above force school and system leaders to ask two important questions: 'What, in today's context, constitutes excellence in a Catholic school?' and 'Who decides?'

Articulating and defending a conception of excellence

Posing such questions in the present condition of ecclesial and cultural liminality is to invite a range of responses, depending on which frame of reference—denial, traditionalist, transforming or critical—the respondent employs to make sense of the situation. The faith dynamics these questions tap into reveal a spectrum of possible responses. At one end of this spectrum people seek to use power to impose a specific meaning on the situation, while at the other end they seek to open up what they see as a necessary dialogue in order to create a degree of consensus about core meanings. Most responses will lie somewhere between these poles, depending on how open people are to engaging in dialogue and what form this takes.[237] In such cases engaging in dialogue is living out the mission of the school or system in real terms.

Given the pressures that now impact directly on Catholic school and system leaders from both the culture (including parents and government) and the Church, and taking note of the forces driving change in the cultural and ecclesial contexts, it seems absolutely necessary that school and system leaders be able to *articulate and defend the school's or system's conception of excellence*. Schools need to be clear about what it is they aspire to achieve. This is an exercise in meaning-making that they simply cannot avoid. It is a primary test of their credibility and authenticity. Furthermore, they must be able *to translate this conception into concrete effectiveness indicators*.

The problem of meaning: religious and secular construction of mission

The religious conception of mission opens up a range of possibilities which render the day-to-day work of teachers meaningful in a way that its secular counterpart cannot. These transcend the often narrow understandings staff hold about what 'being Catholic' means. The Kingdom of God perspective which the contemporary Catholic understanding of mission provides, challenges all attempts to narrow the Gospel message and impose a correspondingly narrow meaning on 'being Catholic'. In this context, frameworks—as outlined above— provide *important and useful boundaries* within which necessary processes of consultation and dialogue can and should occur.[238]

While it is always possible for a leader to impose meaning on a situation, it is not possible to impose ownership of that meaning. Ownership of meaning comes from participation in the meaning-making process. *A crucial skill in effecting mission is, therefore, leading the meaning-making process in such a way as to engender ownership.* This is where shared theological reflect can play a role.

Models and the pursuit of excellence: some Inherent limitations

The NSW experience has been that a management model is effective *only if there is the critical mass of people in the organisation who have the capabilities needed*

---

237 As we have seen previously (Chapter 7), in the context of mission, dialogue can take a number of forms: dialogue of life, of action, of exchange, and of spiritual experience.
238 One of the most complete attempts to address this challenge currently occurs in the Archdiocese of Hobart where the Archbishop's charter for Catholic schools is linked to the Catholic school system's school improvement framework.

to operate it. That such a critical mass does exist can never be presumed. It must be developed, and the practical way to do this is to *involve people in the development of the model itself*. The development of frameworks and processes is an important exercise in learning as well as in collegiality and co-responsibility. However, it also needs to be recognised that this strategy provides only the first generation of users. Writers on leadership, such as Robert Starratt, recommend the need to 'institutionalise the change' so that succeeding generations growing up within it come to take it as the norm, as part of the culture.[239]

Renewal of frameworks and processes in this context is an important strategic priority. Precisely because they come to be taken for granted, when models are institutionalised there is a downside. People lose contact with the meanings the models had for the first generation of users, and begin to question them as a meaningful response to the demands of *their time and their context*. There is some evidence in the Sydney experience that this is already happening due largely to changes in school leadership.

The lesson from the Sydney experience seems to be that *meaning has to be continuously recreated*. The erosion of meaning, as contexts and people change, makes processes vulnerable in that they can date quickly, particularly if they lack adaptive flexibility. They can become a form without substance. On the other hand it needs to be recognised that, because the careers of people working in CEOs are often tied to the implementation of certain processes, these can acquire a longevity that exceeds their usefulness.

The *development of frameworks* is an important innovation because these provide the parameters within which a variety of processes can emerge with the degree of flexibility needed to sustain a school improvement model. The lack of prescription generally associated with a framework allows processes to be progressively adopted, adapted and replaced—a necessary condition in meeting *the human need for variety* which tends to put a 'use by' date on all processes.

In NSW the MBO model has been progressively translated into 'system processes' via the development of frameworks which over time have become institutionalised. In some instances these have become quite inflexible, raising attendant problems and tensions that had to be addressed. A major learning from this experience is that *the collective meaning needed to develop and implement a model is often lost once the model is institutionalised*. A new generation of leaders, who were not part of the initial development, quickly lose ownership of processes under these circumstances. The rate of

---

[239] Robert Starratt 'Leadership, Vision and Dramatic Consciousness' in *The Drama of Schooling/The Schooling of Drama* (London: The Falmer Press, 1990), 98–107.

turn-over in designated leaders is a critical variable in determining the life-span of a process, and sometimes of a framework as well.[240]

The Sydney, Melbourne and Hobart experiences highlight the *importance of developing meaning frameworks* that can provide guidance and direction in the development of processes, whether these are in leadership development, school improvement or system improvement. Frameworks have a longer life expectancy than processes. The experience suggests that a sound management model is one that ensures that there is a close alignment between frameworks and processes at both school and system levels. It also ensures that this is continuously monitored, because alignment tends to fall off over time due largely to ongoing changes in leadership personnel.

Mission thinking requires strategic thinking

The processes developed by the Sydney CEO became integral to the model within which the system sought to achieve its mission objectives. The way the model was developed illustrates how, within a centralised culture, the principles of subsidiarity and co-responsibility can work out in practice. What has emerged as the experience has unfolded, and was in many respects unexpected, is the vulnerability of processes needed to implement a model. This vulnerability has to be taken into account in the development of a model if the model itself is to be sustainable. Mission thinking can result in good frameworks, but by itself is insufficient. It must be balanced by the strategic thinking required *to sustain processes as people change*. This is an insight that the Sydney experience offers other Catholic school systems.

PRIORITIES IN LEADING FOR MISSION

PRIORITY 14.1 In leading for mission it is always necessary for leaders to balance the demands of being a local community with those of being part of a system.

Being a Catholic Church means being caught up in the tensions inherent in the culture of the Church. Central among these is that between the Church as community and the Church as institution. The tension arises from differences in focus. The mission of a faith community is to make the Kingdom of God present in local contexts while that of the institution is to sustain the life of faith communities across time from within a finite resource base.

---

240 Five to seven years seems to be the life span of a process in Catholic education. By that time the meaning it had for the developers and first users has either altered or in some way been compromised by circumstance.

Continuing the Conversation

The community/institution tension translates into Catholic education as the CEO/local school tension. How this is experienced depends on the way in which the relationship is understood and how it works out in practice. Some forms of relationship aid particular schools in formulating and achieving their mission; others simply cause frustration. How the balance point between community and institution is set and where it is set become important issues. The situation can be analysed in terms of 'drivers' and 'pushers' and the way in which power is distributed between them.

- What are the main drivers in the life of your school which seem to shift power in the direction of the CEO?
- What are the mains pushers which balance the influence of these drivers?
- What processes exist so that these influences on school life can be addressed and an appropriate balance point negotiated?
- How does the CEO seek to shape the way 'being Catholic' is interpreted within the school system? In what ways is this appropriate/inappropriate given the context of your school?
- Does your school system have a 'school improvement/learning framework'? If so, how were the criteria of excellence proposed in the framework developed? What level of ownership do these have in your school?
- Can you outline the principal elements (frameworks and processes) which make up the school improvement model that shapes your school's understanding of excellence? How is this understanding aligned with the school's stated mission?
- How sustainable is the model given the context of your school/school system?

Part E
LEADING FOR MISSION:
Processes and priorities

In the exercise of theological reflection, the aim in bringing the wisdom of one's faith tradition and that of one's cultural tradition into 'conversation', is to discern the 'heart of the matter' with regard to human experience. This is *the vital step* towards formulating an adequate response. The conversation as pursued in the preceding chapters has focused on leading Catholic schools and school systems in a liminal era. As we showed in Chapters 3 and 4, this experience is not new to the Australian Church, and indeed we have argued, following Raymond Brown, that the New Testament writers themselves created their texts in response to the challenges of leading in situations of liminality.

How then do we actually identify and respond to the 'heart of the matter' when it comes to leading Catholic schools and systems, given the nature of the present era? Our argument has been that Catholic education leadership in a liminal era requires a premium on mission thinking, which demands a shift in emphasis from the situation in which operational and strategic thinking are centre-stage in educational leadership. In our view, the 'heart of the matter' in leading for mission in the present circumstances, is *raising both the quality and scope of mission thinking*. Our argument is that, in order to do this, the response needs to be formulated at three levels—responding to the immediate challenge, responding to the strategic challenge, and responding to the enduring challenge.

The *immediate challenge* is to address the cause of a pervasive anxiety that is characteristic of the present era in Catholic education, viz. the fear that

Catholic schools and school systems are becoming progressively secularised, as many of the parents who support them move further away from active membership in the worshipping Church community. This challenge is taken up in Chapter 15 which focuses on the role mission thinking plays in negotiating the balance point between secularisation and evangelisation in a Catholic school.

The *strategic challenge* is to ensure that school and system leaders acquire basic skills in mission thinking – that they develop as organisational meaning-makers in terms of Catholic education's core religious and cultural purposes. For this to occur, school and system leaders need to master the fundamentals of theological reflection. This is a project which is both strategically important and demanding in that it requires sustained effort. In Chapter 16 we outline a model of theological reflection which contains both a framework and a well-tried method. The aim is that, ultimately, such thinking will become a habit of mind and heart, rather than simply a process to be used with regard to isolated issues or events.

The *enduring challenge* is to ensure that Catholic schools remain Catholic, as Church leaders—clerical, religious, and lay—negotiate the change from a religious culture responsive to the aspirations of modernity, to a religious culture that can also incorporate the aspirations of young people growing up with a post-modern mindset. This mindset is formed by a pervasive culture that has largely lost confidence that truth can be established in any objective sense. Rather than 'the truth', there is just 'your truth' and 'my truth'. This mindset is a by-product of increasing pluralism, and relentless exposure to 'spin' which operates on the principle that truth is ever only a matter of interpretation. School leaders who deal with recalcitrant students are well aware of how the 'my truth/your truth' dynamic plays out once the post-modern mindset takes hold.

The Catholic Church community stands with those who offer an alternative way of seeing the world. It holds that an important function of education is to educate young people away from a mindset that rejects, often implicitly, the notion that truth can be established objectively. It does this by offering an alternative construction of truth based not only on what is best in its religious tradition, but also on the best in the community's culture, in our case the enduring legacy of the Western intellectual tradition with its passion for excellence in the pursuit of truth.

This project defines the scope of mission thinking which has traditionally embraced passing on the faith, creating life chances, and committing to social transformation. Today it also encompasses, to a greater degree, promoting the wellbeing of students, creating a positive relational environment, and forming the personal worldview of students as they make sense of the world and of their life within it.

The enduring challenge is that, with regard to truth, schools be both Catholic and catholic. If this is to occur, the quality of mission thinking needs to be high, which brings us to the final question: What are the characteristics of mission thinking? We conclude the study, and Chapter 17, by identifying six characteristics of quality mission thinking.

15
EVANGELISING THE CULTURE OF CATHOLIC SCHOOLS AND SYSTEMS

Those charged with the leadership role in Catholic schools and school systems have to contend with two opposing forces. On the one hand there is the secularising tendency which has the effect of muting the religious message of the school. On the other there is the evangelising imperative originating from the school's identity. Secularisation and evangelisation now stand as theme and counter-theme in many Catholic organisations, and the location of the balance point plays a significant role in defining their culture. This is particularly true of Catholic schools and Catholic Education Offices. In this chapter we explore both of these terms and the relationship that exists between them. The bottom line is that, if a school or school system does not have specific evangelising strategies in place, then the secularisation of its culture is the inevitable consequence, and the mission of the school or system is compromised.

EVANGELISATION IN CATHOLIC DISCOURSE[241]

In Catholic discourse the term 'evangelisation' has a long history dating back to the apostolic era. Not surprisingly, for a term that has been around so long, it has acquired a range of meanings, and it is these that we wish to explore.

Negative stereotype: evangelisation as 'preaching' to others

From the first eras of Christianity, those who proclaimed the message of Jesus to new audiences were called evangelisers. The term has its roots in classical Greek. After major victories generals would send an *euangelion* (carrier of good news) to announce the victory at home. The term was

---
[241] For an insightful treatment of the topic see J. Gorski 'From "Mission" to "New Evangelisation": The Origins of a Challenging Concept' at http://www.maryknollvocations.com/Mission.pdf

also used with reference to the reward given to the bearer of the good news. It was subsequently applied by Christians to those who announced the Gospel, seen as the good news par excellence. This usage has a long history in all Christian denominations, and equates with what we earlier called 'proclamation by word'. Catholics have tended to view this form of ministry with suspicion, seeing it as 'something that Protestants do'.[242] This attitude often sits behind comments such as 'I am not here to evangelise' meaning 'I am not here to preach at you'. Australian Catholics generally do not construe their relationship with colleagues in a way that permits overt proclamation, because this is not seen as culturally appropriate[243]. Some Catholics now challenge this position.[244]

Evangelisation as a stage in coming to faith

A second understanding of evangelisation emerges in the study of faith development. The insight from such study is that people come to faith in stages.[245] Three such stages are usually differentiated: pre-evangelisation, evangelisation and catechesis. Pre-evangelisation is a preparatory phase in which a potential Christian encounters people of faith, and shares in the life of a faith community. Such experiences raise questions and hopes, thus providing the ground in which the seeds of faith can be sown. Evangelisation is a second stage that involves hearing the Good News of Jesus and responding in faith. It encompasses all those processes by which the seeds of faith are gradually stirred into life. Catechesis then becomes a third stage in the process. Here the seeds of faith, nurtured into life by evangelisation, continue to grow, develop and bear fruit as the new Christian comes to share his or her faith with others and is caught up in the mission of the community.

At the time of the Second Vatican Council, this usage was common. It raised important questions for Catholic educators: Is the school best thought of as a context for pre-evangelisation, or for evangelisation? Is it possible, or even realistic, to continue to think of the Catholic school as a context for catechesis, given the range of faith responses encountered among staff, parents and students? The answers to such questions were

---

242 Until the mid-1950s 'evangelisation' was not part of modern Catholic discourse. It re-entered the Catholic lexicon as the kerygmatic approach to religious education gathered momentum in the 1960s.
243 See John Thornhill *Making Australia: Exploring Our National Conversation* (Newtown: Millennium Books, 1992), 167ff.
244 This tradition of 'proclamation by word' is being reclaimed in the way some Catholic groups now interpret the practice of what is termed the 'new evangelisation'.
245 Pope John Paul II in *Catechesi Tradendae* (##18–20), 1979, speaks of catechesis as a stage in a person's coming to faith, distinct from the initial proclamation. He also reiterates that evangelisation is a 'rich, complex and dynamic reality, made up of many elements, or one could say moments' (*Catechesi Tradendae* #18).

fought over as the transition was made from the second to the third era of Catholic education. It is a moot point as to whether they were ever decisively answered as the concept of evangelisation developed in new directions in the post-conciliar period.

Evangelisation as the 'new evangelisation'

Mission *ad gentes,* as discussed in Chapter 7, has a long history in the Christian churches. It is a history of dedicated missionaries moving across cultural and geographic borders to proclaim the Gospel to those who have not yet heard it, and then to establish Christian communities. In modern times, until relatively recently, these were people from the northern hemisphere, and particularly from Europe. However, beginning in the 1960s, this pattern began to change as Europe grew increasingly secular in its outlook. A major decline in institutional affiliation became a concern to European Popes such as John Paul II and his successor Benedict XVI. John Paul II saw the need to proclaim the Gospel anew to those in whom the light of faith had grown dim, and who had distanced themselves from the Church and its mission.(*Redemptoris Missio #33)* In 1979 he attended the meeting of Latin American bishops (CELAM) at Puebla. At this meeting discussion turned to 'new missionary situations' which included the cultural and social conditions created by urbanisation and large-scale migration, which were redefining human life in large cities. The conference called for a 'new evangelisation' to address the needs of people caught up in these evolving situations. It was out of these two mission concerns—that in South America and that in Europe—that the broad parameters of a 'new evangelisation' began to take shape.

This conception did not correspond to traditional Catholic missionary activity operating within clear territorial boundaries. So serious had the situations in Europe and South America become,[246] that a new Vatican department was established in 2010, (the Pontifical Council for Promoting the New Evangelisation), and a general synod of the Church was held on the theme in 2012. What seemed called for was not only renewed vision and commitment, but also new methodologies in evangelisation.[247]

Those promoting the 'new evangelisation' quite legitimately looked back into the Christian tradition seeking inspiration there, and adopted the methodology of proclaiming how God is present in their own lives, utilising the witness value of 'testimony'.

---

246 Part of the background here has been attempts to exclude any mention of God in the European Union Constitution. This was taken as symptomatic of how pressing the need for a new evangelisation strategy actually is in Europe and other secularised countries.
247 While this is a methodology in the new evangelisation, it by no means fully defines the field in meeting the challenges the Church faces in bringing the Gospel to individuals, societies and cultures in which the Gospel has previously been announced.

Evangelisation as the mission of the Church

Missiologists also use evangelisation in a fourth sense. This usage was developed by Pope Paul VI in drawing together the themes of the 1974 Synod on Evangelisation. In *Evangelii Nuntiandi* he identified evangelisation with the mission or vocation of the Church (##14–15). He pointed out that the Church exists to evangelise, and went on to speak of two conceptions of evangelisation, a partial view and a fuller view.[248] The partial view understands evangelisation in terms of proclaiming the Gospel to those who have not yet heard it, and establishing the Church among them. The fuller view flows from the theology of the Kingdom of God which the Pope then outlines. In doing so, he wrestles with important implications of this theology. For example, if the coming of God's Kingdom means living in right relationship, how does one interpret this in a world becoming more complex and interrelated? What function does the Church serve in such a world? How should Christians, as followers of Jesus, relate to it?

Pope Paul VI's conclusion was that, in order to enter into right relationship with the contemporary world, the Church *has first of all to evangelise itself*. Secondly, its members have to *work at the task of communal and social transformation*. This task involves two important elements: building and strengthening relationships in a way consistent with the teaching of Jesus, and helping to restore and heal relationships when they are fractured. For this to occur, it is necessary to 'evangelise cultures', that is, to challenge aspects of culture that stand in the way of these projects. Christians need to be committed to promoting and supporting those initiatives that free people from all that oppresses them, particularly in societies where the physical basics of human dignity may be only minimally present.

For many Catholics, thinking about mission as the building up and restoration of right relationships, and all that this implies, is quite new. Associating this with 'evangelisation' requires something of a mental jump for those whose customary stance is 'I am not here to evangelise!' From a missional perspective this is equivalent to saying 'I am not here to do anything about building up right relationships nor to help others to do so!' and 'It is no concern of mine if fractured relationships remain fractured!'

When Paul VI spoke of 'evangelising cultures', he meant bringing Jesus' teaching about right relationships to bear on the frameworks of meaning, feeling and judgement that people use in making sense of their lives (*Evangelii Nuntiandi* #19). Used in this sense *it is possible to evangelise the*

---

[248] See discussion in *Evangelii Nuntiandi* ##25–39.

Church itself, and to evangelise the bureaucracies and institutions that are a central feature of all contemporary cultures. Leading for mission is integrally related to evangelisation when used in this sense.

The evangelising mission of Catholic education

Each of us lives in a life-world that is defined by key relationships: with the society in which we live; with our immediate community (which includes family, friends and peers); with the natural world; with the faith community into which we are born. Education seeks to orient young people within this matrix. Our understanding of these relationships is influenced by how we understand our relationship with God. Evangelisation understood as helping people to live in right relationship, and so make God's Kingdom present in time, presents Catholic educators with a major challenge; it also gives great significance to what schools and school systems seek to achieve. Catholic educators not only teach the next generation about society, the community, the natural world and their faith community, they also assist students to acquire the tools needed to explore the inter-relationships that exist between them, so that they can situate themselves meaningfully within this matrix. Theirs is a Kingdom project *par excellence*. However, they do this in a cultural context that is secular, and the impact this has on their efforts has to be taken into account. It is important therefore to understand secularisation and how it functions.

SOURCES OF SECULARISATION

Secularisation developed in the sixteenth and seventeenth centuries as a repudiation of the exaggerated sacralisation of ordinary life that had occurred in Europe in the late Middle Ages. When the impulse for reform surfaced, it divided European kingdoms along religious lines, and resulted in wars that devastated the region economically and psychologically.[249] An aspiration grew that, in the interests of the common good, religion should be separated from politics. This became possible once people developed confidence in the power or reason to solve human problems.

As a contemporary phenomenon, secularisation has two primary sources. The first, which occurred in early modernity, is the *secularisation of politics*, a process which gave rise ultimately to the modern democratic state. The other is the *secularisation of knowledge* which led to the development of the academic disciplines and their methods of enquiry as we know them today.

---

249 John Thornhill *Modernity: Christianity's Estranged Child Reconstructed* (Cambridge: William B Eerdmans, 2000), 181.

Secularisation of politics

As modern states emerged on both sides of the Atlantic, the determination grew among leaders to limit the influence of religious authority and affirm the *autonomy of the secular order* in making political decisions. As a direct consequence, the churches lost their privileged status and authority in the political realm. Politics was secularised.[250] The theory is that political decisions result from people making the strongest case. In practice however, vested interests more often than not carry the day, and 'spin' is then used to justify decisions.

A consequence of excluding the authority of the churches from public life was to relativise the place of religious institutions in providing public services such as health, welfare and education—areas which had once been the preserve of the churches' and integral to their mission. Public services are now primarily the responsibility of the state and, in consequence, have become a contested area. Secularisation used in the political sense has resulted in a progressive decline in the influence of the Christian religions on public life within Western countries.

Unique form of political secularisation in Australia

Sociologists often fail to note the *unique form* that political secularisation takes in this country. In consequence, they are prone to misinterpret sociological data dealing with religion in Australia.[251] Political secularisation entered public life here when liberal-minded colonial administrators tried to implement a universal system of schooling. 'Public' schools were to offer an education that was 'free, compulsory and secular'. The Australian bishops had a moral objection to public education being 'secular' because, to their minds, it was unthinkable that religious practice and religious knowledge would be excluded from a proper education.

The decision of colonial administrators to opt for a secular public education system was driven *as much by pragmatism as it was by principle*, and this has remained a unique feature of political secularisation in this country. It was practically impossible in a society riven by sectarian tensions to build a public school system based on Church schools. Secularising the school system made sense in the context of sectarianism and growing pluralism. It also made sense in terms of the efficient use of very limited public funds. However, while the administrators took the pragmatic route in developing the public school system, they did not immediately follow

---

250 In the process churches also lost considerable wealth in the form of properties which were confiscated, often to fund the development of institutions in the newly formed states.
251 In our view, an Australian example of this is *The Generation Y Report* compiled by Mason et al (2006) which takes secularisation theory as its starting point.

this same route in areas such as health and social welfare, which for a longer period remained largely the responsibility of the churches.

The combination of principle and pragmatism is a distinguishing feature of secularisation in Australia. Australia did not follow the United States which established a constitutional 'wall' between Church and State. In doing so its framers sought to free people 'for religion'—theirs was a 'soft' secularism. Neither did Australia adopt any of the various ideological forms of political secularisation found in Europe at the time, which aimed to free people 'from religion'—'hard' secularism. Decisions made in Australia reflected the pragmatic nature of Australian politics and of Australian culture more generally. Primary criteria in the Australian cultural mindset are: 'Does it work?' and 'Will it succeed?'

Secularisation of knowledge

The secularisation of knowledge began when it was realised that truth can be pursued using a variety of methods of human enquiry. In this pursuit religion does not hold a privileged place. It took leaders of the Catholic Church in pre-modern Europe some time to come to this realisation. Galileo (1564–1642), who was kept under house arrest for the closing eight years of his life, was a victim of this failure on their part, as was Descartes (1596–1650) who was forced to move from Catholic France to Protestant Holland, and then to Sweden. Today we accept that there are many legitimate academic disciplines with a defining methodology. 'Truth' arrived at by one discipline needs to be respected by others, even as it is contested. This realisation sits as the heart of Western intellectual achievement.

In the modern period science replaced theology in having a hegemony over the construction of knowledge. This has in turn been undermined by the post-modern critique which points out that *all knowledge structures are based on axioms that cannot be proved*. All involve an act of faith. What distinguishes one from the other is where this faith is placed. The post-modern critique also shows how knowledge and power are related, reversing the modern conception that knowledge is power, and making the point that those with power define what knowledge is, not least by controlling the process by which knowledge is accessed, and also constructed.

The secularisation of knowledge also comes into play in Catholic education through the way it controls discourse in the various disciplines taught in the school. Since the academic disciplines are framed in secular terms, students learn to interpret the basic relationships of their life-world in secular language. The school, if it is not sufficiently careful to ensure a different result, reinforces in its learning program the discourse students encounter in everyday life in secular society. This is a challenge for teachers trained in modern academic disciplines who tend to take the modern construction of knowledge and its discourse for granted leaving many students without the language needed to articulate any form of spiritual experience. Secondly, it can mean that the language used in Religious Education classes is perceived as foreign.

Secularisation of social institutions

As societies have become more complex, their cultures adapt to meet new needs. The institutions of society then multiply as knowledge expands. Where there was once a hospital, now there is likely to be a public and a private hospital, a research institute, a university campus delivering medical education, and so on. The driving force behind the development and multiplication of institutions is the development and application of specialised secular knowledge and technologies. The dependency of social institutions on the application of specialised secular knowledge drives the secularisation process in social institutions.

The secularisation of social institutions encompasses an important dynamic. In a complex society few institutions can acquire the knowledge, expertise and technologies needed to fulfil their mission, while at the same time complying with the complex legal and statutory obligations under which they now operate. As a consequence, institutions tend to network together and are mutually supportive.

This trend applies as much to the institutional Church as to other institutions and, by implication, to schools as well. For instance, a diocese now needs to access an array of other institutions - financial, legal, insurance and so on - if it is to function effectively. It can find itself legally bound by the advice it receives from these institutions, and this may run quite counter to the message of the Gospel. This creates a dilemma that is now endemic in modern institutional life. The consequence is that Church institutions become secularised as a consequence of the networks on which they depend, and through uncritically adopting the leadership paradigms and practices of secular institutions. In some cases these paradigms are mandated by government as markers of excellence. Catholic education, in both NSW and Victoria, where processes which are aimed at *Catholic* school improvement have been largely wound back in favour of more neutral approaches, is a case in point. This is the secularisation of social institutions at work. Readers can no doubt add other examples of this form of secularisation from their own experience.

SECULARISATION AND EVANGELISATION

The relationship between secularisation and evangelisation can be conceptualised in two major ways: *as in competition*, so that any advance in one comes at the cost of the other;[252] or *as theme and counter-theme* existing in a creative tension within the school culture.[253]

The post-modern model of culture suggests that the second of these options is helpful. When it seeks to ensure peace or justice in a multi-faith community, secularisation achieves a public good.[254] However, since the Catholic school has broader aims, this is not a sufficient goal. The Catholic school seeks to empower students to evangelise the culture in which they live in a way that makes the Kingdom of God more strongly present within that culture.[255] This is an element of the unique mission of Catholic schools. The processes of empowerment and evangelisation go hand in hand. Failure in one leads to failure in the other, and so to a failure in mission.

How school and system leaders respond to the multi-dimensional challenges that secularisation presents in a Catholic school depends on the level of sophistication in their understanding of it as a phenomenon. The relationship between secularisation and evangelisation can be visualised using the diagram below.

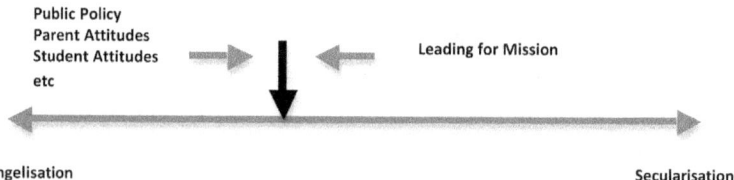

FIGURE 15.1 Relationship between Secularisation and Evangelisation

---

252 This understanding seems implied in the theoretical model that sits behind the Melbourne Scale developed by Professor Didier Pollefeyt and Mr Jan Bouwens of the Catholic University of Leuven as part of the *Enhancing Catholic School Identity Project* (Catholic Education Commission of Victoria).
253 This approach is that of Ronald Rohlheiser et al in *Secularity and the Gospel: Being Missionaries to Our Children* (New York: The Crossroad Publishing Company, 2006).
254 For instance, in both Ireland and Australia it has been the secular government that has called Church leaders to account over justice issues that have arisen from their solicitous care of delinquent priests and their lack of understanding of the damage caused to victims. In this matter the Church is seen as acting little differently from secular institutions, and this provides a counter witness to its evangelising mission.
255 The Kingdom of God is present in every culture, including Australian culture, through the work of the Holy Spirit. This is a fact not often found acknowledged in the Religious Education curriculum of Catholic schools but which has important mission consequences.

The cultural force of secularisation is balanced by the opposing force represented by efforts to evangelise the culture of the school or system. Once these efforts wane, or are taken for granted, secularisation shifts the balance in its favour.

In Western societies secularisation is a defining cultural characteristic. It is our major strategy in enabling many groups to live and work together in a peaceful way, the necessity for which is rooted in Western historical experience. While secularisation is not of itself 'the enemy' in Catholic schools and school systems, some of its consequences are problematic, particularly when educating communities do not have in place an evangelising strategy sufficiently well developed to counter-balance those consequences.[256]

EVANGELISING CULTURES: IMPERATIVE IN LEADING FOR MISSION

Our contention is that, if a school or school system does not actively seek to evangelise its structures and processes (for example, its curriculum and its pedagogy), then the relentless nature of secularisation in our society almost inevitably ensures that relationships within the school, and between the school and its client groups, will evolve around secular principles. Schools need specific 'evangelisation' strategies *to balance this secularising tendency and bring the project of the Catholic school securely under the influence of the Gospel*. Otherwise, because it has deep roots in culture, secularisation prevails. This situation requires soundly-based mission thinking.

In this chapter we have focused on secularisation as a dynamic with the ability to limit and constrain a Catholic school or system's mission. *Secularisation is a fact of modern cultural life that has to be consciously managed in Catholic schooling.* The danger of secularisation is that it suppresses religious expression, and once it becomes people's default frame of reference in making sense of the world, it imposes its limited imaginal horizon on how they understand who they are and what life is about.

The central argument of this chapter has been that, if Catholic schools are to be effective as 'Catholic', then they need to *develop specific strategies to evangelise the school's culture* and so address the otherwise limiting effects of secularisation. These strategies must address the secularisation of knowledge, particularly in the way the school curriculum is presented.[257] They must address the secularisation of politics through the way in which Catholic

---

256 In part, the commitment which the Catholic University of Leuven brings to the *Enhancing Catholic School Identity Project* being undertaken with the Catholic Education Commission of Victoria, springs from a desire on the part of the researchers to prevent a repetition of the secularisation of Catholic schools in Victoria that has occurred in Belgium.
257 Jim and Therese D'Orsa *Catholic Curriculum: A Mission to the Heart of Young People* (Mulgrave: Garratt Publishing, 2012).

social teaching is presented and lived out in school life. They must address the secularisation of social institutions by ensuring that *the school functions as a community* with a distinctive faith-based relational environment. They must also raise awareness of how secularisation creeps into the organisation as a consequence of institutional networking. In seeking to limit the effects of secularisation, it is important to identify how various factors in school life shift the secularisation/evangelisation balance point, and in which direction. Such information is essential in formulating the mission strategy of a Catholic school or system.

Different schools and systems will interpret and pursue the challenge outlined in this chapter differently, depending on the resources available. In concluding, the point we wish to emphasise is that evangelising the life of the school is not an option for school leaders; it is a pressing priority.

PRIORITIES IN LEADING FOR MISSION

PRIORITY 15.1 In leading for mission in Catholic education, it is important to understand both the positive and the negative values at work in the process of secularisation, particularly in the secularisation of knowledge.

Secularisation is a multi-valent concept that is not well understood even whilst its effects are felt. It finds particular expression in the modern worldview and enters education via the influence this has had on the construction of knowledge, and what are generally held to be legitimate methods of human enquiry. During modernity, for many people, science replaced religion as the legitimator of what was true. In post-modern times the position of science as legitimator of knowledge is challenged by the post-modern critique that holds that all knowledge systems are based on sets of axioms that, in the end, cannot be proven.

Continuing the Conversation

- Teachers rarely think about the worldview that lies behind the subjects they teach and the construction of knowledge implicit in that worldview. This is a taken-for-granted aspect of their professional training. They can easily form the unwitting 'cheer squad' for the modern worldview without being aware of its limitations. This uncritical stance sells students short in the sense that they come to regard some forms of knowledge and of human enquiry as inherently more valuable than others in the creation of meaning.
- What value do you place on the forms of knowledge your school seeks to introduce to students? What does this say about the worldview that you bring to teaching?

- What value do you place on the methods of human enquiry included in the school's curriculum? Which are the most important ones for students to grasp, and why?
- What do you know about the modern worldview and the post-modern critique of this worldview? What impact is this critique having on the attitudes students now bring to class? And on the way teachers seek to engage students in learning? How do such developments shape the possibility of bringing the worldview of faith and that of our culture together in the student's search for meaning?

PRIORITIES IN LEADING FOR MISSION

PRIORITY 15.2 Leading for mission provides a counterbalance to the secularisation process by employing strategic approaches in evangelising the culture of the school. Such approaches need to be seen as integral to the school's mission.

Evangelisation stands as a counter-theme to secularisation in the life of any Catholic school or school system. As we have seen in this and earlier chapters, evangelisation can be construed in a variety of ways, some quite narrow, some broad. The meaning a school gives to being Catholic depends on the nature of the strategies it employs to resist those forces which result in the school becoming a more secular environment.

Continuing the Conversation

- If a school or system is to counter the impact of secularisation by adopting specific evangelising strategies, then its leaders need to be able to articulate what these are. They must also be able to articulate the strategic choices they make in seeking to evangelise the culture of the school (or school system). This is crucial in assessing the quality of the mission thinking of Catholic educational leaders.
- What are some of the specific strategies that your school (or school system) uses to offset secularisation of the school culture? What understanding of being Catholic is implicit in these strategies? Is this adequate to the mission situation of the school?
- What resources are currently available in your school system to help leaders adopt a coherent model of evangelisation and develop a strategic approach in combating the negative impacts of secularisation? As it appears in the classroom? In school policy? In the way decisions are made at the school?

16
'DOING THEOLOGY':
A PROCESS OF MEANING-MAKING

The process of theological reflection, popularly termed 'doing theology', is a method of theological enquiry that addresses the challenge of meaning-making. It seeks to bring together human experience, faith and culture, in dealing with the pastoral problems that lie at the core of mission in a local context. It is therefore regarded as a form of local, and also contextual, theology. Mastering the skills involved in doing theology is an important priority in leading for mission. In exploring the topic, we draw together many of the insights from earlier sections. While theological reflection is often used for addressing pastoral problems within a community, it has equal utility in dealing with issues arising from the relationship of the Christian community with the wider world.

Doing theology is both a skill that is integral to religious meaning-making and one which has been undervalued in the Catholic tradition. For many leaders, theology is not something you do, but something you learn. However, as we have shown in Chapters 5 and 6, the various leadership heritages in the New Testament all grew from leaders actually doing theology in creative ways, in the face of pastoral and missional challenges. 'Doing theology' explores the religious significance of our actions. 'Doing theology' and 'mission' are therefore allied concepts because it is mission that gives religious significance to the actions of a leader.[258]

At the outset it needs to be made clear that *there are many ways of doing theology*, and every hard-working Christian leader is likely to have at least an implicit method within his or her leadership skill set. However, the aim here is to provide an *explicit method* readily accessible to all leaders.

When practical theologians talk about theological reflection, they do so in terms of model and process.[259] The model identifies the elements

---

258 For an introduction to theology as something leaders do, see Clemens Sedmak *Doing Local Theology: A Guide to Artisans of a New Humanity* (Maryknoll NY: Orbis, 2002).
259 This usage is different from that used in discussing models in earlier chapters where a model is thought of as a composite of framework and processes, in which the framework makes

Doing Theology

that need to be brought together so that the process leads to meaningful outcomes. While a model can give rise to a number of processes, in this chapter we focus on a particular process which has proved its value as a good starting point for school leaders.

MODEL FOR DOING THEOLOGY

A sound model for theological reflection needs to respect two matters: the nature of *the meaning-making process; and the people involved*. It is accessible to both individuals and groups. Theological reflection is not confined to what the leader does, but often needs to involve the leadership team as well. It is a skill to be shared.

Respecting the meaning-making process

If a model is to respect the meaning-making process, then it has to bring together the worldview of culture and the worldview of faith, as trusted traditions of meaning, into critical dialogue in making sense of human experience. James and Evelyn Whitehead, in their seminal study, Method in Ministry, present a model which meets this criterion.[260] This is set out schematically in the diagram below.

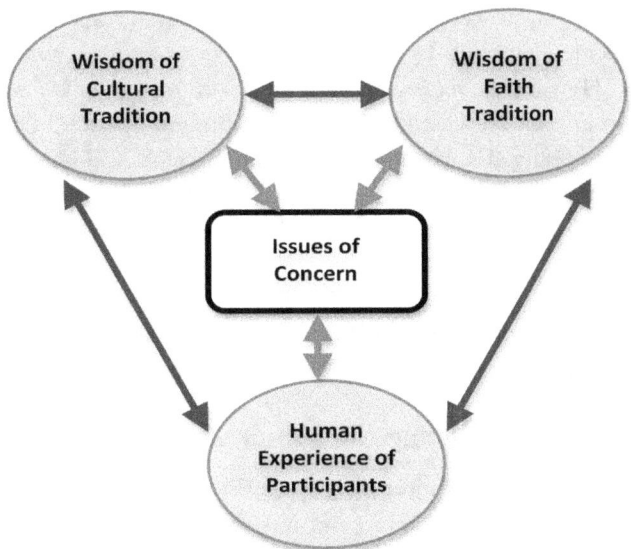

FIGURE 16.1 Model of Theological Reflection (After Whitehead and Whitehead 1995)

---

the processes meaningful.
260 James and Evelyn Whitehead *Method in Ministry: Theological Reflection and Christian Ministry*, revised edition (Kansas City: Sheed and Ward, 1995).

The model suggests that, in trying to make sense of any pastoral situation, it is necessary to bring the human experience of those involved into a critical engagement with the interpretive systems of both culture and faith, being aware that these are related, rather than independent, sources of wisdom. It is important to keep in mind that the starting point in theological reflection is *the human experience of the participants*. Theological reflection is a method of human enquiry into the complex problems of life. It stands as a resource comparable to other forms of enquiry used in the search for meaning, and has generated a vast body of theological knowledge. However, theology is too often understood as this actual body of knowledge, that is, as a product, while the process by which it was created goes largely ignored. In leading for mission, it is particularly important for the lay Catholic educator, as a new class of leader, to reclaim this aspect of the Church's theological heritage.

The model represented in Figure 16.1 indicates that, in looking at an issue of concern, any useful process of theological reflection will acknowledge the human experience of the people involved in the issue. Secondly, at some point in the process, it will seek to access the wisdom of the faith tradition—what does the Gospel or Catholic teaching say to this experience? Thirdly, it will explore what the knowledge base of our culture has to say as well—are there sociological, psychological, historical, anthropological or other issues being played out here that we need to consider? How do the frameworks and processes used in these disciplines help us to understand what is going on? Exploring the matter in this way opens up the issue and tends to highlight the strengths and limitations in the different worldviews that participants bring to making sense of the issue of concern. In a group situation the model requires that people enter into dialogue about the matter, conscious of the biases they bring to this process. At the practical level, the model suggests that, if the leader is to escape being trapped in the hermeneutical circle, discussed in Chapter Ten, he or she will generally *require a dialogue partner*.

Respecting the people involved

Theological reflection is something in which all leaders must engage if they are to be meaning-makers, and is a skill that needs to be shared with others. The process we have outlined below is an adaptation of the See–Judge–Act process which has a long history in Catholic Action where it has proved both accessible and very helpful. While theological reflection is important in individual reflection, *its power is best seen in a group situation*. There it can serve to open up dialogue among people who hold a variety of views, and help them understand one another, which is often a condition of working towards a consensus on important matters.

While consensus is often taken to mean people agreeing on everything, this is a limited understanding. In complex cultures where people value and pursue competing 'goods', consensus often has to do with establishing conditions under which groups can pursue a good without people holding different views interfering with or opposing their efforts. Building consensus is about respecting people and creating a space for difference. Being able to access a formal process to move in this direction is an important resource in leadership. Theological reflection (doing theology) is vital in mission thinking, precisely for this reason. Mission is a term that bridges difference. We echo Jesus' words - 'in my Father's house there are many dwelling places' (Jn 14:2) in saying that 'in God's mission there is scope for all'. Leaders often have to work with staff to discover what this scope actually is!

See-Judge-Act as a paradigm in theological reflection

As we have introduced school leaders to theological reflection, we have trialed a number of processes to find one that they can readily use. Having grown up with the See-Judge-Act model introduced by Cardinal Cardijn, we have learned, across a career in Catholic education, to appreciate its utility. The model has a long pedigree in Catholic social thought. It was endorsed by Pope John XXIII in his encyclical *Mater et Magistra* (1961) as a means of 'reading the signs of the times', which in Catholic discourse is often longhand for 'doing theology'.

There are three stages which should normally be followed in the reduction of social principles into practice. First, one reviews the concrete situation; secondly, one forms a judgement on it in the light of these same principles; thirdly, one decides what in the circumstances can and should be done to implement these principles. These are the three stages that are usually expressed in the three terms: look, judge act (#236).

The model is still widely used around the world by the Young Christian Workers (YCW) and other Catholic groups with a focus on those forms of evangelisation that deal with justice issues requiring the restoration of fractured relationship.

As used by the YCW, the process is sometimes reduced to nine questions:

SEE

- What exactly is happening?
- What is this doing to people? (the consequences)
- Why is this happening? (the causes)

JUDGE

- What do you think about all this?
- What do you think should be happening?
- What does your faith say?

ACT

- What exactly is it that you want to change? (long-term goal)
- What action are you going to take now? (short-term goal)
- Who can you involve in your action?[261]

As is the case with many models of theological reflection, the emphasis is on applying faith to life. This is good as far as it goes. However, many models *ignore the role culture plays in how people make sense of life*. For instance, this problem exists in the Christian praxis model of Thomas Groome, which Catholic educators have used for many years to help students make sense of their life experiences in the light of faith. There is a major danger in taking culture for granted. When this occurs, processes of theological reflection ignore the biases (good and bad) that culture brings to any discussion. Cultural biases shape how a leader 'reads' situations—what he or she sees, or fails to see. While it can be argued that culture is dealt with implicitly in a process such as the one above, the process fails to address the key criterion that a sound process respects the meaning-making process.

In a secular society, culture provides people with a default frame of reference that is secular. This is the starting point for how most people interpret situations. Secularity frames what they see and do not see. What theological reflection invites us to do is to acknowledge this, and to critique its adequacy as a starting point. It does this by exploring what the wisdom of our faith tradition has to say. However, the wisdom of our faith tradition also has its limitations. It contains biases which are cultural in origin, since the faith of an individual or community always develops within culture and has to be expressed through the medium of culture.

The dialogue between faith and culture therefore needs to be two-way. Theological reflection opens up the possibility that faith can grow, and culture can be evangelised *as human concerns are addressed*. For this to happen, as the Whiteheads point out, it is necessary to 'befriend' both the wisdom of our faith tradition and the wisdom of our cultural tradition, that is, to

---

261 This version of the process was promoted in Australia by the chaplain to the YCW, Fr Hugh O'Sullivan. See http://www.hughosullivan.com/home. The website also gives a broad introduction to the model and to the life of its originator and links to other websites. One link http://cardijnresearch.blogspot.com.au/2012/10/seek-judge-act-sertillanges-side-of.html traces the model back to the teaching of Thomas Aquinas on the virtue of prudence.

engage with them critically, but loyally.[262] To 'befriend' is to take what Paul Sharkey, in Chapter 11, has called a post-critical stance to both faith and culture. This requires study as well as experience.

PROCESS FOR DOING THEOLOGY

Theological reflection was reclaimed as an important element in theological education in the late twentieth century. This development began in Catholic circles under the rubric of pastoral theology, and in Protestant circles under the rubric of 'practical theology'. It is now an established part of ministry training in both Catholic and Protestant churches.[263]

Theological reflection as practical theology

The process outlined below draws on the work of Richard Osmer[264] (Protestant) and Patricia O'Connell-Killen[265] (Catholic). The basic framework, breaking the process of theological reflection into 'moments', derives from Osmer. We have added to this the 'focusing moment' which is pivotal in the work of O'Connell Killen and de Beer.[266]

Process in outline

The process endeavours to bring faith, culture and life together in six 'moments', each of which has a defining question. First we set out the process in overview and then expand this in detail.

- STEP 1 The Descriptive Moment. Guiding question:
  What is going on here?
- STEP 2 The Interpretive Moment. Guiding Question:
  Why is it going on?
- STEP 3 The Evaluative Moment. Guiding Question: What should be going on? What is the preferred future we want to achieve?
- STEP 4 The Focusing Moment. Guiding Question:
  What precisely do we need to respond to?
- STEP 5 The Response Moment. Guiding Question:
  What actions/steps do we now need to take?
- STEP 6 The Review Moment. Guiding Question: How effective has our response been?

---

262 Whitehead & Whitehead, 9 ff.
263 See for instance Australian Catholic theologian Terry Veling *Practical Theology: 'On Earth as it is in Heaven'* (Maryknoll N.Y: Orbis, 2005) and from the U.K. Elaine Graham, Heather Walton & Frances Ward *Theological Reflection: Methods* (London: SCM Press, 2007). These outline a range of processes for doing practical theology.
264 Richard Osmer *Practical Theology: An Introduction* (Grand Rapids: W. B. Eerdmans, 2008).
265 Patricia O'Connell Killen and John De Beer *The Art of Theological Reflection* (New York: Crossroad Publishing Company, 1994).
266 O'Connell Killen and De Beer, 63.

The final step leads back to the first, particularly when the response does not lead to the outcome that people had initially hoped for. The method is a form of *praxis* that may run over several cycles. The process can proceed iteratively until the preferred future or some re-negotiated form of it is achieved. There is no assumption that a concern will be resolved first time around.

Process in detail

The process of theological reflection is compatible with the see-judge-act model. In outlining the process in detail below we have superimposed this model over it.

When set out in detail, the process can look daunting, but then, so too does swimming or skiing for adult beginners! As with most skills, the process has to be mastered, but once it is, then it becomes more or less automatic. *A leader learns to do theology by doing it.* Reading about how to do it is simply getting to the starting block!

SEE

STEP 1 The Descriptive Moment (What is going on here?)

Comment

This is the *pre-critical* stage. The aim is to describe the situation, including the feelings generated among the participants and the values at play. This description needs to be done, as far as is possible, *in non-judgemental terms*. Most people find that this is quite difficult. Very often, from the outset, they automatically impose value judgements on their interpretation of events. The process aims to stop this happening, or when it does happen, to identify the subconscious biases that are being brought to the table. The 'moment' seeks to establish 'the facts of the matter'.

Process

Look at the situation and describe its key features.

STEP 2 The Interpretive Moment (Why is it going on?)

Comment

This is the *critical stage* in which faith, culture and life have to be brought into dialogue so that the meaning of what is happening is clearly articulated. In dealing with any issue of concern, people subconsciously bring a perspective to bear in making sense of it. In a secular society this perspective will draw on secular sources, because our primary frame of reference in making sense of life is our culture. Step 2 seeks to surface this initial bias and to critique it, not with reference to faith, but with reference to what else the culture might have to offer. Having established this, Step 2 then brings faith into play *as a qualifying factor*. The wisdom of our faith tradition has something more or different to offer which may be helpful. This creates the possibility of dialogue between faith and culture in making sense of human situations *for the benefit of those caught up in them*. Theological reflection seeks practical outcomes using the best resources available.[267]

Process

Consider the following questions:

A. How are people currently making sense of the situation? What frameworks are being brought into play in making sense of this situation, and what are the strengths and weaknesses of these?

B. What other frameworks could be brought into play, sourced in our cultural knowledge base? For instance, anthropology suggests exploring the role culture may play in the situation. Psychology suggests making sense of situations by taking into account human development issues. Sociology suggests the need for careful social analysis in making sense of the situation.

C. How can we make sense of the situation using the resources of faith? For instance, what relationships are compromised by the situation, and what could 'bringing the Kingdom to bear' mean in improving the situation? Or again, who is being marginalised in this situation? How? Why? Where are faith and culture aligned/misaligned in the way the situation is being interpreted?

JUDGE

Step 3 The Evaluative Moment (What should be going on? What is the preferred future we should strive to achieve?)

Comment

In Step 3, the aim is to bring imagination and feeling (in the form of hope) into the reflection so that it can move from the head to the heart. Most people bring to the discussion some conception of what should be going on, usually based in their experiences. This could be a resource, but needs

---

[267] This orientation is why it often carries the name 'practical theology'.

to be tested. One way of doing this is to see if it will facilitate movement towards what people imagine the preferred outcome to be. Again, having established what culture has to offer, the process provides a dialogue partner and a challenge to the imagination, by bringing the wisdom of faith to bear as a qualifying factor. The genius of Jesus' Kingdom of God motif is that it remains a permanent challenge to the human imagination.

Process

Consider the following questions:

A. What outcomes do we want to achieve in addressing this situation? What is the preferred future?
B. When we analyse this preferred future, what norms are being implied in the way we imagine this?
C. What do faith criteria suggest should come into play in addressing this situation?
D. How do faith and cultural criteria align/misalign with each other in deciding what the preferred outcome should be?

STEP 4 The Focusing Moment (What precisely do we need to respond to?)

Comment

Any process of theological reflection involves discernment, in which there is a sorting out of the essential from the non-essential. O'Connell Killen and De Beer call this getting to 'the heart of the matter'.[268] In discernment the aim is often to see through symptoms to causes, so that actions can be directed to what really counts. In this the leader has to be prepared to sense that God is at work when people of good will set out to address significant human issues. As we have seen earlier, this belief has been part of the Christian leadership tradition from the sub-apostolic age. Prayer has an important place in theological reflection. It often gives leaders the confidence to trust their intuition in discerning what lies at the heart of complex issues. While it is possible to arrive at the heart of the matter through logical analysis, this by no means exhausts the possibilities.

O'Connell-Killen and De Beer suggest an alternative method. To sit with the results of Steps 1 to 3 and wait for an image to arise. Then to put questions as to why that particular image arises. This can be quite powerful. In one of her seminars, O'Connell Killen led a group of female leaders involved in Catholic ministry in theological reflection. As one of them

---

268 O'Connell Killen and De Beer, 80.

reflected on the heart of the matter, the image that arose was of herself standing in a river, dying of thirst. One can only puzzle at the meaning this image held for her.[269]

Having discerned what the heart of the matter is, it is important also to discern what the first step should be in addressing it. Sometimes this involves estimating people's readiness to respond. The first step may involve creating the conditions under which direct action will become possible. Readiness is an important issue in planning effective action. It often requires consciousness-raising.

Process

Consider the following questions:
A. What is the heart of the matter? Start with your own intuitions and test these out against colleagues who have shared in the reflection.
B. What is the first step that needs to be taken in formulating a response?
C. Does the situation warrant direct action or are there readiness factors that need to be addressed before this can be affected? What are they? What strategy do we need to adopt to prepare the way for direct action?

ACT

Step 5 The Response Moment (What do we need to do?)

Comment

The aim in this step is to identify the steps that have to be taken to arrive at the 'preferred future'.

Process

Consider the following questions:
A. What is the plan?
B. Who needs to be involved in developing it?
C. Who needs to be involved in adopting it?
D. What resourcing will be required in implementing the plan?
E. Who needs to be involved in implementing the plan? When? How?

---

269 O'Connell Killen and De Beer discuss the role that feeling and image play in theological reflection, 37. See also Patricia O'Connell Killen *Finding Our Voices: Women, Wisdom and Faith* (New York: The Crossroads Publishing Company, 1997).

Step 6 The Review Moment (How effective has our response been?)

Comment

All interventions have an outcome, and this needs to be assessed in the light of original intentions. This can then be used to reformulate the intervention.

Process

Consider the following questions:
A. What outcomes did our action produce?
B. In what ways do these outcomes move us towards the preferred outcome? In what ways has it become more achievable? More elusive? Why is this the case?
C. Has our discernment of the heart of the matter proved accurate?

In addition to reviewing the process and revealing the sometimes unstated assumptions that lie behind it, the last step also leads back to the first. As set out above, the model can appear daunting at first sight, as we acknowledged earlier, but with practice it becomes relatively easy.

Key features of this model are:

- drawing attention to the innate biases leaders often employ in reading 'the facts of the matter' (Step 1)
- getting to the heart of the matter. The leader formulates a response based on structured questions, and putting trust in his or her own intuitions and the guidance of the Spirit. Prayer is an important component in Step 4.
- bringing together the resources of culture and faith. The process does this at two important levels. Firstly, in making sense of the situation (Step 2) and, secondly, in determining the criteria required to frame an adequate response (Step 3).[270]
- bringing imagination to bear both in framing a preferred outcome and in getting to the heart of the matter. While the process certainly uses the head, it also seeks to involve the heart.

The above process can be used by the leader in attempting to make sense of a complex situation. It can also be used by a leadership group, or as a structured way to work through challenges and conflicts. With experience it can be abbreviated, but initially people find that it is necessary

---

270 The process can be used by the leader in attempting to make sense of complex situations. It can also be used by a leadership group, or as a structured way to work through conflicts. With experience it can be abbreviated, but initially people find that it is necessary to cover all steps.

to cover all steps. The model has the advantage of being anchored to a sound hermeneutical base. However, we repeat, that it is one of many methods which leaders have found useful in bringing faith and culture into conversation in addressing life issues.

In Part C of this study (Chapters 8–10) we explored three questions: How do we make meaning? What roles do faith and culture play in meaning-making? How can educational leaders employ these understandings in real life situations? In answering the first two questions, we have utilised moderate hermeneutics as a guide to making meaning. However, it is in answering the third that we see why meaning-making in context lies at the heart of mission thinking. It is also why we argue that theological reflection, as a method of human enquiry, lies at the heart of leadership in Catholic schools and school systems. It provides a key skill both in evangelising culture and moderating the negative effects of secularisation.

PRIORITIES IN LEADING FOR MISSION

PRIORITY 16.1 In leading for mission, it is necessary that leaders master the skills of 'doing theology'.

A condition of doing theology is that those involved in the process have developed a post-critical understanding of both their faith tradition and their cultural tradition. This implies that opportunities for achieving this are structured into the planning of school system authorities with regard to the development of their leaders, and not left to chance.

Continuing the Conversation

Return to the Case Study at the end of Chapter 10 and use the method of theological reflection outlined above to explore it.

- What, in your analysis, is the 'heart of the matter'?
- How should the Principal respond to the situation?

17
SECURING MISSION: THE ENDURING CHALLENGE

As Catholic school leaders stand on the threshold of a new era in Catholic education, the enduring challenge they face lies in securing the quality of mission thinking in the communities and organisations that they lead. In liminal eras meaning is an issue that moves to centre-stage. The pervasive sense of anxiety which characterises human communities at such times arises because *older meanings lose their interpretive power and, with this, their capacity to direct action*. Taken-for-granted assumptions, those on which a group's culture has been constructed, are challenged by historical developments and consequent changes in human aspiration. In liminal eras new mission needs arise which demand a change in mission thinking. These needs may be sourced in religious concerns, or in cultural concerns. In our time they are driven by the confluence of both.

Irrespective of the source, in all liminal eras there are calls for change by those seeking to return to clear and certain ground. These calls are often strident and unpredictable. With regard to Catholic education in our time, the shape of the changes sourced in cultural movements is beginning to emerge more clearly. However, those which emanate from the religious outlook of parents and students are not as well understood, and are yet to be sufficiently confronted. How these two manifestations of deep change will intersect and interact in shaping the culture of Australian Catholic schools into the future is still an open question, but one with which the present group of predominantly lay leaders will have to deal. Negotiating the challenges of the times will create some major changes in the culture of Catholic schooling, if history is used as a guide.

RECONTEXTUALISING MISSION

In a liminal era schooling, which is the means through which society has access to all young people, becomes a battleground for those wishing to project particular agendas into public and ecclesial policies. At the present time, for instance, secularists have been particularly active within society, as have those within the Church seeking to restore a previous way of 'being Catholic' as normative (sometimes dubbed 'restorationists').

The presence of contested meanings in the public arena has set the scene for a wider debate about the mission of schooling and the place of schools in a multi-cultural and multi-faith society. This, in turn, drives change in the culture of schooling across the board. As a consequence, many teachers are only too aware that, in recent years, there has been a substantial change in 'the way things are done around here' (school culture) as the 'education revolution' introduced by the Australian government has taken shape. Schooling has been projected into the commercial world as a marketable service with parents and students cast in the role of the school's major 'client' groups. Marketing has increasingly become an integral element within the operation of Catholic Education Offices and, in schools, the Principal is called upon to act as the chief 'salesperson'.

We have argued that, during threshold periods, as one era of Catholic education has given way to another, the mission of a school can no longer be presumed. In the two case studies we set out in Chapters 3 and 4, significant developments occurred in the culture of Catholic education as one era gave way to the next. In the first case the result was a clearer conception of what is meant by 'a Catholic school' as distinct from 'schools for Catholics' (that is, schools whose clientele were predominantly Catholic, but which existed within, rather than separate from, the mainstream provision for schooling at the time).

In the second case study, as the transition period came to a close, and government funding began to flow thus ensuring the survival of Catholic schools, an identity crisis was precipitated by the change of personnel from religious to lay. This was resolved by Catholic schools becoming overtly mission-conscious, with all that this implies, and articulating purpose in terms of mission directions to be consciously pursued by their communities over time. This could not have happened without the emergence of unique forms of inter-dependence between schools and system authorities as Catholic school systems developed their characteristic cultures.

The lesson from these case studies is that those who lead school systems have a responsibility to do all they can to understand the contours of the religious and cultural landscape, and to recognise the particular mission needs which these contexts present. In doing so they also need to keep in mind that mission is not something that exists in the abstract, but is *specific to the human contexts in which people live.*

Certain mission needs in Catholic education are defined by the Catholic community, others by the immediate school community, and still others by government. Our faith alerts us to the fact that God is at work in the best of human aspirations from whatever origin, as these are generated and reshaped by change, and leaders are called to be sensitive to the ways in which God is at work in particular communities.

Mission thinking which is concerned with making sense of the mission demands—educational, religious and cultural—of particular contexts, *requires the capacity for discernment and so for making space for God*. Secular management systems on the other hand, tend to place power and responsibility for mission predominantly in the hands of the leader. This has never been the Christian way. *Mission is the responsibility of every member of the community,* assumed through baptism when the Christian attaches him/herself to Christ and to his mission which is to bring about God's reign in all aspects of life—personal, interpersonal and societal. For disciples who seek to imitate Jesus, mission is at the heart of discipleship. It is about people, what they do and why they do it. It exists in the sphere of action, not abstraction.

Discernment in Catholic educational leadership

The Catholic school or school system finds the primary source of its mission thinking in Jesus' own mission. He went about creating 'Kingdom spaces' in the lives of people and in their human arrangements in such a way that his hearers understood what he said, and interpreted his message in terms of his actions. Word and witness worked together in the fulfilment of Jesus' mission. As we saw in Chapters 5 and 6, reflecting on the emergence of leadership heritages in the New Testament, Jesus' mission is continued through the Church community, but also through the role that the Spirit plays in the formation and transformation of cultures.

From this perspective, God has been at work over time in the life of many Catholic school communities, and God's presence is made accessible by examining the community's narrative. The consequence of the Spirit's action is that there are already significant 'Kingdom spaces' in the life of a school. The challenge for leaders is to sustain these spaces, enhance them, and create new ones as mission demands change.

Two important Kingdom spaces are *a positive relational environment* and a curriculum that is Catholic in the influence it has on the way students *develop a personal worldview through their work in the classroom*.[271] The relational environment sets the ambience for learning and personal growth and is an area in which Kingdom values need to be experienced if the school's central

---

[271] These two Kingdom spaces are explored in some detail in earlier volumes in the Mission and Education Series. *Explorers Guides and Meaning-makers: Mission Theology for Catholic Educators* (Mulgrave: John Garratt, 2010) and *Catholic Curriculum: A Mission to the Heart of Young People*. (Mulgrave: Garratt Publishing, 2012).

messages are to have credibility and effectiveness. This Kingdom space grows in importance as schools become more limited in their capacity to 'create life chances', and re-focus their educational efforts on the wellbeing of students, many of whom will be faced with the prospect of long-term under-employment, and possibly unemployment, despite completing their schooling successfully. How does the school adapt its mission to meet this emerging contingency?

Leaders also have important responsibilities with regard to how the school's curriculum assists students to access the public worldviews standing behind all meaning-making. As Paul Sharkey has argued earlier (Chapter 11), this means helping students move beyond a critical understanding of faith and culture, which often leaves them intellectually paralysed. As far as is possible in a school setting, they need to be intellectually equipped to take a post-critical stance to both their faith and cultural traditions, a project that cannot be left to chance in the school's curriculum planning. Helping students understand the fundamentals about how knowledge and meaning are constructed, and so about how people customarily make sense of life, is an important 'Kingdom space' for post-modern youth. It is a major mission need recognised by Catholic and Protestant missiologists alike.

The above considerations highlight the fact that 'the heart of the matter' in leading for mission in a liminal era is to improve the quality and scope of the mission thinking that guides leaders in Catholic schools and school systems. This is essential to sustain and also create Kingdom spaces that can transform the lives of students, teachers and parents.

MISSION THINKING, STRATEGIC THINKING, OPERATIONAL THINKING

Catholic school and system leadership involves three distinct sets of thinking skills: *operational thinking* is concerned with the day-to-day performance of the organisation and how effective this is in practice: *strategic thinking* is concerned with the effective use of resources and personnel in sustaining operations within specific timelines; and *mission thinking* is concerned with both why and how choices are made at the operational and strategic levels. The relationship is illustrated in the diagram on the opposite page.

The three forms of thinking are interdependent. Mission thinking must inform strategic thinking if the school or system is to pursue its mission in a sustainable way. At the same time mission thinking is shaped by the review of operations, and whether strategic and operational goals set in response to mission thinking have actually been achieved in practice (or need to be re-negotiated). Strategic thinking seeks to translate mission goals into sustainable projects and programs within agreed resource limits

FIGURE 17.1 Mission Thinking, Strategic Thinking and Operational Thinking

and timeframes. As such it sets the timelines and resources within which operations are planned and implemented. The day-to-day experience of running a school or school system also influences strategic planning which has to take into account the readiness and willingness of staff to implement policies, projects and programs.

Mission thinking, strategic thinking and operational thinking clearly require different types and levels of skill. These skills exist, or need to exist, at various levels in the organisation, and the wise leader sets out to ensure that there is a critical mass of people in the organisation with the requisite skills. This is the necessary price that must be paid to ensure the organisation can pursue its mission in a sustainable fashion.

On the other hand, if mission is presumed, that is taken for granted because the school is 'Catholic', then the thinking that goes on in schools and school systems changes. Strategic thinking quickly becomes geared to sustaining operations rather than mission, and so operations often take on a life of their own. The new situation is set out in the diagram below which charts the present reality in too many Catholic organisations, a situation which is often the by-product of history!

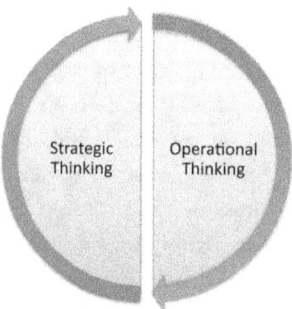

FIGURE 17.2 Leadership Thinking When Mission is Presumed

MISSION THINKING: VITAL ELEMENTS

How then can mission thinking be delineated? We suggest that mission thinking includes the following elements:

Mission thinking is interpretive

The mission thinker is aware of the movements of thought, feeling and aspiration that have currency in the cultural and faith contexts in which the school or school system exists, and how these movements impact on the educational, relational and religious domains of group life.

The mission thinker is also aware of Jesus' strong words to the Pharisees and Sadducees, and by extension to those Christian disciples to whom the *Gospel of Matthew* was addressed, about their inability 'to read the signs of the times' (Matt 16:3). In official Catholic theology, 'reading the signs of the times' is equated with discerning the Spirit at work in societies, in human history and in the life of Christian communities.[272] The skill of reading the signs of the times has an associated knowledge base that leaders need to master. This includes such areas as mission theology, the fundamentals of hermeneutics (how people come to make sense of their lives) and cultural anthropology (how culture functions and how it can be shaped), and the capacity to reflect theologically. These are not areas that feature prominently in Catholic school leadership programs currently.

The interpretive element in mission thinking comes into play when leaders set out to recognise and create 'Kingdom spaces' within the cultural milieu of the school so that students, staff and parents can actually experience the reality of God at work in the life of the community. This experience then becomes their invitation to create, in their turn, Kingdom spaces in their own lives, in those of their families, among their friends, at the local parish, and in the wider community. For this to occur, young people need to develop confidence in their own worth, recognise that they have talents, and be encouraged to develop a mindset in which they see that their talents are best put to use in the service of others, and experience the joy and satisfaction of doing so. The relational environment of a school provides an important context in which this can happen.

The present reality is that the Catholic school remains the *only plausibility structure for faith* that many young people and their parents encounter. How long this situation will hold is uncertain. In the face of this extraordinary mission situation, Catholic schools, systems, parishes and dioceses need to develop and strengthen forms of inter-dependence

---

272 For example *Pastoral Constitution on the Church in the Modern World (Gaudium et Spes)* #4.

that see appropriate pastoral models formulated. This is a clear mission need which is often neglected when mission, be it of school, parish or diocese, is taken for granted.

Mission thinking is imaginative and intuitive

While mission thinking requires the tools of analysis and deduction, it is not confined to them. Mission thinking is the by-product of a worldview, a characteristic way of making sense of and being in the world, in which the leader has to trust his or her own hopes and intuitions, as well as those of others, aware that these are areas in which the Spirit acts. Our belief is that the Spirit acts through the best of human aspiration so the leader has to be sensitive to movements in his or her own aspirations, those of the community, and those of the age.

Mission thinking also challenges the leader to push out the imaginal boundaries within which colleagues usually think. A focus on operational matters tends to limit imagination. The need for stability can overpower the need for development. In many cases pushing out the imaginal horizon means challenging some of the assumptions on which strategic and operational thinking are customarily based. To do this the leader, by monitoring where excellence lies in Catholic education, has to develop his or her own vision of what the 'preferred future' of the school or system can be. As an imaginative mission thinker, the leader is also aware of the power that images, rituals and symbols have in group life, and works to develop this aspect of the school modus operandi. In particular he or she employs the image of mission as journey to a preferred future in telling and re-telling the narrative of the community.

The great spiritualities of the Christian tradition provide leaders with a powerful resource in imaginative and intuitive mission thinking, one whose authenticity and utility have been tested over time. Br Michael Green has highlighted this in Chapter 12.[273]

Mission thinking is integrative

Mission thinkers are aware of the need to set balance points with respect to the major themes and counter-themes that define the life of any Catholic community. In Chapter 15 the evangelisation/secularisation tension was discussed as a culture-defining aspect of Catholic life in schools. Other tensions that shape the culture of Catholic organisations

---

[273] It is planned that this aspect of Catholic school leadership will be taken up in a later volume. *New Ways of Living the Gospel: Spiritual Traditions and Catholic Education* is due for publication in the Mission and Education series in 2015.

include community/institution, stability/development, inclusiveness/exclusiveness, local/global, and system authority/local autonomy. It is the capacity of mission thinkers to hold these tensions as 'both/and' rather than 'either/or' that makes mission thinking integrative. Quality mission thinking does not seek to polarise people or dichotomise responses to complex phenomena.

For example, school leaders like to think of their schools as communities—as groups committed to achieving agreed goals within the limits determined by shared values. This ideal draws the school to articulate its mission in a way that is contextualised, that is, matched to the needs of the immediate group. This is an important way of building a cultural identity, one that distinguishes that which is 'us' from that which is 'not us'. However, the community, despite a complete change in membership, survives over time not because it is a community, but because it is part of an institution—the Church. Without the institutional Church there would be no ongoing school community. Communities need institutional backing to survive and vice-versa. Mission thinkers are post-critical in their awareness that, not only is the Church both community and institution, but that with this come both *costs and benefits*.

Mission thinkers are also aware that local considerations, while important, do not map the universe of mission. Schools are part of a system, part of a diocese, and indeed of a universal Church, and with this comes responsibility to contribute to the mission of each. This responsibility is best met when the mission of the system is *jointly developed* and clearly articulated so that ownership is shared. This, however, is more easily said than done.

While many dioceses now have well-developed pastoral strategies in which school systems and individual schools find a ready frame of reference, this is not always the case. It has often been that there is a mismatch between the quality and focus of pastoral and mission planning at the diocesan and school levels.[274] A similar mismatch can occur between the Catholic Education Office and a school, particularly when CEOs adopt a generic rather than a contextualised approach to mission.

Mission thinking seeks to address another tension point within the faith community—that of inclusiveness/exclusiveness—by realising that, while God works through Church authorities and the Church community, God is not confined by this. Mission thinkers are able to operate 'outside the square' in engaging members of the broader community in the mission of the school. This is made possible because of the diverse forms mission can

---

274 The problem is even more acute in the mismatch that often exists between mission thinking at the parish level and the local school level, particularly when the mission of the parish is unstated.

take. In our experience, those teachers and parents in Catholic schools who are totally alienated from the institutional Church, for whatever reason, are often drawn into the Church's work by the prospect of contributing to Jesus' mission of making present the Kingdom of God. In this respect, mission thinkers are committed to dialogue in the rich way this is understood within Catholic mission theology. They are prepared to be with people, to work with people, to pray with people, and to exchange ideas, all in the interest of realising the mission of Catholic educational institutions viz to create Kingdom spaces in people's lives.

Mission thinking is contextual and future-oriented

Mission thinking is both needs-driven and values-driven. Because schools are focussed on the educational and developmental needs of young people as they progress through the school, mission thinkers are concerned with the *total effect the school has on students*, and so must be future-oriented. In reading the signs of the times, the leader seeks to identify the mission needs that exist in a particular environment, and the characteristic ways in which God works in that community as reflected in the values which underpin its culture. Needs and values are the currency of mission thinking.

Values provide sources of motivation in addressing mission needs because their articulation resonates with the aspirations that drive teachers to strive for excellence. They also tap into the lived experience of God at work empowering people in the service of the Kingdom. Local cultural values are lived by the members of a community, and are shaped by, and also shape, the attitudes and beliefs shared by the community across time. Being able to identify and articulate these values and the Kingdom spaces they create is an important element in mission thinking.

Contextualising the mission of a school is the prelude to setting mission directions and developing a strategic plan, enabling mission needs to determine the directions for the school's development. Understanding the context requires both data processing support and interpretive skills. In this the *Enhancing Catholic School Identity* project (Chapter 11) has much to offer Catholic schools in this country. The fact that, in recent years, school staffs have developed greater facility in interpreting and using data in developing and adapting school programs means that these skills can also be applied to analysing the mission context of the school and identifying the school community's mission needs.

Many schools have yet to identity the positive values that are embedded in the culture of the school as a resource in mission thinking. Getting in touch with school culture and the 'seeds of the Word'[275] buried within it, is a prelude to transforming the culture of the school as a Kingdom space. This is what we meant when we talked of 'evangelising the culture'.[276]

Mission thinking understands Catholic tradition as plural and inclusive

For mission thinkers the richness of the Catholic tradition lies in the fact that it is a plural tradition, despite the fact that it is often presented in monochromatic terms. It is plural in its sources. God does not choose to communicate with humanity using a single voice. Even when God communicated with the people of Israel, they experienced this through a number of means and circumstances, so that different traditions of understanding arose within the one overall Tradition. The Torah was the authoritative 'voice' in the community, for the preservation of which the religious leaders carried responsibility. God also spoke through the prophets who, more often than not, delivered the message from the margins of society, or on behalf of those who lived on the margins. God's word from the margins was usually one of hope. God also spoke as the personification of Wisdom drawing from both the culture of Israel and from the wisdom of other cultures with which Israel came into contact. As scripture scholar, Walter Brueggemann has pointed out that the reason that Israel has been able to maintain its identity across millennia of turbulent history has been its ability to keep these three 'voices' (or forms of religious consciousness) in conversation and balance.[277]

Catholic theologian, Stephen Bevans and missiologist, Roger Schroeder, follow Church historian, Justo Gonzalez, in arguing that a similar dynamic is reflected in the development of Catholic theological traditions.[278] They trace three distinct ways of interpreting the Christian message that date back to the first century of the Christian Church, and go on to show how these subsequently find a voice in contemporary theological debates, creating a range of unresolved issues. In different ages one or other of these interpretations becomes dominant.

Mission thinkers are aware that there are always theological currents at work in the background of Church life. While they know that God speaks

---

275 A phrase attributed to Justin Martyr in the second century of Christianity (circa 100–165).
276 Echoing Pope Paul VI in *Evangelii Nuntiandi* #20 with regard to societal cultures.
277 A thesis developed in Walter Brueggemann *The Creative Word: Canon as a Model for Biblical Education* (Philadelphia: Fortress Press, 1982), 11ff.
278 Stephen Bevans and Roger Schroeder Constants in Context: *A Theology of Mission for Today* (Maryknoll NY: Orbis Books, 2004), 32–72. Bevans and Schroeder acknowledge indebtedness to Justo Gonzales *Christian Thought Revisited: Three Types of Theology* (Maryknoll NY: Orbis Books, 1999).

through the authoritative voice of the Church, they also listen to the voice of the prophet and discern God at work shaping the aspirations alive within cultures. They are aware that the wisdom of their faith tradition is to be encountered in all three sources.

Mission thinking is grounded in action

Leaders create meaning and interpret situations in order to effect action. As we saw earlier, theological reflection as a necessary technique in mission thinking is geared to action. In fact, mission thinking which does not lead to committed action loses its authenticity.

This unfortunately has too often been the case in Catholic school systems which adopt the generic approach to mission as discussed in Chapter 1. A pattern develops in which schools are encouraged to use generic school improvement models to develop a mission statement and strategic plan. The resulting mission statements, often beautifully produced, soon lose their authenticity, due to their lack of contextualisation, and have little salience in directing what happens in the school. Such a system strategy, while well-intentioned, circumvents rather than facilitates, mission thinking, and in practice contributes to the hegemony of operations over mission. When such a mission statement is reinforced by an appraisal system, the damage is amplified. *Mission thinking at the system level cannot replace the mission thinking that needs to occur at the local level.*

Mission thinking should not be equated with mission statements. The two are related in that the mission statement seeks to articulate and give formal expression to the mission thinking of leaders and their communities at a point in time, but 'the game moves on'. In this sense, as with strategic plans, mission statements can soon become dated. This is more likely than not to happen if mission is a topic that comes up at best once every planning cycle, and is not a frequent focus of attention.

If mission thinking is to be an ongoing characteristic of leadership, then Catholic system leaders need to formulate a way in which school leaders are *continuously compliant* in implementing a contextualised local mission. This would require a new approach to developing school improvement processes for use across a system of schools. At the heart of this endeavour lies the task of CEO and school leaders *working together* to develop a model (framework and processes) of Catholic School Improvement that is 'uncompromisingly Catholic'. The dialogue necessary to complete such a task, particularly determining what 'uncompromisingly Catholic' means in our present mission context, would have the immediate effect of elevating the quality of mission thinking. The task of implementing the model would have a similar effect over the longer term. The dialogue at this stage would have to deal with the secularising effect that government-mandated 'school review' and 'school improvement' agendas could have on the model, and how best to obviate or minimise these effects. It is our belief that this is a crucial area where action needs to take place in school systems, and where mission thinking, with a 'hard edge', must connect with school life.

In conclusion it must be said that mission thinking is not the outcome of a process. Mission thinking is what goes on in leaders' minds and hearts, day in and day out, in the ongoing quest to create Kingdom spaces in school life, given all that this can mean for a particular group of students, teachers and parents. As Jesus' mission engagement shows us very clearly, mission is about people and how they experience and make sense of their lives. Leadership and mission come together in the influence that people have on other people in establishing and nurturing God's reigning presence. Kingdom spaces continue to be created and re-created as people find meaning and purpose in their lives through their service to others. The dignity of leadership in Catholic education is that leaders co-operate with God in bringing this about. The challenge of leadership is much greater in a liminal era when no one really knows how and when the process of transformation will end, or indeed what may be its outcome. What they do know from New Testament times, and from our own Catholic educational story, is that: when quality leaders collaborate with those who treasure the community's mission as they do themselves, and move intelligently forward trusting in God's providential Spirit, the outcomes can be extraordinary.

INDEX

NOTE: page numbers followed by 'n' refer to footnotes

A

abuse 228n
action, in mission thinking 254–5
Acts of the Apostles *see* Luke–Acts
Ad Gentes (Vatican II) 101
Address to Aboriginal Peoples and Torres Strait Islanders (Pope John Paul II) 104n
ambiguity 200
American Revolution 31
anthropology, post-modern
    anti-functionalist 130–1
    post-structuralist 130–1
apostolic period 67
    duration of 64n
    leadership in 71–8
Aquinas, St Thomas 236n
Arbuckle, Gerald 131
    on liminality 20
    on social dramas 29
Archbishop's Charter for Catholic Schools (Archdiocese of Hobart) 213n
Australian Catholic University (ACU) 189–202
Australian Centre for Educational Research (ACER) 3
authenticity 161
authority 86–7

B

balance points 132–40, 250–2
Baldridge Education Framework 208
baptism 246
Barth, Karl 103
beloved disciple 89–90
Benedict XVI, Pope 162–3
    on being Christian 162–3
    on presentation of Catholic tradition 170
Bevans, Stephen 66n, 103n, 253
biases 149–50
    cultural 124–5
    in high culture 116–17
Bible
    interpretation of 73
    reading of 36, 38, 48, 163
bishops
    role of, in relation to Catholic education 2, 36, 38–9, 41, 43, 44, 46, 47, 62, 194, 225
Bishops of NSW and ACT 4, 169n
Blair, Tony 117n
Bligh, Governor William 32
Bosch, David 66n, 103n
Bouwens, Jan 165, 169n
Brisbane *see* CEO Brisbane
Britain in 18th–19th centuries 31, 32, 33
British Colonial Office 31, 32–3, 34
Brown, Raymond 64, 68, 69
    on authority in Matthew 87
    on Christians' heritage 82
    on discipleship 90
    on struggle between synagogue and early Christian community 88–9
    on triumphalism 83
Brueggemann, Walter 253
Burns, James McGregor 111
Byrne, Thomas 34

C

Canavan, Br Kelvin 204
Cardijn, Cardinal Joseph 50
Carroll, Auxiliary Archbishop James 54n
Castle Hill Rebellion (1804) 31n
Catechesi Tradendae (Pope John Paul II) 221n
catechesis 221
Catholic, being 12–13
Catholic Action 48n, 49, 50
Catholic Building and Finance Commission 54
Catholic chaplains *see* clergy
Catholic Church in Australia
    first recorded Mass 31n
    official establishment of 31n, 35n
Catholic culture 47–8, 49

Index

changes in 23–4
see also Catholic identity
Catholic culture, post-modern 139
Catholic education
  in 18th–19th centuries 30–34
  in 1960s and 1970s 52–59
  culture of 52
  demands impinging on 57–8
  evangelising mission of 224
  founding mythology of 28–45
  fundamentals of 36, 43–4
  implementation difficulties relating to 36–7
  and life chances 49–51
  mission as integrating agent in 95–110
  mission of 48, 49, 50, 58
  moral purpose of 200
  in New South Wales 53–4
  notion of 36–8
  planning of 52
  as social drama 16–63
  tenets of 38–9
  transition eras in 2–5
  in Victoria 55–7
Catholic Education Advisory Committee (Melbourne) 55
Catholic Education Commission of Victoria (CECV) 3, 56, 158, 228n
Catholic education leadership
  discernment in 246–7
  profile of 195
  see also education system leadership
Catholic Education Offices 194
  Brisbane 3
  development of 62
  Melbourne 55, 56, 57
  New South Wales 54, 57
  Sydney 203–15
  see also Catholic Education Commission of Victoria (CECV)
Catholic education systems
  changes in 193–4
  diversity in 194
Catholic ethos 196
Catholic identity 12–13, 58–9, 158–72, 195–6
Catholic life in the 1960s 48–52
The Catholic School (Congregation for Catholic Education) 9, 59
Catholic school cultures
  evangelisation of 220–31
  shaping of 25–6
Catholic school leaders, questions for 25

The Catholic School on the Threshold of the Third Millennium (Congregation for Catholic Education) 169n
Catholic school systems
  cultures of 24
  effectiveness of 208–12
  first system 39–41
  management in 204–5
Catholic schools
  and Catholic tradition 158–72
  challenges for 176–8
  diversity in 166–8
  effectiveness of 208–12
  emergence of, from denominational schools for Catholics 28–45
  identity of 59, 158–72
  leadership of, in 1970s 59
  mission of 17, 60
  renewal in 61
  and service 139–40
  see also Catholic identity
Catholic Schools at a Crossroads (Bishops of NSW and ACT, and CEO Sydney) 4, 169n
Catholic separatism 47–8, 50
Catholic Social Studies Movement 48
Catholic tradition
  and Catholic schools 158–72
  in mission thinking 253–4
  see also Catholic identity
Catholic University in Leuven 3, 158, 228n
'Catholic wall'
  collapse of 62
  life beyond 49–59
  life within 47–8
CEO Brisbane 3
CEO Melbourne 55, 56, 57, 211
CEO Sydney 4, 169n, 203–15
  management model of 205–6
  system development model of 206
  challenges, and mission thinking 217–19
Champagnat, St Marcellin 180, 182, 183
change, critical response to 22, 23
  see also liminal eras; liminality
charismic
  application of term 175n
charismic culture, building and sustaining of 184–6
'charismic gap' and Catholic education leaders 179–80
charismic movements and liminal eras

257

173–87
Christian Brothers 191, 194
Christian identity 71
   see also Catholic identity
Christology 88
Church 164
   as faith community 139
   as global institution 139
   and God 9
   institutionalisation of 81n
   and Kingdom of God 8
   meaning of 68, 81n
   and mission 7–9
   nature of 9
   role of 103
The Church and Cultures (L. Luzbetak) 114n
The Church the Apostles Left Behind (R. Brown) 64, 68
'civilisation' 115
clergy 35, 62
   role in early 19th century 32–3
   see also bishops
co-education 54n
collegiality 214
Colloquium on the Ministry of Teaching (Jesuit Secondary Education Association) 61
colonisation 96
'command and control' regimes 199–200
'Commandments of the Church' 47
common good 133
communio 176
communism, rise of 47–8
Community of Faith (J. and E. Whitehead) 108n
complex adaptive systems thinking 197–200
Congregation for Catholic Education 9, 169n, 175n
   on living encounter with Christ 177
Connolly, Noel 97n
Conolly, Fr Philip 31n, 33
Constants in Context (S. Bevans and R. Schroeder) 66n
contexts
   influence of 26
   in mission thinking 252–3
   see also recontextualisation
control 199–200
conversation and meaning-making 165–8
   see also dialogue

co-responsibility 214
counter-themes in cultures 132–4
Covey, Stephen 111
creative adaptive systems 198, 200
The Crisis of Authority in Catholic Modernity (M. Lacey and F. Oakley, eds) 170n
crisis of meaning, addressing 25
critical engagement 164–5
Crudden, Fr Pat 56
cultural bias 124–5
cultural change
   and dialogue 126
   and leading for mission 126
cultural configuration, changes in 135–7
cultural leadership 125
cultural myths 119, 123
cultural narratives 124–5
cultural reproduction 116
cultural values 119, 132
cultural worldviews 119–20, 132
culture
   as ally in meaning-making 25
   approaches to
      functionalist 128–9
      post-modern 131–2
      structuralist 128–9
   concepts of
      anthropological 114
      empirical 114
   constructions of
      modern 113–27
      post-modern 128–41
   counter-themes in 132–4
   critiquing of 123
   dimensions of 118–20
      diachronic 132
      synchronic 132
   educational 203–4
   elements of 184
   and faith 204–5
   high 116–17
   iceberg model of 121–3
   and imaginal horizons 122–3
   in leadership 124–6
   as liability in meaning-making 26
   meanings of 9n13, 113–15, 117n, 131
   models of
      empirical 134
      modern 112, 117–20, 128–9, 130
      post-modern 112, 129–31, 134–40
      working 128–31
   and objectivity 115

organisational 114–15, 132
origin of 115
reproduction of 116
themes in 132–4
transmission of 117
views of
   classicist 115–17
   modern 114
Curriculum Improvement Process (Jesuit Secondary Education Association) 61

D

De Beer, John 237, 240
Declaration on the Relation of the Church to Non-Christian Religions (Vatican II) 101, 106–7
Decree on Christian Education (Pope Paul VI) 60n
Decree on the Missionary Activity of the Church (Vatican II) 101
denial in response to change 21, 23
denominational schools 28, 37, 38
Derrida, Jacques 129
Descartes, Rene 226
dialogue 105–7, 118, 150
and cultural change 126
inter-religious 106–7, 117n
and leading for mission 126
and meaning-making 165–8
in theological reflection 234–5
Dialogue and Proclamation (Pontifical Council for Inter-religious Dialogue) 106n
Dickenson, Fr 53n
discernment 83, 246
discipleship in John 89–90
Dixon, Fr James 31–2
Dogmatic Constitution on the Church (Vatican II) 101, 174
'doing theology' 232–43
processes for 237–43
Dominicans 174
Doyle, Fr Tom 59
Drucker, Peter 205
Duignan, Patrick 191
Duncan, William 35n

E

Ecclesiam Suam (Pope Paul VI) 106n
ecclesiology, post-conciliar 176
ECSIP Melbourne scale 169
ECSIP Victoria scale 166–8
Edinburgh World Mission Congress (1910) 103
Educating Together in Catholic Schools (Congregation for Catholic Education) 177n
education, as opposed to indoctrination 166–8
education, public *see* public education
Education Act 1852 39
Education Act 1880 42
Education Act 1961 (NSW) 53, 203
Education Act 1990 (NSW) 203–4
'Education Question' 35, 39
education system leadership 189–202
formation for 195
key matters for 200–1
teaching of 189–202
effectiveness indicators 209, 210, 213
development of 208–9
see also excellence: in schooling
effectiveness of schools and systems 229
evidence-based approaches to 208–12
see also evangelisation; secularisation
Egan, Gerard 6n6, 128
empowerment 228
enculturation 121–2
see also inculturation
Enhancing Catholic School Identity Project (ECSIP; CECV and Cath. Univ. Leuven) 3, 158–72, 228n, 252
history of 158
Enlightenment 173
eras in Catholic education *see* foundation era in Catholic education; principal eras in Catholic education; transition eras in Catholic education
'ethic of authenticity' 160–2
Evangelii Nuntiandi (Pope Paul VI) 7n8, 102, 105, 107n, 223, 253n
evangelisation 101, 105, 167, 181–2
of the Church 223–4
of culture of Catholic schools and systems 220–31
of cultures 223
and leading for mission 229–30
as the mission of the Church 223–4
and the 'new evangelisation' 222
as 'preaching' to others 220–1
and secularisation 228–9
as a stage in coming to faith 221–2
excellence
concept of 212–13
and mission thinking 212
models of 213–15

in schooling 209–12
  dimensions of 212–15
experience
  and hermeneutics 159–72
  and religion 159–72

F
Faber, Frederick 46
'fair go' 133–4
faith 204–5
  categories of 163–6
  and culture 204–5
  see also Catholic identity; 'doing theology'
faith community, pluralism within 23–4
faith development 221–2
'Faith of Our Fathers' (F. Faber) 46
faith stances *see* faith: categories of
First Fleet 31
Flagship for Creative and Authentic Leadership (ACU) 191
flocking 198–9
Fogarty, Ronald
  on Catholic denominational schools 37
'foreign mission' 99
forgiveness 87
Foucault, Michel 129, 131
foundation era in Catholic education 30–8
Framework for Leadership at the System Level in Catholic Education 191
frameworks 232n
  for learning 211–12
  in school improvement 203–16
Francis of Assisi, St 105
Franciscans 174
freedom, personal 133
French Revolution 173
Fullan, Michael 199
  on forming system thinkers 195
future, preferred 6
'The Future for a School System' (F. Martin) 56
future orientation in mission thinking 252–3

G
Gadamer, Hans-Georg 112, 158, 159–60, 163, 166, 168
Galilei, Galileo 226
Gallagher, Shaun 150
Gamble, Ian 208, 209, 210
games and meaning-making 165–8

Gaudium et Spes (Vatican II) 100–1, 117n, 249n
Geertz, Clifford 130, 160
general education *see* public education
The Generation Y Report (M. Mason et al.) 225n
Geoghegan, Bishop Patrick 36n, 39–40
Gilroy, Cardinal Norman 54
God
  and Church 9
  love of 162–3, 164
  mission of 8–9, 102–5
  power of 77
God's Mission and Post-modern Culture (J. Sivalon) 103n
Gonzalez, Justo 253
Good Samaritan Sisters 36n
Goold, Bishop James Alipius 41
Gospel, proclamation of *see* evangelisation
Gospels *see particular Gospels*
Goulburn 'strike' 54n
governments
  and education 2, 4, 21, 28–45, 52–3, 56, 58, 62, 193–4, 203–4, 208, 213, 245, 255
  see also particular Education Acts; particular governors; public education
Grace, Gerald 181
Grattan Institute 197
Gravissimum Educationis (Pope Paul VI) 60n
Greenleaf, Robert 111
  on servant leadership 78
Gregory XV, Pope 97n
Groome, Thomas 236

H
Hall, E.T. 60n
Heidegger, Martin 159
herding 198–9
hermeneutical circles 131, 149–50
hermeneutics 163
  definition of 159
  and experience 159–72
  and mission of Catholic schools 158–72
  moderate 142n, 159n
  and religion 159–72
  and strangeness and familiarity 168–71
  of suspicion 148n
  see also interpretation, in mission

thinking; meaning-making; understanding
Hermes 159
Hiebert, Paul 112, 118, 132, 144
high culture 116–17
Hine, Fr 53n
historically decisive events 45
historicising 45
Hobart, Archdiocese of 213n
Hoge, Dean 151
Holy Spirit, the 77, 78, 104, 135, 174, 187, 228n, 246
   role in Luke–Acts 82, 83
horizons of meaning 168
How Effective Is Our Catholic Education Office? (CEO Sydney) 212
How Effective Is Our Catholic School? (CEO Sydney) 210, 212
How Good Is Our School? (I. Gamble) 209
Hughes, Philip 160, 161–2
Hutsebaut, Dirk 165

I

identity 161
   Catholic 12–13, 58–9, 158–72, 195–6
Ignatius of Loyola, St 96
imaginal horizons 25–6
   and culture 122–3
imagination
   and Master of Educational System Leadership (ACU) 196–7
   in mission thinking 250
   and teaching of education system leadership 189–202
inclusivity 43
inculturation 164
   see also enculturation
indoctrination, as opposed to education 166–8
integration, in mission thinking 250–2
interdependence, intelligent 199
interpretation, in mission thinking 249–50
   see also hermeneutics; meaning-making
inter-religious dialogue 106–7, 117n
intuition, in mission thinking 250
Ireland
   in 18th–19th centuries 30, 31
   education in 36
   in mid-19th century 35

Isaiah, prophet 73, 74, 76
Israel, community of 73, 74
   exercise of power within 76–8

J

James, Anne 39
James, William 39
Jansen, C., et al. 198, 199
Jesuit Secondary Education Association (JSEA) 61
Jesuits 174
Jesus 183
   and ambition 72
   and critique of truncated understanding of God's purpose 77
   in Emmaus story 72
   Messiah 71–3, 74, 76
   mission of 6, 246
   personal relationship with 90–1, 163, 177
   prophet 77
   servant 78
   Son of God 89, 91
   and washing of feet 72
   the Jews in John 89
Johannine tradition
   themes and counter-themes in 138
   see also John, Gospel of; Letters of John
John, Gospel of 72, 235
   leadership heritage in 80–1, 88–91, 92
   polemics in 88–9
   themes and counter-themes in 138
John XXIII, Pope 235
   on presentation of Catholic tradition 170
John Paul II, Pope 221n, 222
   on dialogue 105, 106n
   on the 'Dreaming' and God's Spirit 104
   on inculturation of faith 164
   on Kingdom of God, and Church 8, 104
Johnson, Richard (Anglican chaplain) 31, 32
Josephite Sisters 40, 96n
Justin Martyr 253n

K

Kelly, Anthony 162
Kelly, Fr John F. 56
King, Governor Philip 32
Kingdom of God 6, 8–9, 78, 86, 89, 92,

101, 103, 228
  and Church 8, 104
  and mission 102, 213, 223
Kingdom spaces 246–7, 249
kings of Israel 76–7
Knights Templar 174
Knox, Archbishop James 55, 61n
Kouzes, James 111

L

La Chaise-Dieu Abbey, Le Puy 173, 186–7
Lacey, M. 170n
Law (Torah) 77, 253
lay ministry 62
  lay teachers 28, 30, 34, 39, 42, 44
  recognition of role of 52
leaders
  as keepers of the story 124–5
  as meaning-makers 142–54
leadership
  capacity for 186
  Christian traditions of
    apostolic period 71–8
    emergence of 68–71
  cultural 125
  and cultural change 126
  and culture 124–6
  and dialogue 126
  of education systems 189–202
  heritages of
    emergence of, in New Testament 67–79
    in John 80–1, 88–91, 92
    in Luke–Acts 80–4, 92
    in Matthew 80–81, 84–7, 92
  issues of
    in New Testament 70–1
    present-day 70–1
  in a liminal era 155–216
  and meaning-making 25–6
  for mission 1–15
  as service 192
  transformational 72
Learning-Centred Schools (CEO Melbourne) 211
legislation *see particular Education Acts*
Letter of Peter, First 108
Letters of John 88
  see also Gospel of John
liminal eras 19–27, 41
  in Catholic education 21, 41
  and charismic movements 173–87
  leadership in 1–5, 143, 155–216
  and meaning 5
  and mission 11
  responses to 21–4
liminality 16
  definition of 1
  experience of 19–21
  in Master of Educational System Leadership (ACU) 193–7
  and mission 25
  and spiritual families 175–80
Lismore, Diocese of 54n
'living systems' thinking 197–200
Luke, Gospel of 72, 73, 76, 182
Luke–Acts
  leadership heritage in 80–4, 92
  as narrative theology 81–2
Lumen Gentium (Vatican II) 101, 174
Luzbetak, Louis 114n
Lyotard, Jean-Francis 129

M

MacKillop, St Mary 40
Macquarie, Governor Lachlan 33
Management by Objectives (MBO) model (P. Drucker) 205–6
management in Catholic school systems 204–5
Mannix, Archbishop Daniel 48, 55
Maréchal, Claude 175n
marginalised, the 43, 86
Marion, R. 198
Marists 173–87, 191
  association of 183–4
  education by 180–6
  re-imagining life and mission of 180–6
  spirituality of 179–83
Mark, Gospel of 72
marketing 245
Martin, Fr Frank 52n, 56–7, 60n
Mary, Blessed Virgin 182
Mason, Michael 225n
Master of Educational System Leadership (ACU)
  evolution of 190–3
  and liminality 193–7
Mater et Magistra (Pope John XXIII) 235
mateship 134
Matthew, Gospel of 7, 249
  leadership heritage in 80–1, 84–7, 92, 138

mission in 84–5
pluralism in faith community 85
themes and counter-themes in 138
McKinsey Company 197
McKinsey Report 199, 208
McLay R.S.M., Sr Anne 57n
meaning
  addressing crisis of 25
  frameworks of 215
  and liminal eras 5
meaning-making 8, 65, 132, 209–12
  and dialogue 165–8
  and leadership 25–6
  and Master of Educational System Leadership (ACU) 196–7
  models of 148–52
  and play 165–8
  process of, in theological reflection 233–4
  and religion 160–2
  role of leaders in 142–54
  skills required for 26
  and teaching of education system leadership 189–202
  and theology 232–43
  in view of a dead Messiah 71–8
  see also hermeneutics; horizons of meaning; interpretation, in mission thinking
Melbourne *see* CEO Melbourne
Messiah, death of 71–6
Method in Ministry (J. and E. Whitehead) 233
migrants 51
missio Dei 103n
see also God: mission of
missiology 6
mission
  in Catholic school systems
    contextual understanding of 10–11
    generic understanding of 10–11
  and the Church 7–9
  beyond the Church 104–5
  as a construct with interpretive power 98–100
  and crisis of meaning 25
  cross-cultural 99
  cultural construction of 6
  and dialogue 10
  dimensions of 9
  expansion of, in transition eras 28–30
  forms of 98–9, 107–8, 109
  as God's mission 8–9, 102–5
  holistic notion of 99
  as integrating agent in Catholic education 95–110
  key question for 112
  leadership for 1–15
  in liminal eras 11, 25
  in Luke–Acts 81–82
  meaning of 96–7, 102, 103, 213
  modalities of 105–7, 109
  in Protestant Churches 97, 114n
  recontextualising of 25, 244–7
  as religious construct 7–9, 95–110
  securing of 244–55
  and spiritual families 178–9
  see also mission theology; mission thinking
'The Mission' (film) 98n
'Mission: Mother of the Church and of Theology' (N. Connolly) 97n
mission *ad extra* 99, 100
mission *ad intra* 99, 100
mission command in Matthew 7, 84–5
'mission drift' 178
mission framework *see* mission thinking
'The Mission Has a Church' (S. Bevans and R. Schroeder) 103n
mission *inter-gentes* 99, 100
Mission Matrix 109–10
mission statements 6, 254
mission theology
  Catholic
    before Vatican II 97–8
    in Vatican II documents 100–1
    since Vatican II 101–2
  Protestant 103, 114n
mission thinking 2, 11, 26, 95, 215
  in Catholic education systems 204–5, 209–12
  challenges for 217–19
  contours of 5–9
  elements of 249–55
  and operational thinking 247–8
  scope of 218–19
  and strategic thinking 212, 247–8
missions, the 97
models 232n
  in school improvement 203–16
  for theological reflection 232–7
moderate hermeneutics 142n, 159n
modern age 160–1
modernism 47
  see also culture: constructions of: modern

Moloney, Francis 6
  on mission command in Matthew 84–5
Morley, George 34
Murphy, Bishop Francis 39
MY SCHOOL 208
myths 119

N

NAPLAN 208
narcissism 161
narrative 84
  as limited tool in relation to leadership 83
narrative theology in Luke–Acts 81–2, 83n
narratives, cultural 124–5
National Catholic Education Association (Washington) 61
National Catholic Education Commission 191
National Civic Council 48n
national schools 41
  see also public education
needs 252
new ecclesial movements 175, 176
  see also charismatic movements and liminal eras
new evangelisation 7, 179, 221n
  see also evangelisation
New South Wales, educational culture of 203–4
New South Wales Board of Studies 203–4, 204
New Testament
  leadership heritages in 69–70
  liminality in 69
  themes and counter-themes in 137–8
Nostra Aetate (Vatican II) 101, 106–7

O

Oakley, F. 170n
objectives 205–6
objectivity and culture 115
O'Brien, Anne 52n
  on Catholic education in Victoria 55
O'Connell-Killen, Patricia 237, 240
O'Flynn, Fr Jeremiah 31n, 32–3
On Catechesis in Our Time (Pope John Paul II) 221n
On Christianity and Social Progress (Pope John XXIII) 235
On Evangelisation in the Modern World (Pope Paul VI) 7–8, 102, 105, 107n, 223, 253n
On the Church (Pope Paul VI) 106n
On the Permanent Validity of the Church's Missionary Mandate (Pope John Paul II) 8, 104, 105, 106n, 222
One Body, Many Parts (CEO Melbourne) 211
online communities 161
operational thinking 11
  and mission thinking 247–8
  and strategic thinking 247–8
organisational culture 132
Osmer, Richard 237
O'Sullivan, Fr Hugh 236n

P

Paraclete, the 77
Pastoral Constitution on the Church in the Modern World (Vatican II) 100–1, 117n, 249n
pastoral theology 97, 99, 237–43
Paul VI, Pope 7n8, 60n, 101, 102, 107n, 223, 253n
  on dialogue 106n
  on witnessing 105
Paul the apostle, St 74, 81, 96, 102
personal freedom 133
personal worldviews *see* worldviews: personal
Peter the apostle, St 81
Philippians, Letter to the 74, 76
play and meaning-making 165–8
pluralism 106n, 135, 166–8, 196
  in Matthew 85
  and post-modern model of culture 138–40
Polding, Archbishop Bede 35, 36, 37, 43
politics and Catholic Church 48n
Pollefeyt, Professor Didier 158, 165, 169n
Pontifical Council for Inter-religious Dialogue 106n
Pontifical Council for Promoting the New Evangelisation 222
Posner, Barry 111
post-critical belief 162–5
Post-Critical Belief (PCB) scale (D. Hutsebaut) 165
Postgraduate Certificate in Educational Leadership (ACU) 190, 192
post-modernism 146n, 148n, 218, 226, 228

see also culture: constructions of: post-modern
power
    in post-modern model of culture 137
    use of 132
practical theology 237–43
pre-evangelisation 221
preferred future 6
pre-understandings 149
    see also traditions of meaning
priests of Israel 77
principal eras in Catholic education
    1st (foundational) 28, 30–8
    2nd (of the religious) 28, 39–44, 46
    3rd (of the Catholic lay teacher) 28, 52–62
    4th (imminent) 29, 244–55
priorities in leading for mission 26, 44–5, 62, 79, 93–4, 109, 126–7, 140, 152–3, 171–2, 187, 202, 215, 229–31, 243
processes 232n
    in leading for mission 217–55
    in school improvement 203–16
    for theological reflection 232–3, 237–43
Propaganda Fide 97n
prophets of Israel 76–7, 253
Protestant Churches 33, 34
    mission theology in 97, 114n
Psalms 73
public education 28, 32, 33, 37, 41, 225
    birth of 34–5
public worldviews *see* worldviews: public
'pulling your weight' 133–4
Putting Life Together (P. Hughes) 161–2

Q
Quinn, Bishop James 41

R
randomness 200
reconciliation 77
reconfessionalisation 169
recontextualisation 169
Redemptoris Missio (Pope John Paul II) 8, 104, 105, 106n, 222
reign of God *see* Kingdom of God
relationships 77, 86, 92, 246
    personal relationship with Jesus 90–1, 163, 177
religion 162
    and culture 160–2
    and experience 159–72
    and meaning-making 159–72
religious (sisters and brothers) 52
    and encounter with the modern world 50
    role as teachers 42, 43, 44
    vocation levels of 51
religious congregations 62
    reformulation of missions of 60–1
    renewal in the teaching congregations 60–1
    see also charismic movements and liminal eras
religious education 62
    within the 'Catholic wall' 48
    since the 1970s 58–9
renewal, and spiritual families 178–9
'revolution of expressive disorder' 51–2
Ricoeur, Paul 112, 158, 164, 172
    hermeneutics of 163
righteousness 77, 86, 92
Roddy, Ambrose 53n
Rolheiser, Ronald 228n
Roman curia 32, 33, 35

S
sacraments 90, 246
Santamaria, B.A. 48, 57n
Schneiders, Sandra 162
school improvement 203–16, 254
    and CEO Sydney 205–7
school improvement in NSW 207
school improvement model 210
school management in NSW 207
school objectives 205–6
School of Educational Leadership, ACU 191
schools
    development of 61
    functions of 19
    mission of 19
'schools for Catholics' 245
    changed to 'Catholic schools' led by religious 28–45
    growth of, in mid-19th century 34
Schroeder, Roger 66n, 103n, 253
Scripture
    interpretation of 73
    reading of 36, 38, 48, 163
Second Vatican Council 11, 52, 57, 59n, 174
Secondin, Fr Bruno

on lay involvement in Church 187n
sectarianism 33, 43
secular education 38
secularisation 44, 167, 246
   and evangelisation 228–9
   of knowledge 224, 226
   of politics 224–6
   of social institutions 227
   sources of 224–7
Secularity and the Gospel (R. Rolheiser) 228n
See-Judge-Act method 50
   as paradigm in theological reflection 235–43
Sergiovanni, Thomas 125
servant leadership 72
   as eschatological and cultural ideal 78
Servant Songs 73–7
Service Organisation Leadership Research (SOLR) Project (P. Duignan et al.) 191
Sevenhill 40
shared direction 200
shared meaning 200
Sharratt, L. 199
Sheil, Bishop John 40
Sheil-Woods model of Catholic education 40, 41
signs of the times *see* contexts; recontextualisation
The Silent Language (E.T. Hall) 60n
Simonds, Archbishop Justin 55
Sisters of Charity 194
Sisters of St Joseph 40, 96n
Sisters of the Good Samaritan 36n
Sivalon, John 103n
Slater, Edward 35n
Slowey, Fr John 53
social advancement 49n
social change 50
social dramas 16–17, 20, 29–30
social engagement 49, 50, 51
   see also politics and Catholic Church
social media 161
social transformation 223
Songs of God's Servant 73–7
Spirit, the *see* Holy Spirit, the
'spiritual capital' 181–3
spiritual families
   and liminality 175–80
   and mission 178–9
   and renewal 178–9
spirituality 162, 184–6
   Benedictine 173

Marist 179–83
Starratt, Robert 214
State Aid campaign 54n
State funding 42
   see also governments: and education
Stewart, Bishop Bernard 57n
stories *see* narrative
strategic planning 207
strategic thinking 11, 215
   in Catholic education system 204–5
   and mission thinking 247–8
   and operational thinking 247–8
sub-apostolic period 67, 68–71
   as a liminal era 70–1
sub-cultures 114
subjectivism 161
Suffering Servant 67–79
Sydney *see* CEO Sydney
Sydney Plan 54
symbols 119, 163
system objectives 205–6
systems in Catholic education 193–4
   improvement in 203–16
      CEO Sydney 205–7

T

Tacey, David 162
Taylor, Charles 160–1
tensions *see* balance points
themes in cultures 132–4
theological reflection 232–43
   as practical theology 237–43
   processes for 237–43
theology, pastoral 97
   see also practical theology
Therry, Fr John 31n, 33
threshold experiences 20–1
   see also liminality
Tony Blair Faith Foundation 117n
Torah 77, 253
traditionalist response to change 22, 23, 198
traditions 163
   critiquing of 164
   elements in 159–60
   see also Catholic tradition
traditions of meaning 150
   alienation from 152
   befriending of 152
transformative leadership 84
transformative response to change 22, 23
Transforming Mission (D. Bosch) 66n, 103n

transition eras in Catholic education
    1st (1870s) 2, 28–45
    2nd (mid-1960s) 2–3, 46–63
    3rd (mid-2000s) 3–5
    mission expansion in 28–30
triumphalism 83
Turner, Victor
    on liminality 19–20

U

Uhl-Bien, M. 198
Ullathorne, Dr William 32n, 35
uncertainty 4–5
understanding 163, 165–6
    see also hermeneutics; interpretation, in mission thinking; meaning-making
United States of America
    Church and State in 226

V

values 6, 162, 252
    cultural 119
values education 169
Vatican II *see* Second Vatican Council
Vaughan, Archbishop Roger 41–3
vision 6
Vision and Values (National Catholic Education Association, Washington) 61

W

webs of significance 130–1, 135, 160
    building of 134
Western culture 51–2
Whitehead, Evelyn 108n, 152, 172, 233, 236
Whitehead, James 108n, 152, 172, 233, 236
Who's Coming to School Today? (CEO Brisbane, and ACER) 3
wisdom
    of Catholic tradition 64–110, 253
    of our cultural tradition 111–54
witness 90, 105
women in the Church 91
Woods, Fr Julian Tenison 39, 40–1
works of the Church 176
worldviews 119–20, 146n
    modern 148, 151
    personal 246
        dimensions of 144
    role in meaning-making 143–5
    post-modern 146n, 148, 151
    public 145–8, 247
        of the age 145–6
        community mediation of 147
        of culture 145
        of faith 146
        inter-relatedness of 147–8
Wyndham, Harold 53
Wyndham Scheme 53–4

Y

Young Christian Students (YCS) 50
Young Christian Workers (YCW) 50, 235

www.ingramcontent.com/pod-product-compliance
Lightning Source LLC
Chambersburg PA
CBHW061345300426
44116CB00011B/2002